The Foreign Policies
of the Powers

Edited by F. S. NORTHEDGE

FREDERICK A. PRAEGER, *Publishers*

New York · Washington

BOOKS THAT MATTER

Published in the United States of America in 1969
by Frederick A. Praeger, Inc., Publishers
111 Fourth Avenue, New York, N.Y. 10003

Library of Congress Catalog Card Number 69–12697

This is the first volume in the series
Studies in International Politics

Printed in the United States of America

PREFACE

This book is the first in the series *Studies in International Politics*, to be published by Frederick A. Praeger, which will consist of writings on modern international relations by British and foreign authors to serve both as part of the growing academic literature on this subject and as expositions of contemporary problems for the general reader.

The present work consists of a group of essays on the foreign policies of seven major states – the United States, the Soviet Union, the People's Republic of China, Britain, France, Federal Germany and India – with an introductory chapter on the general nature of foreign policy and its analysis. The contributors are all teachers at the London School of Economics and have based their essays on lectures which they have given for the last few years at the School under the heading of the Foreign Policies of the Powers.

The essays have been conceived less as historical surveys of foreign policy or detailed accounts of these countries' current foreign policy problems than as attempts to describe the general forces, including traditional national attitudes, economic and social structure, interests and commitments, and techniques of policy formulation, which help to make these foreign policies what they are. Although the contributors have varied in their choice of which of these aspects is to be the primary focus, they have all set themselves the question, not so much how these seven Powers react to this or that world problem, but what accounts for their habitual style of reaction to the succession of international problems confronting them. The emphasis, in other words, is intended to be analytical rather than historical or descriptive.

F. S. NORTHEDGE

The London School of Economics and Political Science.

Contents

1·THE NATURE OF FOREIGN POLICY

F. S. Northedge

The framing of foreign policy is a necessary activity of the modern state. It arises from the circumstances, firstly, that the state is, as Lenin remarked, not an immured island but a member of a society of states participation in which is inescapable, and, secondly, that in this society political power is not centralized but distributed among the states in unequal measure. While foreign policy resembles any other state activity, like maintaining educational or medical services or upholding law and order, it differs from these examples in that the state has, if any, only very imperfect control over the world society in which it lives. Domestic policy, according to Roscoe Pound, is social control through law; foreign policy is the use of political influence in order to induce other states to exercise their law-making power in a manner desired by the state concerned.

In this sphere the Minister cannot command success; the most he can do is to try to earn it. The Parliamentary candidate at an election may propound a foreign policy; but this can never be more than an undertaking to negotiate with other states, and whether they will agree even to that is for them to say. Accordingly foreign policy has been compared to gliding rather than to power-driven flight; to sailing as opposed to managing a steamship; to gardening, in which luck and the chances of favourable weather play their part, as distinct from the process of manufacturing an article which extends in direct line from drawing board to retail shop. In international affairs we must never overlook the force of the unpredictable, of what H. A. L. Fisher once called 'the play of the contingent and the unforeseen'. To which may be added what can only be described as the perverse logic of international events, the tendency for situations to arise which were not only not anticipated, but which states devoted their best efforts to avert. That an

American Secretary of State in 1965 should speak of his country having a common interest with the Soviet Union in resisting two-thirds majorities at the United Nations formed by states 'which pay less than their fair share of UN contributions' would have seemed sheer fantasy ten years ago. That, twenty years after the Second World War, Britain should be competing with the United States to sell arms to Germany would have seemed more fantastic still to the generation which fought Hitler.

It follows that such procedures as long-range planning will have less of a place in foreign than in domestic policy; improvisation, adaptability, the capacity to take advantage of swiftly changing circumstances, will always have their weight. The difficulty about the long-range plan in matters of external policy is that it may fail for want of the co-operation of other states, perhaps of only one other state, as President Kennedy's Grand Design for Europe and the United States failed perhaps principally for want of French co-operation, leaving the planners without alternatives to fall back upon. This does not mean that a state's foreign policy, reviewed over a period of years, does not exhibit a certain unity of purpose and direction; but to be true to the conditions in which it has to work, it will generally seek to combine stability of long-term purpose with a certain flexibility, one might say opportunism, of method.

Continuity and change

Here is the paradox of foreign policy: that its aims, the product of interaction between pressures internal and external to the state, have a certain perennial quality about them – a Castlereagh or Bismarck would be more at home at a modern Cabinet discussion of international policy than if prices and income controls were at issue – and yet the implementation of these aims in the concrete circumstances of the times has to bow to ever-changing realities. The factors which place a premium upon adaptability are obvious enough: the uneven military and economic development of the states forming the international system; the immense technological and social revolutions of our times; the alterations in climates of opinion and the fortune of politicians and political parties in the hundred or so states of the present-day world. Britain has won the name of *perfide Albion*, but what country's external policy is not subject to daily pressures which call into question its alliances, the common interests it professes with friendly states, the sacrifices it is prepared to make on behalf of accommodations with hostile Powers? The price of effectiveness in foreign policy is eternal vigilance to the changes restlessly at work in world politics.

Yet inevitably the forces making for continuity and sameness require their emphasis too; foreign policy constitutes an endless dialogue between the powers of continuity and the powers of change. There is, first, the persistence through time of the general features of the international system in which the states live and to which, late or soon, their external behaviour must conform. The international incendiary, such as Bolshevik Russia in 1917, may aspire to destroy the international system and replace it by another. So, too, in her own way and time, has the United States, and so, if Mr. Bullock is to be believed, did Hitler's Germany.[1] The striking feature, however, of these states' encounters with the international system is that, in course of time, they are found to be adjusting to its requirements, practising for example the balance of power which their ideologies may have taught them to reject, or, if they will not conform, going down in defeat and leaving to their successors the duty to practise diplomacy better than they. Within this system moreover the geographical situations of the different states and their space relations with one another remain on the whole changeless, though technology may shift the implications of physical factors. That the Soviet Union is a vast land mass straddling Europe and Asia; that Britain is an island, anchored off a politically restless Continent which from time to time threatens to unite without, if not against, her; that the United States, even in a missile age, is detached from Europe as much as from Asia—all these shape the approach of successive Foreign Ministers to their tasks.

[1] *Hitler, a Study in Tyranny*, Odhams, London, 1964, p. 319.

Perhaps too the *ethos* of a nation, the thoughts and feelings which come natural on the particular piece of earth which they inhabit, with neighbours which, generation after generation, live out their lives beside them, across the river or over the mountain, all dispose a state to take the same things for granted about foreign policy, to indulge the same prejudices, dream the same dreams. Traumatic shocks, such as the First World War or Pearl Harbor, may blast a country out of its entrenched illusions, but these are not surrendered easily, and, when they go, are often succeeded by new myths which are merely resuscitated forms of the old. Have British Ministers since 1945 been very different from the Lord Derby of a hundred years ago who said 'we can trust none of these European governments'? Has not American intervention in world politics since 1941 been pursued with much of the isolationist wish to settle once and for all with the oppressors of the innocent and then retire into the American way of life? 'The ghosts of immemorial policies,' wrote Herbert Fisher of Clemenceau, 'of Richelieu, Mazarin, Danton, lived on again in this brilliant and fiery Republican.' Has not de Gaulle his unforgettable ancestors too?

Hence we should not too much hope, or fear, that changes of government or ideology, or even domestic revolutions, will change the way in which a country conducts its foreign relations; or, if it transforms its manner of diplomacy, it will do the same to its real substance. To adapt an old saying, there is more in common between two English politicians one of whom is a Conservative and the other a Socialist than between two Socialists one of whom is English and the other French. The history of party politics is the record of vast pretensions to change the country's foreign policy out of recognition when the party achieves power, followed by the adoption of all, or almost all, that the former regime stood for. Stalin in 1942 invoking the spirit of Ivan the Terrible and Dimitri Donskoi; the British Labour Party taking the country in 1949 into an Atlantic alliance for balance-of-power reasons which all their previous philosophy had led their rank-and-file to abhor–and against Russia, of all countries; President Eisenhower and Mr. Dulles in 1956 accepting the Communist Revolution in Eastern

Europe which Mr. Eisenhower had been elected in 1952 to 'roll back': all are examples of the truth that in foreign affairs the view of the road changes when one moves from the passenger's into the driver's seat.

Much the same may be said of ideology, the prevailing political orthodoxy of a state. We may distinguish between various functions of ideology in foreign policy: to bind the country together psychologically, to provide a scale of values by which its people may know what to strive for and what to repudiate; a frame of reference enabling people to make sense of the otherwise bewildering world they inhabit and justify their government's efforts to grapple with it; a prism through which states perceive the international realities on which their foreign policy must work. Without ideology a nation does not exactly perish, but it can hardly know what to approve and disapprove. In ordinary circumstances one may expect rational calculation of national interest and ideological prescription to march hand in hand; most modern ideologies are infinitely malleable and, as Stalin showed, terms like 'nationalism' and 'internationalism', 'aggression' and 'defence', 'imperialism' and 'self-determination', can be rendered interchangeable by the skilled ideologist if the will is there. If, however, a sharp breach occurs between interest and political creed, one may assume that the former will generally win out for the simple reason that the state must survive and somehow prosper. The ideologist may say, with Hitler in blazing Berlin, 'après moi le déluge', but in the final resort the nation's will to survive is irresistible; or, if it is not, and the nation commits suicide on its ideology's behalf, its territory will be inherited by a new nation–or a new generation–which knows better than to ignore the first axiom of foreign policy: *primum vivere, deinde philosophari*.

How then, if so much is fixed and ordained in foreign policy, is the government of any state, great or small, a free agent at all? We need not enter here into the age-old controversy as to the limits of free will in public or private life, but it can be said with some confidence that the eternal experience of Ministers is to find that their choices are pre-determined, in domestic but to a far greater extent in foreign affairs, more than they believed, or wished their constituents to believe, when they were aspirants to office. Behind them are the demands of their party supporters, the various organized pressure groups in the country, the public at large; before them the intractable facts of international life, the world's diplomats who can say 'no' in so many languages; at their elbow the officials and advisers who have the ungrateful task of laying on Ministers' desks what Bagehot called 'the facts that live in the office'. It may be thought that, the greater the state, the larger its freedom of choice, but this is no universal rule. In an age of nuclear weapons quite small countries are able to back their fancies because the super-Powers, like climbers in Alpine country, are afraid to raise their voices for fear of precipitating an avalanche. The nuclear Leviathan, precisely because its potentiality for good or evil is so awesome, tends to be conscious, not so much of freedom, as of responsibilities: a well-trained bull in a china shop, aware of the vast damage it can do by merely turning round.

This is not to say that Ministers are not free to make mistakes, though the amount of rational deliberation which goes into the making of most foreign policy is underestimated by most people. Effective freedom in foreign affairs, however, is capacity to choose between relatively few options. The best image, perhaps, is that of a hand of cards. As in a card game, the government in foreign policy is dealt a hand of cards by circumstances. There is no freedom to play a card not in the hand; it is no good, in other words, asking for a verified disarmament agreement if the other country regards verification as legalized espionage. Of the cards in hand, there is always one card, possibly two, which is the 'right' card to play in the prevailing state of the game. It is 'right' in the sense that when the game is finished, all the hands known, and the entire history reconstructed, that card was the appropriate one to play in the circumstances, given (as, of course, need not be the case) the player is out to win the game. The personality, political or religious faith, or party allegiance of the player may help determine why he failed to play the decisive card at the decisive moment. But that there is a decisive card, that its identity is governed, not by the personal attributes of the player, but by the 'run of the game', is not open to doubt.

The aims of foreign policy

What then is foreign policy about? What effects are its practitioners, that is, the various governments, seeking to achieve? We must beware of thinking that, because states are often referred to as 'actors' in the international system, their foreign policies begin with themselves, their wishes, hopes and fears. Foreign policy, as we have said, is an interplay between the outside and the inside. It is comparable to entering a room in which separate conversations are proceeding between different people; the newcomer may hope that all will stop talking and listen to him; but the experienced talker will take the conversations as on-going concerns and try to move them in his own direction, to switch them on to lines agreeable to himself. So the starting point of the Foreign Minister's work is generally not what he wants to see done, but something already being done by other countries' Ministers, which he must either stop or influence in a manner favourable to his own goals. A government learns, like a bolt from the blue, that Hitler has reoccupied the Rhineland, that President Nasser has nationalized the Suez Canal company, that the Soviet Union has placed missiles in Cuba. These foreign initiatives are in their turn often reactions to events originating elsewhere, or represent the seizure of circumstances created by others. Britain and France are alienated from Italy by Mussolini's Ethiopian war and the remilitarization of the Rhineland becomes practical politics; Britain and the United States refuse assistance for the Assuan Dam and Egypt makes her reply; Cuba and the United States are already in all but name at war and Castro is looking for friends. The Foreign Minister, in other words, has to weave *motifs* dear to his own heart into a tapestry on which many other hands are busily working.

But these *motifs* are not his own; they are the public claims which the country he represents make on the international system, its expectations from international life. The President, Prime Minister or Dictator may bequeath to history a legend of one who shaped affairs; in the case of very exceptional statesmen the image may be correct, but generally a leader becomes a leader by using language which seems to meet the needs of his times and people. In practice, politics is not a matter of a people choosing a leader; it is more a case of a leader choosing a people, electing, that is, to put himself at the head of the accumulated wants of those whose franchise he solicits. In a liberal democracy certainly, in a one-party state hardly less so, the national leader has to identify with his people's interests, or rather with what can be convincingly represented as their interests, and in competition with other skilled, ambitious leaders only too anxious to show their fidelity to, and capacity to promote, that same structure of interests.

In all this we are speaking of interests, rather than the national interest, as the motivational basis of foreign policy, the objectives Ministers seek to insinuate into the unending conversation of international affairs. No one seriously denies that discussion of foreign policy proceeds in a modern Cabinet on the assumption that all the different views are oriented towards the national interest; if Ministers are not avowedly seeking that, they are earning their salaries by fraud. What the debate is actually about is which *interests* are to be defended and which, if need be, sacrificed, in dealings with other states. No business can be done without sacrifice, if only of time and energy. The question is: if some harm must be done to some interests, which shall they be? Hence we arrive at the motivational basis of foreign policy: the hierarchy of interests which a government will strive to advance or defend, or which it will refuse to retreat from, in the continuous conversation between the states of the world. And, if a closer definition is required of what interests are, it must surely be that organization of wants, desires, needs and claims of a state in international affairs which commands a consensus at home strong enough to support Ministers who are to act on the state's behalf in the international system.

The primary task of the policy-maker is to articulate the country's external interests and order them in some scheme of relative importance. The articulation and ordering of interests must be continuously changing through time, but a rough-and-ready pattern in the case of most states might follow the following lines. At the head must come self-preservation, the maintenance of the physical integrity of the country and the unity of its people; to this all else will tend to be subordinated, including as we have seen, ideology, on the principle *salus populi suprema lex*. Next follows the difficult concept of independence, meaning the relative freedom of a country from interference in what it regards as its internal affairs, and some degree of power to express and implement an independent viewpoint on external affairs. It may be that the concept of sovereign independence no longer fits the facts of the interdependent twentieth-century world. Nations none the less have an impression of their independence; are aware of how it may be threatened; are willing to pay a high price to keep it. Following from this is, thirdly, a list of attributes to be grouped together under the heading of influence, authority, status, or simply 'pull' in the international community. When Lloyd George in his famous Mansion House speech in July 1911 called on Germany not to act 'as though Britain were of no account in the Cabinet of nations', he was voicing a vital concern of all countries. This consideration may be of greater weight with states like Britain and France which have fallen from paramountcy in the last half-century; but since a country's standing in the various world capitals is a condition of whatever objects it may set itself in international affairs, it constitutes an interest of the highest moment in its own right.

This brings us to the next interest engaged in foreign policy as we move down the scale of importance: namely, the totality of the country's stake in the prevailing international system, the entire congeries of rights and privileges it exercises beyond its borders, the amenities and assets it enjoys, the commitments and obligations it shoulders. A question of crucial importance to ask of any international event is: who stands to gain or lose if affairs turn out thus or thus, which state's hostages to fortune, scattered throughout the world – in the path of the political cyclone perhaps – are endangered and activate the state to move? We must, of course, include under this heading the interest of all countries in international order itself, which enables their peaceful relations to go forward. Possibly this stake is greater for 'bourgeois' or '*status-quo*' states, but all countries have a greater or less interest in ensuring that tomorrow's world is not plunged into flames against which no one's house is fireproof. And finally come the expectations and demands of the people of a country in relation to higher living standards, which have become so large a feature of political life in democracies and dictatorships alike. Twentieth-century foreign policy has been democratized, not only in the sense that public opinion matters more than it did before 1914, but in that policy must have something to do with the improvement of living standards as well as with the traditional objects of statecraft. There is, however, reason for placing these near the foot of the ladder of interests since it is obvious that in the last resort living standards will if necessary be sacrificed for 'higher' national interests, as experience in wartime or during rearmament drives shows. Logically, in a world in which states must provide for their own security, guns must unfortunately come before butter and the practice of states shows that on the whole this maxim is reflected in their policies.

In the making of foreign policy, as we have stressed, interests of the kind described are incompatible in the sense that, if some are served, others must stand and wait. There is, first of all, the obvious limitation of resources; you cannot give economic aid to your friends overseas, keep your place in the military balance of power *and* make voluntary financial contributions to the United Nations over and above your allotted quota without impinging on the interests of your people in material welfare. Resources may be abstract, such as political influence, as well as material. If influence is used with the governing authorities of another country so as to induce them to serve one's purposes, the effect may be to destroy a corresponding source of influence in yet a third country. Secondly, a conflict may exist between an obsolete or moribund interest and a newly developing one. During her period of decolonization Britain has had to face a choice between continuing to help maintain stability and social justice in an area from which she may be withdrawing and her economic interest in keeping a balance between means and commitments; Rhodesia crucially illustrated the dilemma. There has also been the central problem for Britain in the post-1945 world, the conflict, that is, between her remaining global commitments and her developing interests nearer home. It was no doubt because President de Gaulle decided that Britain had not finally resolved this dilemma in favour of her European interests that he felt justified in January 1963 in excluding her from the European Economic Community. Finally, conflict may exist between the external interests of one section of the population and those of another. Farmers in an international common market will have a different set of interests from those of manufacturers; exporters and importers are not necessarily profited by foreign policies which favour producers for the home market; rich and poor do not both invariably benefit from the same developments outside the country's borders; and so on. A government may be practically certain that whatever move it makes on the international chessboard will evoke a groan from one group at home and a cheer, perhaps, from another. The question it must ask itself is whether the groans mean a greater loss of political support than the cheers mean a gain.

Perhaps the most difficult problem facing a Minister when formulating an appropriate hierarchy of national interests in a rapidly changing world is that of reassessing and overhauling interests in order to see that they accord with newly emerging realities. At all times forces are at work eroding established interests and summoning nations to embrace new ones: the restless configuration of world-wide political power, and of diplomatic alliances and alignments; the shifts in the direction of major tensions dividing the international system into hostile sub-systems; the effects of technological progress with its impact on defence, war, international commerce and investment; movements in opinion and climates of thinking, which governments must somehow make a show of reflecting in their external as well as their internal policies, and changes in social structure, habits and psychology at home, all of which have some effect on the values to which a government must give priority in its foreign policy. Yet there exist for all countries equally powerful forces which stand against the achievement of a corresponding adjustment in the definition of interests. The structure of government, as United States experience has abundantly shown, created to serve the country's interests in one age, is not always readily modified to meet the needs of another. It is doubtful, too, whether even the most energetic politicians have time for the close scrutiny of established interests which their continuous adaptation to changing conditions demands; domestic difficulties have to be attended to, elections to be won, and foreign policy has often to mark time.

We must also bear in mind the resistance which any adaptation of national interests to changing conditions encounters in public opinion and organized groups at home. It is sometimes hard, as the British Government found in 1954, when it decided that the maintenance of a military base in the Suez Canal zone was no longer a vital British interest in view of its vulnerability to nuclear attack, to get this accepted, not least by one's own political party. What 'peaceful coexistence' demanded of the two super-Powers in the 1960s, in the shape of revision of their images of one another and of their own place and vocation in world politics, was never readily agreed to by the ruling political forces in either country, as President Kennedy and Mr. Khrushchev discovered. The compulsions of established interests are strong, yielding not easily to argument.

The domestic background

So far we have noted that, while foreign policy may be described as a means of putting a state into communication with its external environment—an environment only partially under its control—a government's freedom to conduct this dialogue with neighbour states is restricted by pressures originating within the country. The internal political situation, with due allowance for variations from one country to another, will determine how forcefully a government can play its diplomatic hand, what it cannot do for fear of losing support at home, what it must do, or try to do, if it is to hold its own against the Opposition, or to conciliate the Opposition if under attack from its own supporters. The machinery of government, the constitutional channels through which the decision-making process flows, will affect the nature of those decisions. The temper of domestic public opinion, the pattern of organized pressure groups acting as lobbies in Parliament or Congress or as opinion-forming agencies in the country at large, the organs for articulating and shaping opinion on foreign affairs such as press, radio and television, will all have their part to play. There is virtually nothing existing within the borders of a state, from the politics of the parish pump to the literature the nation reads, which does not have some influence on the postures its government assumes in international affairs. The problem for the observer is one of forming a framework of ideas in terms of which these multitudinous and varied pressures can be handled.

One such framework might cover the following three headings: the country's political or diplomatic style, the projection, in other words, into the external field of the characteristic thought processes of the country concerned; the manner in which consensus on political matters is formed; and, thirdly, the sources of internal conflict on foreign policy. These aspects of the domestic background to foreign policy, it will be seen, are arranged in descending order of generality.

'Political style' is the established manner of conducting public affairs in a given country, the political mental habits and inarticulate major premises of a nation coloured by tradition and reflected in government policies, its method (to use Professor Oakeshott's phrase) of attending to the arrangements of society. Style helps to make certain policies sensible in terms of the political setting in which they are framed, though they might make little sense elsewhere. Style, too, provides the observer with clues as to how a given country will react in a particular set of circumstances. The experienced diplomat may be able to say how this or that country will respond to this or that move of his own country, not merely because he has studied the pattern of interests which motivate the other country, but because he is familiar with the habitual manner in which it reacts to situations of this kind.

Some examples of this mental hinterland of foreign policy, though no doubt extremely drawn, may be given. It seems to have been, for instance, almost second nature for Soviet spokemen to talk as though all international relations were a struggle between emerging historical forces, representing the ordinary people's struggle for freedom, and forces of oppression, representing the wealthy and privileged; as though this conflict were a long-drawn-out process in which there might be setbacks for the cause of Right but the latter would emerge triumphant in the long term owing to the championship provided by the Soviet Union and her peace-loving allies. Opposed to such a frame of ideas is the American notion expressed in countless State of the Union messages, that behind foreign policy is nothing so base as national interest or the aggrandisement of national power but only the widest possible dissemination of personal liberty and welfare for all men, the assumption being that the common man, left to himself, is capable of making a paradise on earth. The British style of foreign policy, on the other hand, is more earthbound than either vision. Its characteristic tenet is that, between opposing views, no matter how fanatical, there is always a middle term, to be found, preferably, by expert inquiry and quiet negotiation, and that harmonious relations are possible between ideologically divided nations provided the emphasis is laid on 'practical' matters. The British Minister is not much concerned with whether a given diplomatic formula is moral or consistent with his ideology, or even durable. He is satisfied to pray, with Baldwin, 'Give us peace in our time, O Lord'.

Style is far from being monolithic in any country. The aptest image no doubt is of a skein of different strands of ideas gleaned from the nation's experience; one strand or another will seem to make sense in the particular circumstances of the times and be given prominence as it suits the mood and needs of the moment. Hence style leads to our second aspect of the domestic background of foreign policy, the formation of consensus. Politics is the search for the highest common factor of consensus in the midst of inevitable and natural discord. On some issues there may be virtual unanimity; others may so divide a nation that it is impossible for the government even to attempt to voice the national will in foreign affairs. But on practically all issues of foreign policy there is a certain artificiality about the consensus ultimately reached; in the single position finally adopted as official there will generally be some reflection of views which did not, in the process of debate, prevail.

Some countries may continue to speak with two or more voices, with effects confusing to allies and rival Powers. The United States has historically been recognized as an example of split personality, or imperfect consensus, in foreign policy, the two voices being more particularly that of active intervention in world affairs and that of withdrawal. The two positions have, since 1919, been closely intertwined in the American outlook on world affairs; intervention has often been pursued in order to solve, once and for all, what Americans sometimes call *the* foreign policy problem and make possible a final withdrawal into isolation; isolation has often been blessed by interventionists, as by the two candidates Franklin Roosevelt and Wendell Willkie at the Presidential elections in 1940, in order to win time to press the case for intervention more effectively later.[1] The Middle East, too, has evoked conflicting attitudes from the United States: pro-Zionism and pro-Arabism, the rejection of Western imperialism in the area and pressure for Western-organized military pacts. Behind this heterogeneity of voices on American foreign policy lie the recurrent disharmonies between the various American departments of government: the White House, the State and Defence Departments, the Department of Commerce, the C.I.A., and many other autonomous or semi-autonomous organs each with its own axe to grind in foreign policy and often its own officials acting independently abroad. But imperfect consensus is also a characteristic feature of modern revolutionary states, such as the Communist countries and the

[1] See Charles A. Beard, *American Foreign Policy in the Making, 1932–40*, New Haven, Yale University Press, 1946.

Fascist states of pre-war times. These are required at one and the same time to nourish hope in the world-wide revolutionary cause and maintain stable and mutually beneficial relations with conservative states. Such has been the standing dilemma of the Soviet Union since 1917; duality has sometimes been a distinct advantage, but at least as frequently it had been a handicap, if not a positive danger.

Finally, we must consider, as the third of these broad concepts embracing domestic elements in foreign policy, the sources of internal disagreement on policy, out of which consensus must somehow be forged. There is in the first place the possibility of disagreement at the highest, or Cabinet, level between Ministers having civilian and those having defence responsibilities, the relative force and persistence with which such differences are pressed depending upon the traditional place occupied by the military among the organs of state. The issue may focus on the extent to which military or strategic considerations are being overlooked by civilians and opportunities for the use of military force neglected through civilian lack of aggressiveness; this was the argument pressed by Japanese servicemen against civilian Ministers in the 1930s, by General MacArthur against President Truman during the Korean War, possibly by Defence Minister Malinovski against Mr. Khrushchev at the abortive Paris 'summit' conference in May 1960. But the conflict may take the contrary form of the generals urging caution on the politicians, as the German General Staff did on Hitler at the time of the reoccupation of the Rhineland in 1936. In general it may be true to say that civilian Ministers will tend to bear in mind more far-ranging political considerations than Service Ministers or serving soldiers. At the Paris Peace Conference in 1919, for example, Clemenceau was more sensitive to the need to conciliate Wilson, when the French were already at odds with the British over the Rhineland occupation proposal, than Foch, who could think of little but the technical need to deny the left bank of the Rhine to Germany. Similarly, in Britain in recent years Service Ministers have been opposed, largely on technical grounds, to such ideas for nuclear-sharing in NATO as the multilateral force (MLF), whereas the Foreign Office has recognized the political function of such a force in binding together the NATO alliance, and has realized that for Britain too openly to reject such proposals might cement a Washington–Bonn relationship harmful to the special position British Ministers have always tried to occupy in the American capital.

Another type of internal conflict is between the executive as a whole and the legislature, though this can only be real in countries where the latter is genuinely independent of the government. In countries such as Britain, where the government normally has an obedient party of supporters in the popular Chamber, it can in the last resort have its way in foreign policy. The function of debates in the House of Commons is not really to decide foreign policy, but to give Ministers the opportunity of explaining and defending their policy and the Opposition a chance of arguing their greater fitness for office than the present incumbents. In the United States, of course, the situation is wholly different owing to the constitutional division of powers. In theory, the American President executes a foreign policy which has been given legislative force by Congress, President and Congress being elected separately by different processes and by differently constituted electorates. The spirit of the American constitution, even though under recent administrations this has been muted, is not to make the adoption of national policies easy, but to make it difficult, as a safeguard against autocratic government. But this leads to a further vital difference between British and American practice, with far-reaching results for foreign policy. The British M.P. will normally expect one day to have some Ministerial responsibility, perhaps even to be the Prime Minister. His instinct therefore, even in Opposition, is to make government work, or rather not to make its task impossible, since he hopes himself to inherit its responsibilities. The American Senator, certainly the Congressman, on the other hand, has normally so remote a prospect of becoming President that, with a few outstanding exceptions, this can rarely constitute a realistic ambition; and to be a Cabinet Minister carries with it little prestige in that country. What he can and does aspire to be is a permanent legislator, if possible the chairman of an important committee such as the House of Representatives Appropriations Committee or Senate Foreign Relations Committee. In that capacity, while seeking to influence government policy, he will also tend to act as a brake upon it, a permanent watchdog overlooking the government on his constituents' behalf. The average American Congressman is a professional critic of government as much as the British M.P. is an aspiring member of it. The American system thus tends to maximize conflict between government and legislature, the British to minimize it.

As for the other classic conflict, or tension, out of which national consensus on foreign policy has to be shaped, that between official policy-making elements and the public at large, together with the organized pressure groups within it, analysis must proceed likewise on a country-by-country basis. In Communist China it hardly seems that the views of the 'man in the street' are of great account to the organs of decision in Peking, and recent events have shown that the power of such sub-groups of the population as the intellectuals can sooner or later be curbed; in the United States and Britain it is a different story. Nevertheless, some generalizations may be hazarded. In all states the government tends to experience a tension between the objective requirements of the international situation confronting it and the frame of mind of the larger public on whom the government's tenure of power depends; to act from *raison d'état* and to play to the gallery are not always possible at the same time, nor is it always easy to placate every influential and interested pressure group by the same policy. Secondly, the form which this dilemma takes is often that of the public, or its spokesmen, demanding that resources be used for purposes of domestic consumption which the Foreign or Defence Minister would prefer to apply to international commitments. Thirdly, the wider public may be assumed to be generally concerned with the ultimate objects of foreign policy rather than with means, with desirabilities rather than feasibilities, whereas responsible Ministers are only too conscious of what they must do, or what they cannot do, rather than what they should do, or would like to. The question often raised by the layman about a foreign policy is whether it is morally right; the Foreign Minister, in his daily dealings with many countries, each of which is generally convinced of the rightfulness of its own cause, will tend to be doubtful whether it is ever a case of fulfilling moral laws in foreign policy. The typical problem facing him is how to get through today's problems without doing quite unacceptable damage to his, or his country's, moral standards, and without making impossible the solution of tomorrow's problems on somewhat similar terms.

The formation of foreign policy then represents, on its domestic side, a continuous series of compromises and adjustments between the different elements of government and social structure which we have referred to. It is easy to ignore this aspect since what emerges from the process is that apparently single thing, the country's foreign policy. There is a tendency, too, for officials charged with the implementation of a policy, and of Ministers who publicly defend it, to overstate the singlemindedness of the country in the interests of presenting a united front. It is true that, in any isolated act of foreign policy, it is not always easy to see which of the forces mentioned here have been placated and which resisted, how far Ministers have been swayed by the prevailing state of public opinion, by pressure groups, which may shun publicity and the light of day, by Parliamentary debate or forceful Cabinet colleagues who can lower the government's standing in the country if their will is crossed. What we can say with some assurance is that the precise constellation of these forces may vary from one country to another, depending upon its traditions, political system, social and economic structure and many other variables, but that, except on minor issues which can be settled 'in the office', foreign policy-making will always proceed in the midst of the kind of vortex of conflicting forces we have suggested.

Implementing foreign policy

We may assume then that all these internal hurdles have been overcome and the policy is finally adopted; we must now consider how it is implemented, or rather, considering the highly conditional character of diplomacy, how its implementation is sought. It is useful, at this stage, to think, not so much of a government's policy, as of its 'position'. Foreign policy represents an infinite sequence of positions on the daily flow of international issues reaching the Foreign Minister's desk. Attached to each position is a price, standing for the sacrifice the country is prepared to make in order to secure the implementation of its position. Rarely does a position represent what everyone involved in the decision-making process would like to see put forward on the state's behalf; normally it is the desirable pared down to the politically acceptable. As the price to be paid for the position rises, alternative positions previously rejected in the decision-making process may seem more attractive.

There is naturally a sharp distinction between the implementation of foreign policy and the execution (a more desirable term in this context) of domestic policy. A government can normally ensure the execution of its domestic policy–though the policy itself may fail–owing to its control over the reactions of its subjects. Generally speaking, there are three methods for the execution of domestic policy: law, that is the promulgation of binding rules with sanctions in the event of non-compliance; positive and negative inducements, such as higher pay for soldiers to back a recruiting drive or stiffer taxation to discourage smoking; and persuasive argument. In liberal societies it is commonly accepted that law is an instrument to be used sparingly for the execution of home policies. Moreover, in foreign policy, law, that is municipal law, may for all practical purposes be ruled out as a means for implementing positions since the laws of no state have any validity abroad. Foreign policy has therefore to be put into effect by the second and third methods mentioned, that is, by skilful persuasion backed by positive and negative inducements, or in other words 'carrots and sticks'.

Hence the first stage in the implementation of a foreign policy position is persuasive explanation, that is, the advocacy abroad of a line of action as being in the interests of other states, whose co-operation is essential to success, as well as in that of the state concerned. Effective and clear explanation may be said to be of particular importance at the present day, owing to the fatal consequences which may ensue in a matter of minutes as a result of faulty communication, and to the ideological factor in modern international relations, which increases the difficulties of translating the intentions of one country into meaningful terms within the ideological context of another. Explanation, too, clashes with its opposite, obfuscation or tactical concealment. There may be circumstances in which it pays a country to play the game 'with its cards close to its chest'; this will naturally be the case when a country is preparing a surprise attack against another, or contemplating a diplomatic *volte face* the full implications of which may not yet have been worked out; or when a revolutionary country wishes to enjoy the advantages of peaceful relations with more conservative states while conspiring against the existing world order; or when a state not yet of one mind on an outstanding issue has no interest in having its domestic divisions of opinion trumpeted abroad. Most countries, like buyers in a market, will also wish to conceal the *price* which in the last resort they are prepared to pay in order to secure the implementation of their positions. Nevertheless, we should not exaggerate the extent to which governments normally seek to conceal their foreign policy positions from the rest of the world. 'The art of diplomacy', ran a British White Paper, 'consists in making the policy of H.M. Government, whatever it may be, understood and, if possible accepted by other countries.'[1] Since the implementation of foreign policy is ultimately dependent on the co-operation of other states, it is necessary to go to some lengths to explain what one is up to.

The explanation of policy may at once secure the compliance of the other state, which will end the matter; if it does not, a pause may elapse before the explanation is repeated. On many issues since 1945 the Western Powers and the Soviet Union have stated and re-stated their positions to one another—on Germany, disarmament, Berlin—with scarcely an alteration of one syllable and with the hope that some day the other side will reverse its stand and

[1] *Proposals for the Reform of the Foreign Service*, Cmd. 6420 (1943), p. 2.

accept them. The key question in deciding whether to reach a settlement by compromise on the basis of the first explanation or to wait and re-state the position again is whether circumstances are likely to remain the same during a pause or whether they will deteriorate from one's own point of view. Thus, in May 1955, after ten years of stating and re-stating its position on the Austrian question, the Soviet Government reversed its attitude and settled for lower terms than it had been demanding. The reason for this was presumably that events in Germany were worsening for the Soviet Union, since the Federal Republic had been admitted into West European Union and NATO in the previous October, and it no doubt seemed important to the Soviet authorities to try to entice the Germans away from the Western Powers by holding out the prospects of neutralization on the Austrian model.

Alternatively, the initial statement of positions may be followed by the act of bargaining, in which the attempt will be made to probe for common ground between the two positions, or rather between the highest price the state promoting a certain position is prepared to pay to have the position implemented and the lowest price the other is willing to accept for a settlement. Again, consideration of the flow of time is important, the question being whether it is profitable to settle on the basis of the terms offered or to prolong the talks on the assumption that the situation is improving from one's own point of view. Here it is vital to have a proper relation between agents and principals. It is generally accepted in Western practice that the initial presentation of positions, together with the inquiry into possibilities of middle ground between positions, should be left as far as possible to professional diplomats, since these are generally credited with skill in framing alternative positions and in defining their legal and other implications. The political principals, the Ministers that is, will tend to be drawn in at a later stage when the essentially political decision has to be taken whether to close the gap by sacrificing a portion of the agreed position, or to fall back on an alternative position, or to break off the contact and resume when the situation is more favourable. This is sometimes known as the 'coping stone' function of Ministers. Where, however, there has been a long record of coolness in the relations between two states and arrears of diplomacy have to be made good, Ministers are believed to have a second, or 'thawing out', function. Even here, however, the previous sequence of official and Ministerial interventions will tend to be adhered to after the 'thawing out' service has been performed.

While explanations and bargaining are proceeding, the government advocating a certain position will be bringing to bear its repertoire, or armoury, of inducements and deprivations, or offers and threats, in order to induce an accommodating frame of mind in the other state. The repertoire runs from the more verbal at one end of the scale to the more forceful, including economic and military restraints, at the other. It comprises all that the state has to give or withhold in its relations with other states, but we may assume that the drawbacks of particular inducements and deprivations will rise towards the compulsive end of the scale. We may also assume that the richer and more powerful a state the larger and more varied the repertoire of offers and threats at its disposal. That, after all, is mainly what power in international relations is sought for; it is to enable a state to enlarge the repertoire of inducements and deprivations with which it supplements the verbal exposition of its policy positions. On the other hand, it is far from true that the great Power can in all circumstances compel the weaker to do its will. The United States is a supreme example of a state with immense resources which can apparently do little with such weaker states as France or Cuba.

Limitations exist to the apparent range of rewards and punishments available to the giant Power for implementing its foreign policy. Physical force may be ruled out on moral or legal grounds; or through fear that its use cannot be limited; or because the recalcitrant state is protected by an opposing Power capable of inflicting reprisals, or situated in a part of the world in which one is seeking to establish an image of oneself as a force for peace. In the present-day world, with its United Nations Charter and legal restraints on the use of force, its fear of escalating hostilities and its

systems of alliances, its *tiers monde* and the general sensitivity of
world opinion to anything suggesting bullying by a great Power,
the resort to armed force as a pressure in foreign policy is severely
restricted. Even economic pressures have their drawbacks; the
denial of supplies to another country may cause an outcry at home
from people who stand to lose their jobs or profits, or from allies
who are expected to join in the embargo. The attempt to ostracize
a troublesome country from the world's foreign trade also runs the
risk of making that country a client state of a rival international
coalition whose influence one may be otherwise seeking to restrict.

All this refers to the implementation of foreign policy as between
governments. Something can be achieved, however, and this has
increasingly been the practice since the First World War, by
winning the support of the people of another state more directly.
There are two ways in which this may be done: by organizing
partisans of one's own cause in the other state who will be local
advocates of one's foreign policy, or even may take part in an
actual seizure of power in that country in order to change its
foreign policy in a way favourable to oneself, and by direct verbal
appeal to the people of the other country using all the resources of
mass communication. Both methods have been used, with more
or less success, by Communist and Fascist states in the twentieth
century and, although it was a Western democratic leader, President Wilson, who, in the First World War and at the 1919 Peace
Conference, was a pioneer, at least in the latter of these two
methods, Western governments have generally had mental reservations about such departures from traditional diplomacy. Moreover, in any general resort to these devices, 'bourgeois' societies
have many disadvantages compared with closed and regimented
states built on the totalitarian model.

The direct appeal to another people to co-operate in the fulfil-
ment of one's foreign policy, like the use of forcible pressures, has
its drawbacks and may misfire. Propaganda may have a reverse
effect from what was intended. A menacing tone, as the Nazis
discovered, may produce submission at home but only derision

abroad. The mere fact, too, that propaganda comes from abroad may strengthen support for the home government on the principle 'fear the Greeks when they come carrying gifts'; moreover, it may, somewhat in the manner of an arms race, stimulate counter-propaganda which offsets much of the value of the original effort. Above all, the effect of any direct approach to another national people as part of a programme for the implementation of foreign policy must at best be long-term; by the time the harvest is being reaped the needs of the state initiating the propaganda campaign may have changed and a favourable response from the other country may be a positive handicap. For years the United States argued for European Union in season and out of season on the assumption that a unified Western Europe would strengthen the Atlantic alliance. But, as European unity developed in such forms as the Economic Community, it was apparent that this was taking place under the hegemony of a neutralist, intensely anti-American France. It looked, at least for a time, as though a united Europe under such auspices might be as much a threat to the Atlantic alliance, and hence to American policy, as the disunited Europe which existed before.

The implementation of foreign policy must always be regarded therefore as the continuous attempt to secure international co-operation with one's own positions, modified as far as may be necessary, on the successive international issues of the day. This co-operation cannot be legally enforced, nor can it, except in rare circumstances, be imposed at the point of the gun. Explanation, persuasive argument, as between government and government, and government and people, play a much larger part than is commonly supposed; international affairs are by no means the proceedings of a primitive society in which brute force alone counts. We have also seen how, as far as the repertoire of inducements and penalties available to states for the implementation of foreign policies is concerned, the price, drawbacks and unpredictability of each of these rise, and may rise sharply, towards the compulsive end of the scale.

The conditions of success

But this leads to our final and most elusive question: what constitutes 'success' in foreign policy and on what kinds of factors does
it depend? What attributes of a foreign policy make it 'effective'?
There is of course the initial problem of saying how we define
'success'. Judgments on foreign policies vary from one generation
to another as the events recede into history. The Munich agreement of 1938 is commonly regarded today as a 'total, unmitigated
defeat' for Britain and France, as Churchill described it, but
history's final verdict has not yet been given, nor ever will be. We
must bear in mind, too, the time-scale chosen. The short-term
success may prove the long-term failure, and *vice versa*; count no
man happy, wrote Sophocles, until he is dead. Hitler's *coups* in
foreign policy were among the most brilliant in the diplomatic
record but their further consequences were appalling, not least for
Germany.

Perhaps it is easier to define failure than success, and hence
arrive at some understanding of the latter by the back door. Most
would agree that a policy has failed if a declared object has not
been attained and no compensating advantages have been secured;
by this test no doubt the rejection of Britain's application to join
the EEC in 1963, two years after the government had committed
itself to enter, was a failure. Failure may also be pronounced when
a declared object has been attained but the country's prestige and
standing have drastically fallen in the process; thus, freedom of
passage through the Suez Canal was established after the 1956
crisis (except for Israel) and to that extent the objects of British
policy were attained, but only at the cost of the virtual extinction
of all British influence in the Middle East. Or there could be said
to be failure when an established interest has been abandoned in
return for the strengthening of no equivalent interest. By this test
Germany's pre-1939 policy of *Heim im Reich* for Germans abroad
had decisively failed by 1945 because her own interest in territorial
integrity had been lost without a compensating advantage, except
perhaps an armistice, having been gained. On the other hand, the
Cuba missile crisis of October 1962 could hardly be regarded as a

failure of Soviet policy because, although the Soviet missiles were withdrawn from Cuba, their presence there could not be regarded as a long-established and settled Soviet interest. Moreover, in so far as the crisis led to a period of Soviet–American understanding profitable to Russia, it could be regarded almost as a success for that country.

Speaking more positively then, 'success' in foreign policy may be broadly defined as the achievement of declared, publicized or recognized objects of state policy, the maintenance or advancement of prestige or influence abroad, and the abandonment of interests only in return for the gaining of comparable or if possible weightier interests. By such a definition it must be admitted that 'success' in foreign policy is the exception rather than the rule; the Foreign Minister experiences an unending encounter with frustration. It is easier to make a list of striking failures of foreign policy, such as France's Ruhr policy in 1923 or British and French policies towards the Dictators in the 1930s, than one of striking successes, such as the formation of the Atlantic alliance in 1949 and President Kennedy's Cuba policy in October 1962. It is evident, from such examples, that it is perhaps easier to say 'no' in foreign policy, and hence to frustrate other countries' policies, than to prevail upon another country to say 'yes' and hence make a success of one's own policy. The most favourable position for a government to be in is where other governments are pressing it to say 'yes' and it can afford to say 'no'. The worst is where it is asking another government to say 'yes' and cannot take 'no' for an answer.

Perhaps the factors making for effective foreign policies, in the sense already given, can best be summed up in a series of questions. In the first place, is the policy based upon a realistic assessment of the facts? Are the policy-makers working with the most accurate understanding of the situation abroad as is humanly available to them? A classic failure of foreign policy, with serious long-term results for all concerned, was the British and French decision in 1917–18 to regard the Bolsheviks as unlikely to hold power because they would be repudiated as traitors by the Russian people, a miscalculation stemming from wishful thinking and politically biased reporting. The correct assessment of foreign situations is of course not merely a matter of accurate factual information; it also requires judgment and capacity to weigh one sets of facts against another in order to discern the drift of affairs. Considering the pitfalls in gathering and interpreting information relevant to foreign-policy making, the problem is not so much how to provide more and better information: it is the more modest one of how to minimize the distortions of facts to which all policy making is inevitably prone.

A second question to ask of foreign policy is: is it timely, both in the broader sense of being in tune with the emerging shape of affairs, the *Zeitgeist*, and in the narrower sense of taking advantage of a temporary, perhaps wholly accidental, coincidence of events? We have already said that failure in foreign policy is often the result of running head-on into the resistance of other states; it follows that successful initiatives must be launched when resistance is weakening or when events are about to take a turn which may lead to greater resistance in future. A model of timeliness of this kind was the initiative of Gustav Stresemann in 1925 when he deflected the tendency towards a bilateral Anglo–French mutual guarantee by proposing a multilateral Western security pact which later became the Locarno agreement. While making a revolutionary concession in accepting the Versailles settlement of Germany's western frontier, Stresemann adroitly prevented a one-sided British undertaking to defend France and at the same time ruled out the possibility of a concerted move by France and her East European allies to crush Germany.[1] A more recent example where the concurrence of two events worked both advantageously and disadvantageously for the states concerned was the Soviet suppression of the Hungarian revolution in the autumn of 1956 and the Anglo–French armed action in Egypt at the same time. The fact that Britain and France were intervening in Egypt was fortunate for the Soviet Union in that it tended to direct attention away from Hungary and confused moral judgments on Russia's

[1] George A. Grün, 'Locarno: Idea and Reality', *International Affairs*, October 1955.

action; for Britain and France, it had the adverse effect of placing their actions on a par, in the eyes of many people, with Russia's doings in Hungary.

The factors of effectiveness may also lie, not merely in the general circumstances in which a policy is pursued, but in the policy itself. Is it, for example, internally consistent or self-contradictory, and if the latter, are the internal self-contradictions sufficient to destroy its credibility? This is a difficult question because some degree of inconsistency is inseparable from foreign policy; governments, as we have seen, have to serve many interests and please many people at the same time. The most common type of inconsistency occurs where the need arises for firmness in the defence of certain interests coupled with the need to conciliate in order to minimize the amount of force required for that defence. The ability to balance these two requirements is said to have been President Kennedy's great strength during the Cuba missile crisis in 1962, in that, while yielding not an inch in his demand that the Soviet Union must withdraw the missiles, he nevertheless allowed that country an honourable means of retreat. Lord Templewood, in *Nine Troubled Years*, calls this blend of firmness with conciliation the 'double line', but in the phase of British policy to which he refers, that is, in the 1930s, the order was reversed: conciliation came first and only when it was evident that it was failing was a policy of strength adopted.[1]

We can proceed to ask other questions of a foreign policy: is it firmly based in public opinion or are its advocates likely to be rejected at the next election or the next *coup d'état*? Above all, are undertakings matched with resources; is the 'Micawber rule'–never allow commitments to outrun strength–being followed? But finally we cannot discard, in foreign policy as in all human affairs, the element of fortune, meaning a favourable concatenation of circumstances which could not have been reasonably foreseen at the time the decision was made, and which was probably not foreseen. Looking back from today on all the circumstances which permitted President Nasser to nationalize the Suez Canal

[1] *Nine Troubled Years*, Collins, London, 1954, Chapter 33.

company with relative impunity in 1956, it is hard to deny that an ingredient we cannot but call good fortune favoured the venture. The unanimous Afro–Asian resistance to forceful reprisals against Nasser; the new strength at the United Nations of these countries, with their passionate anti-colonialism focused especially upon Britain and France; the Hungarian revolution which helped the Egyptians to be identified in world opinion as similarly innocent victims of Great Power politics; the November elections in the United States which provided President Eisenhower with a strong incentive to bill himself as a man of peace; the newly arrived and newly recognized nuclear stalemate between the two super-Powers which gave them both good reasons for wanting the crisis hushed up; all these circumstances comprised a stroke of fate, making Nasser a winner on the international chessboard. Though he may have foreseen them all when he nationalized the canal, it would not be singular in historical experience had he been as much surprised as his adversaries.

If one were to add together all these ingredients in success in foreign policy, one might conclude that such a policy is likely to achieve its aims if it is based as far as possible on an accurate assessment of the facts; if it is timely, in the long-run and short-run senses of that word; if it is as self-consistent as the nature of foreign policy allows it to be; if understood and backed by relevant social forces at home, if supplemented by appropriate resources, and if smiled on by fortune. But, above all, a foreign policy is perhaps most likely to succeed if it is moving with the tide of affairs and weaving itself into the positive volition of other states rather than pitting itself against their resistance.

BIBLIOGRAPHY

BELOFF, MAX. *Foreign Policy and the Democratic Process.* Baltimore: Johns Hopkins Press, 1955. (Paperback ed.: Johns Hopkins.)

BLACK, JOSEPH E., and THOMPSON, KENNETH W. (eds.). *Foreign Policies in a World of Change*. New York: Harper & Row, 1963.

COHEN, BERNARD C. *The Influence of Non-governmental Groups on Foreign Policy Making*. Boston: World Peace Foundation, 1959. (Original paperback.)

CRABB, CECIL V. *Bipartisan Foreign Policy: Myth or Reality*. New York: Harper & Row, 1957.

FRANKEL, JOSEPH. *The Making of Foreign Policy*. New York: Oxford University Press, 1963.

GROSS, FELIX. *Foreign Policy Analysis*. New York: Philosophical Library, 1954.

MACRIDIS, ROY C. (ed.). *Foreign Policy in World Politics*. 2d ed. Englewood Cliffs, N.J.: Prentice-Hall, 1962. (Original paperback.)

MODELSKI, GEORGE A. *The Theory of Foreign Policy*. New York: Frederick A. Praeger, 1962.

ROSENAU, JAMES N. (ed.). *International Politics and Foreign Policy*. New York: The Free Press, 1961.

SNYDER, RICHARD C., *et al.* (eds.). *Foreign Policy Decision-making*. New York: The Free Press, 1962.

WESTERFIELD, H. B. *Foreign Policy and Party Politics: Pearl Harbor to Korea*. New Haven: Yale University Press, 1955.

2·THE FOREIGN POLICY OF THE UNITED STATES

Michael Banks

At the present stage of the development of the study of international relations, to 'explain' the foreign policy of any one country, especially a country of the size, power, range of interests and political complexity of the United States of America, is quite impossible. A satisfactory explanation would require three sets of components. The first would be a complete list of all the factors (or 'causes' or 'variables') contained within American politics, culture, economy and the like which affect the attitudes of the country towards each of the 120-odd other states which make up the international political system. Second, the explanation would need to have an equivalent list of all the pressures, opportunities, provocations and so forth which flow in the reverse direction – into the United States from each of the other countries in the world. Third, there would have to be a set of rules enabling the two lists to be put together: each factor would have to be weighted in accordance with the degree of priority which it is given in the peculiarly American system of making foreign policy decisions. Even these three points give only a hint of the complexity of the final explanation. Allowance would have to be made for the effects of the personality of the individual policy-makers, for example. And the explanation could not be static, for policy is constantly either renewed or modified. So the 'feedback process', or the implications of the way in which a foreign country reacts to previous policies of the United States, would have to be taken into account. All this constitutes an exercise of comprehensive analysis which is well beyond the capacities of either political scientists or government officials at the moment, although something approximating to it may be achieved in some remote future.

Meanwhile, the real world of politics and foreign policy continues, with state behaviour ranging along a wide continuum from co-operation to war, from deliberate actions in a well-perceived and carefully controlled crisis to casual diplomatic mistakes with consequences no expert could have foreseen. Despite its inability to account for these events in any scientific fashion, the study of international relations has nevertheless evolved a technique for describing foreign policy in a way which yields at least some understanding. This involves grouping together what are thought to be the more important causal elements into a series of categories. The present essay can do no more than analyse, or unravel, some of the mysteries of American politics and foreign policy within the framework of this technique, as it has been outlined by the editor in his introductory chapter. Inevitably, some generalizations must be rather sweeping, and some unfashionably imprecise concepts must be employed, when the great mass of information available on the United States is telescoped in this way into a single essay. But as the first lesson of an elementary course in power politics indicates, a great Power has a disproportionately large effect on the course of events in the world generally; even a crude attempt to 'explain' the policies of the United States in the second half of the twentieth century is clearly of profound importance.

American culture and traditions

Foreign policy decisions are made in the context of the political culture, or set of attitudes towards politics, of the society in which the decisions are made. In some countries, like France, the political culture may be diverse, with several sets of values competing for authority. The United States is unique among the great Powers (with the possible exception of Britain) in having a political culture which is the opposite. It is not only extremely homogeneous, but it has also been highly stable ever since American foreign policy began. There is a popular myth, found mainly within the borders of the United States itself, that America is a 'young' country; in fact, compared with each of the other states treated in this book, it is a very old one, in political terms. The continuity, stability, and uniformity of its government, politics and attitudes towards foreign policy mean that an examination of its conservative culture and tradition is perhaps more important than when considering other countries, in which different factors such as geography, size or economic circumstances may go far towards creating a general understanding.

American policy itself appears, on superficial examination, far from being consistent, to have undergone staggering changes during its history. Following the entangling alliance with France during the revolutionary war, there was a century and more of neutralism, succeeded quite suddenly by a switch to hegemony and involvement on a scale which has caused some observers to accuse the United States of attempting to create a world Empire since 1945. The neutralist phase itself was interrupted by the War of 1812, by a burst of imperialism in the 1890s, by enforced intervention in each of the two world wars of this century, and by brief periods of diplomatic leadership, great-Power style, in the 1900s and in the aftermath of World War One. Yet beneath these apparent alternations between active and passive foreign policy, it is possible to discern an entirely consistent pattern, as Professor Hans J. Morgenthau has argued forcefully in his *In Defence of the National Interest*[1] and elsewhere.

In its simplest form, this pattern has consisted, first, of an assertion of United States dominance in the Western hemisphere, comprising the north and south American continents, the Caribbean, and the Pacific Ocean at least as far as Hawaii. This hemispheric hegemony might be described as the 'vital interest' of the United States in a relatively narrow sense, and it was established in a very early stage in United States development. Further, it has been traditional and consistent American policy to support a general balance of power in Europe in order to prevent the growth of any one super-Power there which would be capable of exercising a major threat across the Atlantic Ocean. In the same way, the United States has been concerned to establish and maintain a rough balance of power in the Far East, although the confused evolution

[1] New York, Alfred A. Knopf, 1951.

of events in Asia has given little opportunity for American policy to emerge clearly during the period since its first diplomatic assertion in 1899. This elementary formula, control of the Western hemisphere plus intervention on the side of the weaker Powers whenever the balance seemed to be in danger in Europe or Asia, does give some understanding of American policy, in the period before 1945 particularly. But it is by no means a comprehensive explanation, and it gives no impression of the distinctively American philosophy of foreign affairs which was first expressed in President Washington's celebrated Farewell Address and which is necessary to an understanding of the attitudes of successive generations of Americans towards the world around them. This American national attitude, which in its turn gives to the foreign policy of the country its diplomatic 'style', has its roots in the national character and historical experience of the American people.

National character

The principal elements in American history and culture which created its national character can be summarized under five headings: the ethnic composition of the population; the intensity and variety of the religious traditions established in the country; the revolutionary nature of its origins, together with the constitutionalist doctrines deriving from the Philadelphia Convention of 1787; and the impact of the dynamic frontier on the society as it developed both before independence and subsequently. Each of these components is recognized by interpreters and chroniclers of American civilization, from de Tocqueville onwards, as having made a significant contribution to the distinctive national character which was formed by the nineteenth century, but has become familiar to the rest of the world only in the twentieth. Different facets of the general diplomatic style and flavour, occasional quirks and attitudes, of American foreign policy can be traced back, sometimes to individual roots of the national character, sometimes to the overall pattern which resulted from the mixing together of the varied elements.

43

Historians often remark on the importance of the role which distinct ethnic minorities have played in American foreign policy. Virtually every community of Europe, and large parts of Africa and Asia as well, were represented in the nineteenth and early twentieth centuries by identifiable immigrant groups in the United States. Opposition to Woodrow Wilson's quixotic effort to re-draw the political map of Europe along satisfactory lines of self-determination in 1919 came from vociferous representatives of these groups. More questionable lines of causation are sometimes put forward, such as the proposition that the generous peace treaty signed by the Truman Administration with Italy after the Second World War was influenced by the large number of Democratic Party officials in American cities who were of Italian descent. But if it was true in the past that the Irish, German or other communities were able to make a significant impact, as pressure groups, on particular items of foreign policy, it ceased to be the case once the floodgates of immigration into the north American continent were virtually slammed down in the 1920s, and the minorities became integrated. The one spectacular exception is the Jewish minority, which is now the only recognizable ethnic group with sufficient political importance, firm views on foreign policy, and the necessary degree of organization and leadership to exert effective pressure. Its importance has been demonstrated throughout the post-1945 period in creating ambivalence in an American policy in the Middle East which would otherwise be determined by the economic and strategic importance of the Arab countries. This was shown very clearly in the United States' stance during the three Arab–Israeli wars of 1948, 1956 and 1967. The possibility that the 23 million Americans who show some degree of African descent might influence official policy towards the African continent has long existed, but there is no evidence so far that the Negro community can fulfil the necessary conditions to act as an effective pressure group in this respect.

The major importance of the history of ethnic minorities lies in a different direction. The dominant stock within the American population is labelled by voting-behaviour analysts as 'WASP', or white-anglo-saxon-protestant; true to the imperial record of the United Kingdom elsewhere, the British element retained supremacy long after the successful revolution of 1776. But this supremacy has always been marginal within the pluralist, egalitarian and assimilationist American culture. There has never been a 'mother-country' psychology in the United States to compare with that of Australia or Canada or even the latterday revolutionary society of Rhodesia. Sentiments have always favoured Germany as much as Britain, Russia as much as Sweden. The United States has officially looked with dispassionate impartiality upon the affairs of European countries, at least until ideological fervour came to influence its judgment after the advent of communism in the Soviet Union. The experience of unprecedentedly smooth large-scale ethnic integration (Negroes alone excepted) created one of the many potent myths of American society, that of the 'melting-pot', which gave rise early in American history to the belief that a new, different and in many ways superior civilization was being created on the north American continent. This sense of separateness became a principal cause of the aloof official attitude towards what were seen as the distasteful intricacies and militaristic power politics of European international relations. Isolationism was in part an offshoot of this feeling, and even a generation of embittered involvement in the normal realities of international politics has not wholly removed it from the American political scene.

The religious traditions of the United States have tended to reinforce the sense of uniqueness and separateness generated by the ethnic diversity of the society. Will Herberg's *Protestant, Catholic, Jew*[1] traces clearly the way in which the three principal religious traditions, with protestantism dominant among them but fractionated internally, merged with the political and economic mores of the society to create a uniform ideology of 'Americanism' which shares some of the puritanism of old New England with the liberal spirit of the frontier and the profiteering instincts of big business. The quasi-religious symbols of American nationalism, like the high-school flag ceremonies, are among the most striking features

[1] New York, Doubleday, Anchor Paperback, 1960.

45

of American society to the visitor from the more secular countries of contemporary Western Europe. In foreign policy, the twin strands of moralism and idealism, much discussed in the specialized literature, can each be traced back to the deeply pious traditions of the cultural pattern in which men like President Eisenhower, with his tendency to make ready judgments of the 'good' and 'bad' in politics, were educated.

The individualistic and idealistic stress of the protestant religions in the United States is linked with the intellectual tradition of the revolution. Compared with societies in which revolution has been both more recent, as in China, and more potent, as in the Soviet Union, the war of independence is a remote and relatively unimportant event in American history. Yet it left its legacy, of which the most significant aspect for the student of foreign policy is probably the long record of anti-colonial attitudes, starting with the legend of the Boston Tea Party and continuing down to support for African nationalism as displayed in, for example, United States logistic and diplomatic assistance to the United Nations operation which suppressed the Katanga secession from the Congo, 1961–3. During the series of summit conferences at which Churchill, Roosevelt and Stalin attempted to create a new world order for the aftermath of the Second World War, the British Empire was a serious corrosive factor; it even appears that Roosevelt was suspicious of what he regarded as Churchill's ambitions for a pre-eminent British role in the ruins of the pre-war European balance. The general American distaste for what were thought to be the evils of colonialism meant that its Latin American sphere of influence was subjected to all the force of American power, discussed by native diplomatic historians under labels like 'the big stick' hemisphere policies of presidents like Theodore Roosevelt, without any corresponding sense of responsibility. This compares unfavourably with, for example, the maintenance of civil order which most of the European imperial states operated in their imperial domains of Africa and Asia. The 'good neighbour' policy of the later Roosevelt made little positive impact on the southern American states, and it was not until President Kennedy introduced the 'Alliance for Progress' in 1961 that the United States began to employ constructive international policies within its sphere of vital interest.

A different strand of tradition emanating from the war of independence might be called the doctrine of constitutionalism, or legalism. The political philosophy of John Locke exercised a potent appeal in the original thirteen communities of the USA as, in the eighteenth century, they established their novel constitution with its federal structure, its principle of the separation of powers and its theoretical stress on the government of laws, not men. It seemed to the Founding Fathers, and even more to the subsequent generations who were taught to eulogize their achievements, that the land of North America really had been a wilderness, a state of nature tamed and populated by civilized men who had employed the powers of reason alone to create a prosperous, stable society under the authority of an inspired social contract. The unparalleled stature of the Supreme Court's rulings, as the constitutional system evolved through the nineteenth century, came to symbolize this attitude.

Transferred to international politics, this American reverence for the authority and prestige of law was expressed in this century in what George F. Kennan has called the 'legalistic-moralistic' approach to international problems.[1] There are numerous examples of this tendency in the record: attempts to outlaw war by international legislation; to create 'open diplomacy' and thereby abolish the supposed evils of the European practices of power politics and secret treaties; to lay down clear-cut points of principle upon which wars were to be fought and with which no compromise was possible; to create 'democratic' international institutions in which debating and voting procedures would be used to settle international disputes in the same manner as they are thought to settle disputes within American society. Secretary of State John Foster Dulles, who exercised unusual sway over the whole span of foreign policy during his seven years as Secretary of

[1] In *American Diplomacy, 1900–1950*, Chicago, University of Chicago Press, 1953.

State in the 1950s, was notorious internationally for his legalistic justifications of the policy of non-recognition of Communist China; for his formalistic insistence upon the construction of a neat cordon of states encircling the entire Communist Bloc, with each of them 'signing on the dotted line' an agreement with the United States which would contain communist expansion; and for his moralistic outburst against neutralist states which refused to accept this system, calling them 'immoral'. Dulles was undoubtedly an extreme example of the way in which idealistic beliefs in democratic institutions, the sanctity of law and the purity of United States motives in its foreign policy could be distorted by excessive conviction into becoming dogmas and moralisms. But he was by no means an unrepresentative leader. In the United States there is sincere and widespread support for the view that since 'the great experiment' of government within the country has successfully demonstrated that imperfect man can be ruled with justice and efficiency by the right government institutions, this principle must somehow be transferable to the chaotic international environment. Observers of public opinion often comment on the way in which the American people are perplexed and disappointed when their well-intentioned foreign policy, often stemming from generous motives at least in part–as with the Peace Corps or the aid programme–is received in hostile fashion by the more cynical populations of other countries.

The frontier tradition

The final major source of the American national character to be considered here is the frontier. Life in a society undergoing constant expansion is an experience unique to the United States among the great Powers. The ever-moving frontier was literally present in the physical sense until the close of the nineteenth century, and even as recently as 1960 John F. Kennedy chose to base his presidential campaign upon a catch phrase, 'The New Frontier', intended to evoke the spirit which pervaded the society in more dynamic expansionist days. The social characteristics associated with life in the frontier tradition are those usually found in simple stereotypes of American national character: optimism, materialism, competitiveness, egalitarianism, individualism. The legendary slogans of 'go west, young man', and 'log cabin to White House' epitomize qualities which are still among the most prized values of the American way of life, despite the changes in social structure which have resulted from the urbanization and industrialization of the past century.

As with other strands of the fabric of political culture of the country, it is not difficult to identify specific foreign policy attitudes which appear to stem directly from the frontier experience and mental outlook. Foreign economic aid, for example, became a significant instrument of policy shortly after the Second World War, when it was used through the Marshall Plan to assist in the reconstruction of the economies of France, Italy, Britain and other European countries which were then struggling to cope with the disruption caused by the war. The Marshall Plan was an overwhelming success, and it generated the belief that aid could act, if not as a panacea, then at least as a powerful lever to bring about desired effects not only in the economic life of weak states, but also in their political attitudes. As the aid programme came to be used as a policy tool in the wider arena of third-world developing countries in the 1950s, sceptical observers began to detect an underlying formula on which the policy was supposedly based.

The formula was materialist and simplistic: it assumed that totalitarian political regimes were likely to engage in warlike foreign policies, whereas democratic ones would be more peaceful; that totalitarian regimes were the result of poverty, or more precisely of the inability of representative political leaders to respond satisfactorily to the 'revolution of rising expectations' which was sweeping across Africa and Asia. Therefore, the formula ran, the solution was to inject capital and technical know-how into the developing nations. This would generate economic growth and prosperity, create a middle-class, free-enterprise economic and political system, and a peaceful, pro-Western foreign policy would result. This pattern of thought persisted until a decade of experience with it showed, by the 1960s, that the needs of the underdeveloped countries were far more subtle, and their difficulties much more intractable, than the formula would suggest. The resulting American disillusionment has acted as one of the principal causes of decline in congressional and public support for the economic aid programme in the present decade, despite the fact that no alternative proposal has yet been found for coping with the problems that the aid formula was designed to solve.

Other recent examples of the frontier inheritance are not hard to find. Perhaps the most spectacular of them is the space race. This project began in a wave of public concern at the successful launching, in 1957, of the first Soviet earth satellite. Sputnik aroused a spirit of self-criticism and a competitive reaction in the United States quite unlike the response to any challenge that the country had experienced before, except for the stimulus of military provocations like German submarine warfare in 1916 or the Japanese attack on Pearl Harbor in 1941. A massive effort to develop intercontinental ballistic missiles followed, in order to close what was thought to be 'the missile gap' between the United States and the Soviet Union. It was not until after the Kennedy Administration was safely elected that it was announced, in 1961, that the 'gap' was by no means as wide as had previously been believed.

Attention was then transferred to the exploration of space, using the vast technological resources built up for military purposes. By the mid-1960s the military and civilian space effort was costing annually far more than, say, President Johnson's 'War on Poverty', the urban renewal programme and the foreign aid bill all put together. To foreign observers, noting domestic problems on the awesome scale of those which generated the race riots of the period 1965–7, this exercise seemed to involve a strange scale of priorities for the allocation of public money. Yet there has been little protest along similar lines within the country itself. Successive presidents have justified the enormous enterprise on a variety of grounds, including some which seem reminiscent of the kinds of reasons advanced by mountain-climbers when asked why they pursue their risky avocation. But it seems clear that international prestige is at least as significant a motive for the programme as any other, and concern for prestige appears to stem in turn from the cultural inheritance of the frontier. On the one hand, there is the atavistic spirit of competition stimulated by a project of unprecedented scale and excitement. On the other, there is the nature of the work involved. Unlike the field of politics, with its misunderstandings, its compromises, its interminable need to live with a problem until it evolves to its own solution, space research is engineering–a skill in which Americans have long excelled.

The American ideology of foreign affairs

Perhaps the great utility of the frontier concept as a means of interpreting American national attitudes is in throwing some light on the place of ideology in the country's recent foreign policy. The fervent emotionalism of the response of the public to the existence of communism in the Soviet Union, China and other countries is a relatively new phenomenon in American history, contrasting sharply with traditional attitudes. The characteristic philosophy of foreign affairs which developed early in the nine-teenth century was genuinely isolationist. For the most part, Americans viewed the affairs of other societies with detached unconcern. Their own continent offered more than sufficient pre-occupation for their attention. Although occasional issues like the alleged evils of Spanish colonial rule in Cuba and the Philippines attracted a temporary interest, foreign policy was seen only as a tool for dealing with contingencies, not as an absorbing, routine requirement. From time to time problems arose calling for American action. But once action had been taken, and the problem 'solved', it seemed to the pragmatic American people quite reason-able that their attention should return to domestic concerns. Occasionally the brief spate of activity would become a moral crusade, as when the idea of 'making the world safe for democracy' captured the public imagination as a simple rationale for United States participation in the First World War. But even after that experience the mass of the population returned, to the dismay of its own leaders as well as that of the other founders of the League of Nations, to disinterested isolationism.

Since the onset of the Cold War the American mood has been profoundly different: concerned, watchful, interventionist. A few symptoms of the old isolationist spirit do remain, and could perhaps increase in strength in the future; 'Fortress America' is a potent symbol. The State Department operates an extensive public relations system to guard against the possibility, painfully discovered in the past, that the public, if not kept informed and alert to foreign policy issues, might revert to its traditional attitude and 'go fishing'. But the predominant feature of the contemporary American public mind is the depth and not the superficiality of its feeling of commitment to an activist foreign policy, as the degree of support shown for the dreary and costly war in Vietnam bore witness in the mid-1960s.

Many theories have been put forward to explain this 'revolution', as it is often called, in American attitudes to foreign affairs. The most common explanation is simply that of change in the environment. United States policy is seen as a necessary and reluctant response to the call of history for leadership, or to the immutable functioning of the balance of power mechanism with its minimal requirement in the rule that nation-states act in support of their national interests, whatever their temperamental disposition might be. In 1945 Soviet expansionism put before the United States a threat which could not be ignored. True to its traditional rejection of spheres of influence, balance of power thinking and the use of force on distant continents, the United States did ignore the threat—but only briefly. Within a few years it embarked on a policy of rearmament; it adopted a technique of diplomatic firmness to match the hostile negotiating style of its Soviet antagonist; it based troops on foreign shores for the first time during a period officially known as peace; and it drew around itself a network of alliances more 'entangling' by far than those envisaged by George Washington in his celebrated denunciation of such a foreign policy. The pattern was set for the 1950s, and in its basic essentials this policy of containment, as it came to be known, was significantly modified in the 1960s only by the gradual substitution of the Chinese for the Russians as the principal source of potential aggression from within the Communist Bloc.

Anti-Communism

The United States became the world's leading great Power after 1945 by circumstance, not by choice. It exercised what it perceived to be its new range of world responsibilities with moderation and in a mood of self-criticism, in striking contrast to the confident imperialism of Britain, say, in the nineteenth century. Viewed as a necessary response to the profoundly altered circumstances in which the United States found itself in the postwar world, the constructive and responsible defensiveness of its new posture by the year 1950 was a tribute to the statesmanship of President Truman, Senator Vandenberg, General Marshall, Secretary Acheson and the other leaders who conceived and carried through the revolutionary initiatives of the postwar era. But the pressure of events alone is not a sufficient explanation for the phenomenon of anti-communist feeling which accompanied and bolstered the novel American involvement in world affairs. A clear indication of both the strength and the nature of this feeling was given by the outburst of witch-hunting and hysterical accusation in domestic public affairs in the period 1948–53, known to the outside world as McCarthyism.

A number of historians and political scientists have put forward analyses of American nationalism and political culture which go far towards explaining the twin phenomena of anti-communism abroad and McCarthyism at home.[1] A brief survey can perhaps convey the force of their argument, though hardly its sophistication. The principal feature of American political thought, they observe, is its uniformity. American society is indeed 'pluralist', as

[1] See Hans Kohn, *American Nationalism: An Interpretative Essay*, New York, Collier Books, 1961; Daniel Boorstin, *The Genius of American Politics*, Chicago, University of Chicago Press, 1953; and especially Louis Hartz, *The Liberal Tradition in America*, New York, Harcourt Brace, 1955.

is so often suggested, but only within limits which represent a narrow range of attitudes by international standards. The origins of this situation lie in the historical and socio-economic circumstances of the country, and in particular in the cultural effects of the frontier.

In the eighteenth century, a typical western society was composed of three distinct social classes–rural proletariat, middle class and aristocracy. Political theory and action tended during the industrial nineteenth century to reflect this threefold tradition, with reactionary conservatism representing aristocratic and monarchic interest, Marxist socialism voicing the demands of the now urban working classes, and liberalism speaking for the needs of the modernizing and capitalist middle classes. This simple model has the merit of dramatizing the way in which radically different traditions of thought were created side by side in each of the major western countries. In some, like Britain, they coexisted in reasonable harmony, and a political culture was developed along lines capable of tolerating fundamental differences of opinion without itself disintegrating. In others, instability and friction remained, as in Germany or Italy; or led to conflict and the virtual elimination of all but one tradition, as in Spain or Russia.

During this century of social tension generated by industrial change, the United States stood apart. In colonial America the beginnings of an aristocracy had been established, but it never took a firm hold and in the population explosion of the nineteenth century it became a negligible minority. No philosophy of true conservatism was ever expounded from authority after the attacks of 'factionalism' of eighteenth-century figures like Hamilton and Washington. In the same way, a rural proletariat never really existed, apart from the Negro slaves of the south, who in this as in so many other matters are an exception. An urban proletariat did indeed exist, on a very large scale, but it was remarkable for its uncharacteristic outlook on society and politics. The Marxist predictions of increasing impoverishment and subsequent 'alienation' of the workers were nowhere more confounded than in the United States. Abundance, business opportunity, social mobility and the levelling effects of the open frontier meant that poor immigrants from the more static societies of Europe were converted to would-be capitalists within a generation. Rural progressivism apart, there have never been significant socialist intellectual movements or political parties in the United States.

Cursory though it may be, this analysis does convey some understanding of why political culture became so conformist in the United States that some observers have written of the 'absolutism' of its value system. With only one dominant political tradition, it is not surprising that deviationist beliefs could not be tolerated. The Declaration of Independence made the point with a simple dogmatism: 'we declare these truths to be self-evident'. During the long period of isolationism, the American way of life stood unconsidered, unchallenged and, in the eyes of the people, extremely efficient in meeting their needs. In political matters America became a deeply conservative society, differing only from other tradition-oriented communities in the one, vital, respect that the principles conserved were liberal. A prime liberal tenet is, of course, the right of any citizen to express a dissenting opinion. But rights tend to lose their currency if they are not widely used. The philosophical confusions which mark the pronouncements of contemporary conservatives like the 1964 presidential candidate, Senator Barry Goldwater, are a reflection of this paradoxical inheritance.

When the twentieth century brought ideologically motivated international conflict, and with it a new revolutionary creed which gained adherents even within American society itself, the reaction of the American public was dramatic. The Second World War with its suppression of fascism achieved, it seemed, no reward of peace, but instead enlarged the overseas responsibilities of the United States. Communist doctrines not only challenged the right of other countries to choose their own governments, but attacked the very basis of the American policy. Communism became a scapegoat for all the frustrations that the new tensions of the Cold War engendered. The scapegoat was persecuted not only abroad but at home as well, for the two faces of the alien creed were seen to be linked through the spectral presence of international communism.

American attitudes in the Cold War

One of the numerous difficulties of the study of international politics is the way in which an apparently straightforward concept like the balance of power becomes almost superficial once its operation is examined in detail in any particular instance. It is so with the United States response to the Cold War situation with which it was faced after 1945. Balance of power theory holds that policy should, above all, be pragmatic. Alliances must be made and unmade for reasons of expediency, in relation to the logic of the situation alone and untainted by considerations of prejudice, ideology, morality or other forms of sentiment. In general such rules do account for the overall pattern of American behaviour after 1945. Germany, Italy and Japan, for example, were transformed from their enemy status of 1942 to that of allies in the 1950s in due obedience to the general shifts of the world balance. But there seems to be far more to the underlying attitude of the United States during the Cold War period than a mere accounting of alliances and alignments can reveal. Anti-communism, for reasons already discussed, was one of the principal ingredients of what might be called the domestic input into the American attitude. The other significant ingredients can be identified by a review of the national characteristics with which the first part of this essay has been concerned.

The philosophy of foreign affairs which was developed early in American history was subject to reinforcement and modification by a variety of historical forces and circumstances during the next hundred years. Two of these were peculiar to the United States, and deserve emphasis in order to show how the contemporary American posture can be placed in a framework of consistent attitudes towards foreign affairs. The more important of them is the isolationist experience itself. Today it is obvious that United States isolation was a luxury, a result of a fortuitous combination of circumstances rare in international politics. Throughout the nineteenth century the security of the Western hemisphere was guaranteed, not so much by the Monroe doctrine, as by the British domination of the seas, at a time when naval power was the only means by which any threat could be made. And British interests happened, for the most part, to coincide with United States interests.

Generations of Americans, however, grew up not understanding that isolation was an objective matter of geography plus technology plus power politics, but instead believing that it was a matter of subjective preference. This myth left in the American tradition encouragement for the sense of omnipotence, and for the view that American actions were governed by a different set of standards from those applicable to other nations—both tendencies already present in the outlook of the nation. Isolationism also had the incidental effect of enabling critics to accuse the country of inexperience, when the need for long experience became evident during World War Two. 'Inexperience' is a difficult concept to apply to a nation-state, but it was certainly the case that the Department of State was not built up to substantial strength until the 1920s and did not compare in scale with the foreign offices of other great Powers until after 1945.

The other factor affecting the development of the national outlook from its origins down to the present may be considered more briefly. It is, quite simply, the unique record of unbroken success and expansion of the United States. During the period when the country was isolated from Europe, ostensibly pursuing a static foreign policy, it conquered, bought or colonized a continent. It did so without meeting the obstruction of another great Power, which sets it quite apart from the expansionist experiences of most other states throughout history. In exploiting the resources of its rich territory, it became the wealthiest nation the world has ever seen. The United States never suffered any major disaster of foreign policy, and the only serious disruption of its domestic life, the civil war, was largely undisturbed by foreign intervention and tended to reinforce the stability of its political institutions while accelerating the pace of its economic growth and national integration. In the war which catapulted it to the top of the great Power league, the major burden of occupation, sacrifice and destruction was borne by its allies situated to the east and west of Nazi Germany. When, after that conflict, the Soviet Union tossed down the gauntlet of international confrontation, it was challenging a country which had lost few battles and never a war; which had a profound civic faith in the strength and resilience of its own institutions; and which was accustomed to decisive action rather than to the tedious subtleties of involvement in international affairs.

With these considerations in mind it is possible to conclude this survey of national attitudes by reference to some of the themes in American policy since 1945 which are difficult to comprehend if policy is considered as nothing more than a direct response to external pressures. The general strategy of containment, as already discussed, constituted the overall plan, or 'idea' as Michael Donelan has called it.[1] It began with the Truman Doctrine of 1947, in which the grant of United States assistance to Greece and Turkey was extended to any other countries similarly threatened by subversion or potential aggression from communist sources. In subsequent years containment came to mean the erection of a 'wall' around the entire periphery of the Communist Bloc, with each member state receiving military guarantees, routine military aid and economic 'defence support' to enable it to maintain its independence. In conception this had much of the character of a conventional military alliance system. It appealed to the American taste for a scheme of world politics which stressed mutual co-operation and tidily organized international relationships. And in so far as Soviet policy under Stalin emphasized expansion by direct or indirect military methods, it was highly effective.

However, the Soviet challenge did not consist of a conventional military threat alone, even in the earliest phase of the Cold War

[1] For a detailed account of American policy after 1945 along lines similar to those adopted here, see M. D. Donelan, *The Ideas of American Foreign Policy*, London, Chapman and Hall, 1963.

and certainly not during the Khrushchev period of the fifties. Unjustifiably confident of the technological superiority of their own society, American experts underestimated the pace of Soviet advanced weapon development, and were taken by surprise first by Soviet development of an atomic bomb, then of a hydrogen bomb, and finally of the intercontinental ballistic missile. Even after the first of these shocks had been absorbed by American public opinion, the phenomenon which has been called 'the illusion of American omnipotence' helped to bring the Republican party to power in the 1952 presidential election on a platform which included the concept of 'liberation', never well defined, of countries within the Soviet Bloc. The concept was proved to be an empty one when overt resistance to the satellite regimes broke out in East Berlin in 1953, in Poland in 1956, and in Hungary in 1956. The uprisings were suppressed without any hint of public American intervention, but the vain promise of 'roll-back' remains as testimony to the impatient reluctance with which the United States came to terms with the need to live in frustrated coexistence with the Russian sphere of influence which it found so objectionable.

The military preoccupation of American policy

Even though liberation became a dead letter, the pattern of thought which gave rise to it remained a prominent feature of American policy throughout the height of the Cold War, in the 1950s, and continued in somewhat muted form in the rather different international situation of the 1960s. During the Eisenhower Administration it could be found in the rigid diplomatic posture adopted for high-level dealings with the Soviet Union. In spite of the slight movement towards *détente* in Soviet policy in the middle of the decade, indicated by the Austrian State Treaty and the 'Spirit of Geneva' after the 1955 summit conference, this became the era of the tough line in American foreign policy. Reports of the speeches of John Foster Dulles were redolent with grand slogans expressing the rigidity of the new United States attitude: 'negotiation from strength', 'massive retaliation', and the like.

Perhaps the clearest example of the Dulles spirit was 'brinkmanship', a concept invented by him but so christened by the journalists who found that reporting his declarations made vivid copy. In effect brinkmanship meant that the United States drew a distinct line around the border of the Communist Bloc. If the Soviet Union or China should cross that line in any act regarded by the United States as aggressive, then the response would not be local, but strategic; not limited, but massive, and directed at Soviet cities. The risks inherent in the brinkmanship concept have been widely emphasized, but the fact remains that no territory changed sides across Cold War lines of demarcation during the massive retaliation period, despite a number of crises. Even West Berlin remained, somewhat incredibly, in Western hands.

In the 1960s, in explicit recognition of the dangers of massive retaliation now that the Soviet Union could counteract American strategic power with a nuclear striking force of its own, the United States returned to a philosophy of military strategy which at least began with a rung of conventional warfare on the ladder of escalation. However, it then found itself once again engaged, in Vietnam, in a ground war in Asia on a scale not paralleled since the Korean struggle of 1950-3. Meanwhile, on the upper rungs of the escalation ladder, the United States built up a military establishment of unprecedented scale and power. The acquisition of second-strike nuclear capability meant that the arms race of the 1950s with the Soviet Union was temporarily slowed during the following decade, and for several years after the Cuban crisis of 1962 a *détente* began to emerge between America and Russia, marked especially by the Partial Nuclear Test-Ban Treaty of 1963. But by 1967 the emergence of a defence system against modern nuclear attack, in the form of anti-ballistic missiles, meant that a new and vastly enlarged phase of the arms race appeared to be imminent. It did not seem likely, in the light of the previous American conviction of the need for overwhelming military strength to form a backdrop to its diplomacy, that the expensive temptation to develop this 'ABM' system would be ignored.

Relations with Europe

The preoccupation of American policy-makers with mechanistic solutions to international problems, in line with the traditionally direct and emphatic problem-solving approach of the community to its difficulties, was applied with considerably less success to the delicate task of managing United States relations with the communities of Western Europe. In the aftermath of the Second World War the object of policy was both simple and widely agreed: to rebuild the economies and thus the defensive capacity of the European Powers in order to enable them to carry a larger share of the burden of deterring a possible Soviet attack. Within the NATO and Marshall Plan frameworks, the encouragement of co-operation and of a co-ordinated policy towards the Soviet Union achieved a significant degree of success. But during the fifties a wide range of issues began to generate friction. American policy on colonial issues was always and necessarily ambivalent, reflecting on the one hand the long tradition of anti-colonial feeling and on the other the importance of maintaining alliance ties with the colonialist but anti-communist Powers of the Old World. American pressure for European economic integration under British political leadership was resented on the continent, especially after the United States demonstrated, at the Nassau Conference of 1962, what Gaullist France believed to be a clear indication of favoured treatment for Britain in defence arrangements.

The most serious instances of American mismanagement of alliance relationships, however, occurred in the two related fields of military–political relationships within NATO and the dispersion of nuclear weapons. During the initial decade of operation of the North Atlantic Treaty there were frequent signposts towards the roadblocks which were to appear ahead. Few alliances run altogether smoothly in the varying climates of international politics, and while there is no space here to consider the numerous frictions of the NATO story in detail, it is evident that a number of attempts to 'fix' the workings of NATO in a neat, pre-designed pattern led to political dissension and finally, in 1966, to French withdrawal from the integrated NATO structure.

The most significant early signpost was the EDC affair. As soon as NATO was formed it seemed essential to the United States that it should incorporate the potential strength of Germany. A scheme for alleviating anxieties about the dangers which many Frenchmen thought to be inherent in any newly rearmed Germany was then devised, called the European Defence Community. After tortuous negotiations, French opposition finally killed the project despite threats of an 'agonizing reappraisal' of American relations with Europe, voiced by Secretary Dulles. Yet, nearly a decade later, when Democrats had replaced Republicans in power in Washington and a great deal of water had flowed beneath the bridge of Atlantic co-operation, a new scheme was proposed by the United States, similar in spirit and doomed to meet a similar fate in another period of worsened American–European relations. This project was known as the Multilateral Force, or MLF, and in its essence was designed to forestall any potential inclination of Germany to acquire nuclear weapons of its own by giving it and other NATO members the form, if not the substance, of control over a part of the NATO nuclear resources. Like the EDC negotiations the project collapsed, and official attention in Washington turned away from the organization charts of NATO command and control to the wider issues of nuclear dispersion.

In the mood of *détente* which came about between the United States and the Soviet Union in the mid-sixties the time seemed opportune to devise some worldwide method to enable the two super-Powers to slow down the nuclear arms race, and thus prevent the uncertainties of conducting international affairs in a future world of many nuclear states. By 1967 America and Russia were able to announce together, in the forum of the standing United Nations 18-Member Disarmament Conference at Geneva, that they had devised the text of a 'non-proliferation' treaty. This agreement would, in very general terms, prevent the acquisition of nuclear weapons by any additional Powers, and although the details of the treaty were not immediately announced it seemed to be the intention of the two super-Powers that the only concession they, as nuclear 'haves', would make to the 'have-nots' was the implication that world stability would be maintained by a continuing joint hegemony of America and Russia.

This proposal stood squarely in the spirit of efficient crisis management, far-sighted military planning and a general 'engineering' approach to international problems that Defence Secretary McNamara had brought to American policy throughout the decade. But there were immediate objections on numerous technical and diplomatic grounds. The central difficulty, as the Italians, on behalf of Europe, and the Indians, on behalf of the neutralist countries, were quick to point out, was that the proposed treaty assumed a continuing American–Soviet hegemony, and furthermore was not even realistic in view of the rapid rise of Chinese nuclear power and the likely development of nuclear weapons by small countries, such as those of the Middle East, in the near future. Once again, it seemed, the struggle of the Washington policymakers to bring a pattern of coherent, planned relationships based on law to international politics was about to be frustrated by the lack of a sure diplomatic touch on the part of those whose task it was to soothe the prickly sensibilities of sovereign states.

Relations with the Third World

The deep American yearning for decisive solutions to the problems of world order during the Cold War period was expressed in even more unfortunate fashion in its relations with the countries of Africa, Asia and South America. The long-standing posture of anti-colonialism which ought to have stood to the credit of American policy was doubly compromised: on the one hand, by the requirements of a realistic priority for relations with the colonial states of Europe, and on the other, by the general conservatism of American political attitudes. Thus the United States, after its early support for Indian and Indonesian independence, its energetic sponsorship of the small Powers within the United Nations, its continuing attempts to cultivate good relations with the new leaders of Africa and Asia, and its massive aid programme, nevertheless found itself losing credit in the Third World as the 1950s moved on.

In the United Nations the United States was so much the dominant force during the first decade of the Organization's history that it managed to gain official sanction of the world body for what was essentially a balance-of-power operation in the Korean War, and on most other issues it maintained an automatic voting majority for its favoured policies down to 1959, when the narrow voting on the British–American landings in Jordan and Lebanon finally marked the arrival of an independent Afro–Asian Bloc. But in the later phases of the period it has become apparent that successes gained in instances like American opposition to the British–French Suez landings of 1956, American efforts to 'keep the Cold War out of the Congo' in the 1960s, American support for a 1963 General Assembly resolution boycotting the sale of arms to South Africa, and the like, were more than outweighed by other factors.

Underlying the difficulties of the United States in its dealings with the Third World during the Cold War period was the persistent tendency of American leaders to think in terms of tidy, formal methods of establishing relations with the developing countries. The moralistic impatience of the Republican administration with the studied neutralism of men like Nehru, Tito, Nasser, Nkrumah and Sukarno has already been discussed. The attempt of the United States to apply an 'us' versus 'them' pattern of military alliances to regions like the Middle East and Southeast Asia has also been considered. And even after a more liberally inclined group came to power in Washington under Kennedy in 1961, the abortive Bay of Pigs invasion of Cuba, the stepping-up of the arms race with the Soviet Union, and the increasing revelations of the subversive activities of the Central Intelligence Agency were typical of the incidents which combined to weaken the prestige of the United States among the communities of the world's underprivileged. In the more conservative administration of President Johnson, the challenge to American policy was again seen in Washington as a 'competition' for the 'allegiance' of the Third

World countries, which was itself not a formulation likely to endear the Americans to the hearts or minds even of the new military leaders of Africa and Asia.

Policy towards China

Perhaps the most revealing topic of all for the student of American attitudes is policy towards China. The United States became involved with the giant of Asia as early as the nineteenth century, when its profound isolation from European affairs was balanced to some degree by an awakening interest in the Far East. By the close of the Second World War the United States had developed a fairly strong cultural and paternal image of Chinese civilization, based partly on trade, partly on American support for the Nationalist regime against the Japanese invaders during the war, and partly on the considerable impact of American missionary activities on both countries. The success of Mao Tse-tung in leading the Communist Party to victory over all mainland China in 1949 came as a profound shock to American public opinion, and even to policy-making circles in Washington itself. Throughout the 1950s there was even a continuing tendency on the part of government spokesmen to regard the communist regime in Peking as temporary, something which would in due course be removed by Nationalist forces returning from Taiwan to take the lead in a spontaneous national uprising against the hated communist dictatorship.

It was this illusion which helped to foster a remarkable volume of support for the rigid United States policy of non-recognition, isolation, exclusion from the United Nations, boycott, and generalized hostility towards the new rulers of China. The communist victory came at a time when a number of factors combined in American politics to create a wave of anti-'red Chinese' feeling which made it impossible in the two decades which followed for American leaders to consider any significant modification of the United States stance, whatever the objective requirements of the international situation might indicate to be desirable. Perhaps the least important of these factors, although it has received a great

65

deal of publicity, was the 'China Lobby' operated by representatives of the Nationalist regime in Washington circles. The real importance of the China lobby was that it operated against a negligible opposition; there was no strong voice in Washington in the late forties and early fifties to give any authority to the view, held by some other countries including Britain, that the best means of living in the future with the reawakened dragon of China might be to cultivate good relations with it. The reason for this atmosphere was the McCarthyist climate of the period. The Republicans were making political capital at the time out of what some called the Democratic 'sellout' to the Soviet Union at the Yalta Conference of 1945, an effort to negotiate in co-operative fashion with Stalin which was held to be a substantial cause of the subsequent weak western position in Europe and especially in Berlin. In order to counter this charge, the State Department and the Democrats were forced in their turn to adopt a frozen, anti-communist line on China. Once the basic position had been created, the general tendency of the United States to stand by its commitments and maintain a consistent attitude meant that policy towards Peking was to a considerable extent determined by the moral, legal and political stake in the relationship between Washington and the much less significant regime of Chiang Kai-shek at Taipeh. The legacy of this remarkable domestic input into United States foreign policy was carried on until at least the late 1960s.

American policy formulation

It was in relations with China, as well as with the rest of Asia, that the ponderous machinery for devising and executing American foreign policy was at its least effective. This subject is too large to be considered here in detail, but its basic principles can be outlined. The enormous Washington bureaucracy concerned with foreign policy is a relatively recent development. The Constitution, which is fairly described as an eighteenth-century document still forming the basis for a twentieth-century government, paid little attention to the conduct of foreign relations since most of the overseas activities now undertaken by the United States were not only unforeseen, but not desired, by the Founding Fathers. The major constitutional provision was true to their overall guiding principle that tyranny should be prevented by a separation of powers. It provided that while the Congress should have overall responsibility for laying down guidelines for policy, declaring war, authorizing funds and supervising the activities of the executive branch generally, the President and the administrative agencies under his control should be charged with executing policy. The President and the Congress were to be elected separately by different constituencies, and in the case of the Senate for different periods of office.

What has in fact happened under this system is that the executive and congressional branches of the government, each aware that policy cannot be made without the co-operation of the other, compete and co-operate constantly, with compromise, delay and unevenness of policy measures being typical products of the system. Under some conditions, however, the system does work with great efficiency, the Cuban crisis of 1962 being a case in point. The most effective sections of the government are those which, like the Defence Department, expend large sums within the domestic economy, or like the Central Intelligence Agency are required by the nature of their work to maintain a high degree of secrecy. These factors bring them a degree of immunity from congressional opposition and public examination. The Congress is relatively more sensitive to the vagaries of public opinion than the legislative bodies of other countries such as Britain, and in many ways is made unrepresentative by its own conservative rules of procedure as well as by the federal structure. The net effect of the whole system is that policies which emerge successfully from the formulation process tend to be those which can promise a tangible reward within a fairly short period; which can be easily related to the national interest of the United States, narrowly and sometimes crudely defined; and which can be efficiently costed, measured and controlled. In short, those policies with a military emphasis tend to be favoured, while others, such as the advocacy of the State Department for a different attitude towards Afro–Asia, tend to fail for want of a sufficient volume of support within the intricate network of policy-making. There is no shortage, in Washington, of officials who are fully aware of the shortcomings of American policy, as outlined in this essay and indeed perhaps going far deeper than an academic observer may appreciate. But the point being made here is that would-be root-and-branch reformers are helpless to alter the nature of a governmental system which reflects the political culture of the country which it is designed to manage. It is through the hierarchy of its own governmental institutions that the national attitudes of the American community are transmitted to the outside world, to give to American policy the national stamp which distinguishes it so clearly from the kinds of policies which other nations might adopt, when faced with the same international problems and challenges.

BIBLIOGRAPHY

ALMOND, GABRIEL A. *The American People and Foreign Policy*. New York: Frederick A. Praeger, 1967. (Paperback ed.: Praeger.)

BELL, CORAL. *Negotiation from Strength*. New York: Alfred A. Knopf, 1963.

COUNCIL ON FOREIGN RELATIONS. *The United States in World Affairs*. New York: Harper & Row, published annually.

CRABB, CECIL V., Jr. *American Foreign Policy in the Nuclear Age*. 2d ed. New York: Harper & Row, 1965.

DULLES, FOSTER R. *America's Rise to World Power, 1898–1954*. New York: Harper & Row, 1955. (Paperback ed.: Harper & Row.)

RESTON, JAMES. *The Artillery of the Press: Its Influence on American Foreign Policy*. New York: Harper & Row, 1967.

SAPIN, BURTON M. *The Making of United States Foreign Policy*. Washington, D.C.: The Brookings Institution, 1966. (Paperback ed.: Praeger.)

SPANIER, JOHN W. *American Foreign Policy Since World War II*. 2d rev. ed. New York: Frederick A. Praeger, 1965. (Paperback ed.: Praeger.)

3·THE FOREIGN POLICY OF THE SOVIET UNION

Geoffrey Stern

More than fifty years after the Revolution which swept the Bolsheviks into power in Russia, political analysts are still divided on the question of the intentions and motivations of Soviet foreign policy. Part of the debate stems from political bias. At one extreme there are the 'cold warriors' who detect in Soviet foreign policy a combination of ideological expansionism and traditional Russian imperialism in a relentless quest for 'world domination'. At the other extreme are the 'apologists' who see the Soviet Union as a victim of circumstance and explain virtually every reprehensible act as a response to a largely hostile environment.

But disagreements in accounting for the foreign policy of the Soviet Union flow not only from political partiality but also from differences in study methods. There is the highly lucrative, but still somewhat speculative, school of Kremlinology which sees the main determinant of Soviet foreign policy as the outcome of the struggle between conflicting personalities, factions, and functional groups, such as the Party, the state bureaucracy, the army and the police. At a rather more esoteric level there is the socio-cultural school, which looks primarily to the peculiarities of the collective mentality of the Russian people, that is, their habits of thinking as expressed in their social institutions, customs and traditions. More academically 'respectable' than both is the school of Geopolitics which finds the key to Soviet foreign political behaviour in the interplay of Russian domestic political circumstance with the facts of her external environment.

THE FOREIGN POLICY OF THE SOVIET UNION

'Ideology' versus 'National Interest'

The most pertinent controversy relating to Soviet foreign policy is that between those who emphasize 'Realpolitik' and those who look to 'ideology' as the major determinant. The former see the Russian state as pursuing the time-honoured policies of all states—the pursuit of what is loosely termed 'power' and 'national interest'; the latter relate Marxism–Leninism to Soviet foreign political purposes and hence see something novel about Soviet aims and methods. Some analysts have sought to resolve the 'ideology' versus 'Realpolitik' controversy by establishing that in Soviet foreign policy the two are inextricably bound up. Such a conclusion seems plausible enough. Yet it is of limited value where there is no exploration of the meaning of 'ideology' and 'interest' or the nature of the relationship between the two.

'National interests', as has been pointed out in Chapter 1, are those broad objectives which in a sense all foreign policy is designed to secure. They generally include the preservation of the nation's way of life, the projection on to the international scene of its values and aspirations, and the enhancement of its welfare. They embrace, too, the physical integrity of the state, through which these objectives are secured, and its relative freedom from outside interference. In Russia they have been understood as including, in addition, security of tenure for the holders of political power (though this is not peculiar to Russia). Yet, as has been remarked, the ordering and interpretation of these interests in particular situations are matters for argument. And the debate itself will generally be influenced by ideology–ideology being understood in this context to mean 'a cluster of inter-related ideas relating to the social order and its betterment'. National interests, that is, are usually perceived and evaluated in terms of ideology, official or otherwise.

It is not unreasonable to assume, therefore, that those responsible for the foreign policy of the Soviet Union, nurtured in the works of Marx, Engels and Lenin, act within a framework of Marxist–Leninist ideas, even if these have to be re-interpreted in accordance with events. Although, that is, the view of the universe held by a Communist in 1967 may be somewhat different from that of a

Bolshevik in 1917, there remains a characteristically Marxist–Leninist approach to world problems. The notion, for example, that the Russian Revolution was not an isolated event, that it was the prelude to the eventual collapse of the European-orientated state system and the establishment of a society of a new type persists among Marxist thinkers today. And the idea that it requires a Party of the Leninist type–centralized and disciplined–'correctly' to appreciate and channel the forces to bring about the anticipated global transformation is still widely held in the Soviet Union.

It is this kind of approach, then, which shapes the perceptions and expectations of Soviet foreign policy-makers. But because these policy-makers must act within a given geographical and strategic context and have to adjust commitments to capabilities, they have had to employ some of the foreign political techniques of their predecessors. Because, too, they are Russians who have been nurtured in a domestic and international environment in which pre-revolutionary ideas persist, their 'cluster of interrelated ideas relating to the social order and its betterment' bears also a characteristically Russian stamp. In any case, the leaders have to take account of the patriotic susceptibilities and aspirations of their people if they are to win respect. It is, however, one of the ironies of history that nationalism has received its highest expression in a regime dedicated to 'proletarian internationalism': witness Stalin's patriotic appeals during the Second World War or, indeed, some of the claims and counter-claims in the Sino–Soviet dispute.

Thus, in Russia, as elsewhere, experience is viewed in the light of ideological preconceptions, but these preconceptions are themselves modified by experience. Attitudes in respect of both domestic and foreign policy, therefore, are shaped by the vicissitudes of domestic politics, pressures and personalities, by technological developments, and by the actions and reactions of other states.

But modifications of Soviet ideological attitudes are not, however, always apparent to the observer. This is because the Communist Party's claim to control Russia's destiny depends upon its posture as the unchallengeable interpreter of Marxism–Leninism which in turn rests on the eternal validity of the doctrine. Accordingly, the Party leaders are often reluctant to admit the need for doctrinal revisions, for fear of ultimately undermining the basis of the Party's authority. Hence, they will tend to cling in their public utterances to the language of the Marxist–Leninist texts even when their thinking has advanced beyond them.

Thus, Soviet ideology is an amalgam of Marxist–Leninist thought and traditional Russian attitudes modified by the realities of domestic and international political life. Marxism–Leninism itself provides, firstly, the transcendental objectives of Soviet foreign policy and, in particular, the apocalyptic vision of a Communist world. True, the notion of world revolution may have little immediate relevance to foreign policy, but the ultimate if protracted transformation of the world remains a foreign political consideration. Secondly, it provides the tactics for the furtherance of those objectives, including the formation of Communist Parties and Front organizations. Thirdly, it offers a framework of analysis for the diagnosis and prognosis of social and international forces. The dialectical view of the universe, for example, has predisposed Soviet leaders to expect conflict with an 'inevitably' antagonistic world, thereby prolonging the Soviet Union's understandable dislike of the Powers which intervened, albeit half-heartedly, to crush the regime in its early years. Fourthly, it provides the symbolic language necessary for binding to the Soviet regime adherents of Marxist–Leninist ideology, both in Russia and throughout the world. And it confers legitimacy on the Communist Party's rule and any extension of Soviet power.

But, as we observed earlier, to say that Marxist–Leninist doctrine influences Soviet foreign policy is not to deny a degree of continuity in Russia's policies and attitudes. Indeed, although Marxism has been added to the conceptual framework of the Russian policy-makers, it has, like the adoption by a ruler of Kievan Russia of Byzantine Christianity nearly a thousand years ago, 'passed through the crucible of Russian national tradition and has been remoulded by it'.[1] Since, therefore, post-revolutionary Russia has exemplified some of the foreign policy characteristics of the previous regime, it seems appropriate to examine some aspects of the Czarist legacy.

The Czarist legacy

Undoubtedly the foremost characteristic of pre-revolutionary Russia was its propensity to expand territorially in almost every direction. At the end of the fifteenth century Moscow, having thrown off the Mongol yoke, was in process of consolidating into a centralized, Russian state a number of East Slavic principalities which had similarly suffered two centuries of domination by the Golden Horde. But by 1914 Russia had become the world's largest contiguous inter-continental empire, embracing more than half the land mass both of Europe and of Asia. And only fifty years before the Russian empire had also extended to the North American continent to include Alaska. Well over a hundred ethnic and linguistic groups had been absorbed in this empire of more than 8,500,000 square miles. And even today, only just over half of the Soviet population is of Great Russian stock.

Yet for all its size, and partly because of it, Russia was a country with an acute security problem. There was always the danger of internal anarchy when one or more of Russia's ethnic minorities rose in revolt as, for example, the Poles in 1830 and again in 1863. In addition, Russia's economic weakness, together with her possession of the world's longest and most exposed frontiers to the East, West and South, made her especially vulnerable to attack.

For two centuries after the Mongols had been driven out, the Crimean Tartars under the protection of the Ottoman Empire continued their harassments in the South. And until the late eighteenth century the Russians were continually having to defend themselves against well-organized attacks from their Swedish, Polish and German neighbours. At the beginning of the nineteenth

[1] E. H. Carr, 'The Bolshevik Revolution in Perspective—I', *The Listener*, 21 April 1955.

century the French invader came within the gates of Moscow, and in 1856 Russia suffered a defeat in the Crimea at the hands of a combined Anglo–French–Turkish force. There was the disastrous confrontation with Japan in 1904–5, and in the First World War the Germans made the first of two major incursions into Russia in the twentieth century. As a result, the Russia which emerged in ruins at the end of the First World War was considerably smaller than the Russia of 1900.

Related to the problem of security was the question of Russia's economic backwardness. Because of the ravages of war and her remoteness from the technological and ideological developments of Western Europe, Czarist Russia had remained, despite her wealth of raw materials and minerals, economically inferior to the West.

Russia had responded to her situation internally by centralizing the administration, creating an extensive network of bureaucrats, policemen and censors. Externally she had sought to absorb or truncate her neighbours, weak and strong alike, and extended protection to private traders and adventurers operating beyond Russia's frontiers, especially in Asia. She had been attracted by the prospect of warm-water ports to facilitate trade, and struggled for control of the Baltic through which she could engage in trade with the lucrative markets of North and Western Europe. Later Russia extended her interests to the Black Sea, the Persian Gulf and the Pacific Ocean. But of course such activities merely generated apprehension among Russia's neighbours, sowing the seeds of further instability on her frontiers. However, when faced by determined opposition in any one theatre of operations, Russia tended to switch her attention to another. When baulked in South-East Europe, as in the Crimean War and later at the Congress of Berlin in 1878, her gaze would shift to the Far East or Central Asia. When Russia's Eastern adventures ended in defeat at the hands of the Japanese in 1905, Russian interests turned once again to the Balkans.

But from this concern for her security and the deep conscious-ness of her backwardness in relation to her Western neighbours arose an ambivalence in Russia's attitude to the West which persists to some degree. On the one hand, there was a grudging admiration for the technological successes of Western Europe and for some of the institutions which made possible these developments. On the other hand, there was the resentment at and distrust of the West at whose hands Russia had suffered so many bloody humiliations. Such an attitude explains to some extent the restrictions on travel to the West as early as the seventeenth century and the suspicion attached to Western voyagers to Russia.

This partial rejection of Western culture and values was reinforced by Russia's Eastern Orthodox tradition and by a tendency among some of her influential churchmen and intellectuals to regard Russia as the bearer of a civilization uniquely endowed with a capacity to uplift and ennoble mankind. This 'messianistic' idea had received its most famous expression in the writings of a sixteenth-century monk, Philotheus of Pskov, who saw Moscow as the 'Third Rome'—the final repository of religious truth, Rome and Byzantium having fallen prey to apostasy and error. It followed that Moscow was under an obligation to carry the truth to the unenlightened and assume responsibility for Orthodox Christians. If the 'Third Rome' concept had comparatively little effect on the small 'Westernised' élite which surrounded the Court of Peter the Great and his successors, the same cannot be said of Slavophilism and Pan-Slavism, the nineteenth-century expressions of the 'messianistic' idea.

For the Slavophiles, Russia's mission lay in carrying the benefits of her culture and faith to the West, helping Western Europe to develop a new civilization in which the best of their own and that of Russia would be combined. For the Pan-Slavists who believed that Russian and Western institutions were incompatible since God had created separate, unchanging national types, Russia's duty lay in emancipating, if necessary by force, the Slavs from the Ottoman Empire and from Western Europe, and in creating a Slavic federation under Russian control.

Thus far, 'messianism' had been more a state of mind than a

policy, but by the 1870s the Asiatic Department of the Russian Foreign Office was giving financial backing to Serb, Croat and Slovenian nationalists, helping to foment revolutionary upheavals in the Balkans and filling the diplomatic posts of the Near and Middle East with dedicated Pan-Slavists. The analogy with more recent Russian practice is too obvious to require further elaboration.

But Russia's defeat in the East by Japan in 1905 and in the West by Germany in the First World War had shaken faith in the old 'messianism'. However, the Russia of 1917, humiliated, politically decadent, and industrially retarded was receptive to a new 'messianism', this time from the West—Marxism, with its international implications.

Foreign policy repudiated

For some four years after the revolution of November 1917 the Russians tried to break with traditional ambitions and to repudiate the central objective of statecraft, the pursuit of the national interest. This is not to say that the Bolsheviks were uninterested in the well-being of the citizens of the former Russian Empire, but that they were more concerned with furthering the revolution throughout Europe, of which they believed their own revolution to be but a part. There was little need for foreign policy since foreign policy was conducted between states and these were doomed soon to disappear. To foster this revolutionary transformation the Soviet leaders set aside several million roubles and in 1919 established the Third International, or Comintern, with its headquarters in Moscow, to co-ordinate revolutionary activity and create throughout the world disciplined Communist parties on the Leninist model.

Moreover, the new leaders of Russia refused to accept the established modes of inter-state intercourse. They rejected international law as an instrument by which European bourgeois governments had dominated the rest of the world, and repudiated the international agreements of their predecessors, including the debts and liabilities incurred. Likewise, they had no use for the

League of Nations. And they revived the French revolutionary technique of appealing to peoples over the heads of their governments. For example, on the day after the Bolsheviks took power Lenin, appealing to the belligerent governments to conclude a 'peace without annexations', called upon the peoples of the world to overthrow their rulers. As if to demonstrate the iniquities of the old diplomatic system, the revolutionaries abolished diplomatic rank, threw open the Foreign Office archives, and published the secret treaties of the war years. At Brest-Litovsk in March 1918, when the Russian delegation arrived to conclude a peace treaty with Germany, they exemplified another aspect of this approach by distributing political literature from the train windows to the waiting German officials.

None the less, even during this four-year period, the new Russian rulers could not altogether dispense with the traditional aims and methods of diplomacy. The new Soviet Republic had to be protected, if only because it was the base from which revolutionary activity had to be co-ordinated. Hence they struggled to defend the new state against intervention and called upon Russian patriotism in helping to defeat the invader. They undertook, moreover, to conduct a foreign policy of sorts—if only as a holding operation until Germany and the rest of Europe had sustained a successful revolution. They made economic and political agreements with a number of countries, but always on the assumption that these were merely of temporary validity. As Lenin said, in March 1919:

> We live not only in a state, but in a system of states, and the existence of the Soviet Republic side by side with the imperialist states for a prolonged period of time is unthinkable. In the meantime a series of frightful collisions will occur.

Such then was the Leninist conception of 'co-existence' between the Soviet Republic and the Capitalist world.

But under the impacts of events Lenin modified his views. By 1921 the Soviet Republic had survived its early tribulations and was no longer in a state of siege. Save for the Japanese (who remained in Sakhalin until 1925) the interventionists had gone, and the blockade of Russia had been lifted. Moreover, Russia's retreat from Socialism implied in Lenin's New Economic Policy had rendered her more acceptable internationally. At the same time, however, the revolutionary tide which had flowed towards the end of the war and shortly after it seemed to be receding. Attempts to establish Soviet Republics in Hungary, Austria and various parts of Germany had failed, and the revolutionary impetus in the Middle East was exhausted. To meet the new situation Lenin at the Third Congress of the Comintern in June 1921 advocated adjustments in the policies both of the Soviet Union and of the Comintern. The new approach Stalin was later to describe as building 'Socialism in One Country', that is, the creation of a strong industrialized Soviet state in a non-Socialist world.

That Trotsky could say, in reference to the revolution, 'We used to say, in 1919, "it is a question of months". And now we say "it is a question of years"' indicates that the messianic vision had not faded altogether. Russia would still strive to discredit and weaken all governments opposed to communism and provide support for revolutionaries throughout the world. But in fact as the prospect of world revolution receded still farther the Soviet state came to undertake a foreign policy that was less unconventional than that in the first four years of Bolshevik rule–a policy which in seeking to protect Russia's security, expand her sphere of influence, and establish and retain her status as a great Power was, in some respect, familiar. For like other major Powers, Russia came to pursue balance of power tactics–even, indeed, to the extent of co-operating with virulent opponents of her ideology.

Decision-making

Analysis of the objectives, methods and style of any foreign policy must focus on the decision-making process. This, never an easy task, is made more complicated in the case of a country like the Soviet Union where Foreign Office archives are inaccessible and neither Parliament, press nor public can interpellate leading officials. The few memoirs or biographies which are published in the Soviet Union generally provide little insight into the question. In any case, much valuable information has been buried along with those who were in a position to know. Nonetheless, certain tentative conclusions can be drawn on the basis of (a) records relating to decisions in the Leninist period, when the Russian leaders were somewhat less secretive about them than they are now; (b) information supplied by defectors like Trotsky and Svetlana Stalin, or knowledgeable 'deviationists' like Tito, Nagy, Mao Tse-tung and the supporters of Dubcek in Czechoslovakia; (c) information 'leaked' in the course of in-fighting between Soviet leaders. For example, Khrushchev's 'secret' speech at the 20th Congress of the CPSU in 1956 revealed much about Stalin's methods of arriving at policy decisions. (d) 'intelligence' information from such sources as Colonel Penkovsky and Greville Wynne; (e) accounts by foreign statesmen such as Winston Churchill, James Byrnes and Milovan Djilas, who had had access to leading Soviet officials. And, of course, shrewd observers may also be able to infer something from shifts in the Soviet hierarchy and the purges that generally follow, and from changes in political direction and style.

Since foreign policy making is an aspect of policy making in general, it seems appropriate to investigate what is known of that process in the USSR. But whenever one analyses policy making, it is always important to distinguish theory from practice. In the USSR such a distinction is particularly important since the gap between the two is especially wide.

The powers of the government – in theory and practice

Government power is diffused, political authority deriving in the first instance from the local soviets, that is, rural or town councils, and flowing upward to district, province, republic and finally all-union level. Each body is elected directly by the people and once every four years every Soviet citizen over eighteen is entitled to vote for one of the 750 candidates to the Soviet of Nationalities which together with the 767-member Soviet of the Union constitutes the Supreme Soviet. The Supreme Soviet is, according to the

Constitution, 'the highest organ of state authority'. Responsible and accountable to it are commissions to advise on various aspects of its legislative work, and such organs as (1) the Praesidium of the Supreme Soviet, consisting of 33 members and headed by a chairman who is the President of the Soviet Union–at present Podgorny. Empowered to act for the Supreme Soviet when that body is not in session, it can ratify and denounce treaties, recall diplomats, order mobilization and proclaim a state of war. It also elects (2) the Council of Ministers–the executive branch of government–consisting of about 85 ministers whose chairman is the Prime Minister, at present Kosygin. He, together with the Foreign Minister and several Deputy Prime Ministers, forms an inner cabinet to deal with important matters, including foreign policy. Like every other government body, this works under the broad direction of the Communist Party.

Such is the theory, but the practice is rather different. Firstly, although the local soviets do have some control over the running of local affairs, power does not, in fact, flow upwards. In general, the lower administrative bodies function within the framework of instructions received from higher organs. Secondly, the vote is of little significance since there is always only one listed candidate–in effect the Party nominee, even if not a Party member. The voter may, indeed, register a negative vote by crossing out the name on the ballot form, but this achieves little and comparatively few people risk it. Thirdly, the Supreme Soviet has little real power. It meets generally twice a year for less than a week, and at each session members merely listen to and approve ministerial reports, enact the proposed legislation and endorse the pre-selected names for the Praesidium. 'Debates' and 'discussions' referred to in Soviet literature consist largely of speeches delivered by carefully selected deputies emphasizing the 'correctness' of the government's policy. The role of such bodies as the commission on foreign affairs is at present unclear, but there is little evidence to suggest that they are of more than marginal importance. And, fourthly, the leading government organs are guided, not by the Party as such, but by the central organs of the Party.

The powers of the Party—in theory and practice

In theory the Party, now thirteen million strong, is organized on the Leninist principle of 'democratic centralism' according to which the 'centralist' notion that the decisions of the higher Party apparatus are binding on all members is tempered by 'democracy'. All functionaries are elected, from the lowest to the highest, and Party decisions are preceded by free discussion in which all members may have a voice. The main lines of Soviet political, economic and social development are agreed at the Party Congress, which nowadays meets every four years or so and is attended by some 5,000 delegates. The Congress elects a Central Committee of some 350 members and candidate members to implement Congress decisions, to form commissions on various aspects of policy, including foreign policy, and to meet in plenary session every so often to discuss the reports of these commissions. The Central Committee also elects a Politburo (called the Party Praesidium in the years from 1952 to 1966) of some 19 members to administer day-to-day affairs between plenum meetings and an eleven-man Secretariat, which draws up the agenda for the Politburo and has control over important political appointments.

In fact, however, the 'democratic' element is largely ignored. During Stalin's time there was little free discussion even in the higher Party echelons, and for the last forty years or so the leading functionaries have remained a sort of self-appointed governing bureaucracy. Members of the Politburo, for example, pre-select the Central Committee, partly according to the vicissitudes of power in the leadership and partly on the basis of special-interest groups whose leaders it may want to consult or bludgeon. Generally, members of the professional apparatus of the Party predominate in the Central Committee, but a considerable number come from the government bureaucracy and technocracy. The representation of other interest groups—the cultural intelligentsia, the army and secret police—is usually much smaller. The list of delegates for the Party Congress has generally to be approved by the Party leadership, who often vet the speeches for the occasion.

Even in Lenin's day the central organs were beginning to acquire more power than the Party Congress. By 1920, at the 9th Party Congress of the CPSU, Lenin was able to report that the 9-man Politburo, created the previous year to 'take decisions not permitting of delay', had decided all domestic and foreign problems of substance during the year. Moreover, the decision at the 10th Party Congress in March 1921 to prohibit 'fractionalism', that is, the organization of dissentient groups or factions, undermined the independent voice in Congress and Central Committee and further strengthened the role of the Politburo. By the time of Lenin's death in January 1924 the central organs between them controlled a Party apparatus that was to keep in check all professional and interest groups in the country. No social organization, not even the armed forces, would escape Party control. Close contact, however, with the interest groups enabled the Party leaders to keep abreast of their special concerns and at times to formulate policy with their interests and advice in mind.

The Decision-makers

(a) *Lenin*

Like many other early revolutionary leaders, Lenin combined the tasks of founder, leading ideologist and organizer of the Party with the country's chief administrative post. Nonetheless, while Lenin led the Party, its structure remained oligarchic rather than autocratic.[1] The freedom of discussion which the Central Committee had always enjoyed prior to a decision was for a while to continue after the 1917 revolution. But until 1922, when he suffered the first of his three strokes, Lenin played a persuasive role, threatening to resign if he did not get his way. The extent of his influence on foreign policy is described in an article written for *Izvestia* shortly after Lenin's death by Chicherin, the Foreign Commissar, and significantly called 'Lenin's Foreign Policy'.

Clearly Lenin was largely responsible for the underlying theoretical concepts of Soviet foreign policy as expounded in such

[1] See Robert Tucker's *The Soviet Political Mind.*

works as *Imperialism: the highest stage of capitalism* and *The National and Colonial Theses*. He gave the necessary theoretical basis for adjusting Soviet policy to a world in which the revolutionary tide had ebbed. This included the exploitation of 'contradictions' between Russia's enemies so as to prevent an effective anti-Soviet coalition, and the application of the 'dialectical' principle to her international posture. There was, for example, the dual policy of trying to do business with the very governments the Comintern was designed to destroy. Secondly, Lenin gave Soviet foreign policy its peculiar style, in particular its combination of revolutionary gestures such as the 'peace decree' with more conventional diplomatic procedures. Thirdly, he suggested and directed many of the practical arrangements of foreign policy. Chicherin speaks of him as supervising the details of negotiations with Estonia in 1919 and Finland in 1920, directing by telephone the peace talks with Poland at Riga in 1921, guiding Russia towards a rapprochement with Afghanistan and Persia and laying the groundwork for the Rapallo Treaty with Germany in 1922.

But however influential Lenin was, he did not make policy decisions without consultation, not did he stifle initiative in his subordinates. Indeed Chicherin, and his deputy (later successor), Litvinov, probably enjoyed more freedom in executing policy than does Gromyko today. The extent of their autonomy can be seen in a document dated 25 March 1920,[1] authorizing Litvinov 'to conclude all kinds of agreements and treaties with the inclusion of all conditions and guarantees considered necessary and acceptable to the Russian Republic' for the establishment of trade and diplomatic recognition. It was moreover left largely to Chicherin to create a diplomatic service and a Foreign Commissariat to collect and evaluate reports from diplomats and Party agents abroad, to prepare memoranda for the decision-makers and transmit their decisions to those in the field who were to implement them. Under Lenin, the Foreign Minister had not yet become a mere cipher of the leadership.

[1] *Leninskii Sbornik 34*, Moscow, 1942.

(b) *Stalin*

Stalin's struggle for supreme power in the aftermath of Lenin's death was to have far-reaching effects on foreign policy. He manipulated the notions of 'Socialism in One Country' and of 'peaceful co-existence' in such a way as to discredit left-wing opponents like Trotsky, Zinoviev and Kamenev. Similarly, it was partly for domestic reasons that for some eight years after 1927 there was an apparent intensification of Soviet antagonism towards the capitalist world. For in order to encourage the Russians to make the requisite sacrifices for his agricultural and industrialization programme and at the same time discredit those right-wingers like Bukharin who were critical of his plans, he had to raise the spectre of imminent attack from the 'imperialists', whilst maintaining the search for diplomatic contacts and potential allies. By the end of 1929, however, Stalin had already rendered politically impotent his main opponents in the Soviet Party and government apparatus and throughout the Comintern. Henceforth there were few internal constraints on the Soviet dictator's decision-making powers.

After 1930 the Party Congress became no more than a rubber stamp for Stalin's decisions. Meetings became increasingly rare, and the last discussion of any significance occurred at the 17th Congress in 1934, when Bukharin, though bereft of much of his former power, dared oppose Stalin's conception of Fascism. For Bukharin, Fascism was an especially menacing threat to the Soviet Union and not, as Stalin had supposed, a symptom of the collapse of capitalism. Naturally the Stalin line prevailed, but to ensure that there would be no opposition at the next Congress, he purged over half the delegates at the 17th Congress. According to Khrushchev, 1,108 of the 1,966 delegates were arrested for 'anti-revolutionary activities'[1] and by the time of the next Congress Bukharin had been executed.

The two further Congresses during Stalin's lifetime were important as sounding boards for shifts of line in foreign policy. At the 18th Congress in March 1939 Stalin put out feelers for a

[1] Text released by the U.S. State Department and published in English translation on 4 June 1956.

rapprochement with Germany; at the 19th Congress, which did not meet until 1952, Stalin hinted at a moderation of the Soviet Union's militant posture in Europe, the Middle East and Asia.

Like the Congress, the Central Committee had by 1934 virtually lost all power to discuss and criticize policy. Here, too, Stalin ensured acquiescence in his decisions by eliminating any who had merely expressed misgivings or were suspected of complacency or apathy. According to Khrushchev, of the 139 members of the Central Committee elected by the 17th Congress in 1934, no fewer than 98 were shot. One body of the Central Committee, however, played an important role during the latter part of the Stalinist period—the so-called Special Sector. According to Captain M. Ruslanov, a Russian emigré, 'Through the Special Sector, Stalin directed the foreign Communist parties, received reports on the work of military and political services abroad, gave directions to ambassadors, guided the fifth columns and issued instructions to them such as those on the assassination of Trotsky, the kidnapping of General Kutepov, atomic espionage and so on. . . . Foreign policy was made in the Kremlin by Stalin and transmitted downwards through the Special Sector.'[1]

The Politburo, too, declined in importance and, as Alexander Barmine, another defector, makes clear, had become a mere advisory channel by the early 1930s. 'A thin appearance of collective work is still kept up at Politburo meetings. Stalin does not "command"; he merely "suggests" or "proposes". The fiction of voting is retained. But the vote never fails to uphold his "suggestions". The decision is signed by all ten members of the Politburo with Stalin's signature among the rest. Yet everyone knows that there is only one boss.'[2]

Sometimes the Politburo would be by-passed altogether while Stalin made policy single-handedly, as he did, according to Khrushchev, in the decision to oust Yugoslavia from the Cominform in 1948. There was, however, a small Politburo committee to supervise the work of the foreign commissariat, consisting in the

---

[1] Voskhozhdena Malenkova in *Sotsialisticheskii Vestnik*, Nos. 7–8 (July–August 1953). [2] *One Who Survived*, New York, 1945, p. 213.

later 1930s of Stalin's three closest aides, Molotov as chairman, Mikoyan in charge of foreign trade and Zhdanov in charge of Comintern affairs.[1] During the Second World War this committee on foreign affairs was enlarged, but the Politburo itself fell into decay until 1952 when it was reconstituted as an enlarged Praesidium with a small but powerful inner bureau.

But even if the Party were under control, Stalin's need to bolster the military establishment during the war and the state machine after it in the task of reconstruction, threatened to dilute Stalin's institutional supremacy. In the post-war period, therefore, he demoted or destroyed some of the leading figures in the army and the administration, just as in the '30s he had eliminated those military and security police chiefs who might have posed a threat to his supreme authority.

But if Stalin concentrated the power of decision-making into his own hands, he was not entirely deaf to expert opinion. Indeed, although he reserved the right to dismiss advice proffered – witness his rejection in 1941 of warnings of an impending German attack – and to liquidate his advisers as scapegoats for policy failures, he frequently consulted the experts. He may, for example, as Isaac Deutscher points out, have determined even some of the finer points of military strategy during the Second World War – the Stavka, the Red Army's G.H.Q., was indeed located in his offices in the Kremlin – but not until after discussions with the relevant generals. In the Stalingrad campaign, for instance, he kept in constant touch with Marshals Vassilevsky and Rokossovsky, and the other leading military men in the field.[2]

Moreover, those implementing Stalin's foreign political decisions were often allowed some freedom of manoeuvre. The Foreign Commissar, Litvinov, was given considerable scope to explore the possibilities of Stalin's 'collective security' policy. He, in fact, guided the USSR finally into the League of Nations, whose former Deputy Secretary-General said of him, 'Litvinov

[1] Merle Fainsod, *How Russia is Ruled*, Cambridge, Mass., 1953, p. 282.
[2] Isaac Deutscher, *Stalin, a Political Biography*, Oxford Paperbacks, 1961, p. 496, n.

rarely asked for time to consult his government; he seemed always to decide on the spot when to press his argument, to propose a compromise or to resign himself to accepting the majority view. It was clear that he had at least as free a hand as was generally given to the Foreign Ministers of the democratic powers.'[1] On the other hand, the removal of Litvinov in 1939 when Stalin decided on an accord with Hitler shows the limits of Litvinov's competence. To Litvinov's successors, Molotov and Vishinsky, however, Stalin was to allow less independent initiative, although Molotov was entrusted with the responsibility of the agreement with Hitler.

Although Leninist ideas were still to condition Stalin's outlook to some extent, his own theory of building 'Socialism in One Country' was to be the main prop of his foreign policy. Russia had to be made economically and militarily powerful if she were to survive. And since the dissolution of the Soviet state might spell the end of organized Communism, the primary duty of all Communist parties and their sympathizers lay in giving every possible assistance to the Soviet Union. As Stalin wrote in August 1927,'An internationalist is one who, unreservedly, without hesitation, without conditions, is ready to defend the Soviet Union because it is the base of the world revolutionary movement.'[2] This notion was to be incorporated into the statutes of the Comintern at its Sixth Congress in 1928.

In consequence, Communists could be urged even to temporary self-destruction to serve the real or supposed interests of the Soviet Union–the base of revolution. Between 1928 and 1935, for example, Stalin encouraged Communist Parties to regard the Social Democrats as more inimical to Communism than the Fascists–a policy which, by discrediting the Socialists, facilitated the rise of Nazism. It is not implausible to assume that to Stalin a Germany led by the Nazis was preferable to a Social Democratic Germany, since the Nazis were known to be hostile to the West while the Social Democrats had sufficient Western friends to be able to combine in a formidable alliance against

[1] F. P. Walters, *A History of the League of Nations*, I, London, 1952, pp. 358–9.
[2] J. Stalin, *Sochineniia*, X, Moscow, 1947, p. 61.

Russia.[1] In any case, it is to the foreign policy of Hitler rather than to that of Stalin that we have to look to find the causes of the breakdown in Soviet–German collaboration. When in 1938 Stalin again sought a rapprochement with Nazi Germany in order to postpone an 'inevitable' German attack, he did not hesitate physically to destroy those Communist refugees from Germany, Poland, and elsewhere who might have qualms about any such arrangement with the Nazis. That Russia's pact with Germany might have some chance of survival, Stalin insisted on the sabotage by Communists of the Allied war effort, that is, until Russia was herself attacked.

Loyalty to the USSR remained the primary Communist duty even after the dissolution of the Comintern and the extension of Communist Party rule to much of Eastern Europe. An article in *Pravda* dated 12 January 1949 makes this quite clear: 'In our time one can be a sincere revolutionary and internationalist only by unconditionally supporting the CPSU and the Soviet Union itself, only by basing one's actions on the principles of Marxism–Leninism and proceeding from the experience of the Russian Communist Party–the leading force in the international Communist movement.' Separate roads to Socialism were therefore not permissible and indeed Stalin had given little encouragement to independent-minded Communist leaders, like Tito and Mao Tse-tung. Likewise, the growth of Eastern Europe was to be retarded by Russia's economic exploitation of the region. Terms of trade with Eastern Europe were weighted in Russia's favour, and the Russians took most of the profits of the joint stock companies in the area even though the Eastern Europeans had invested most of the capital. On ex-enemy countries the Russians imposed heavy reparations, which in the case of East Germany amounted at one time to nearly a quarter of the country's total national income.[2] It is entirely in keeping with Stalin's attitude that Tito, who objected amongst other things to Russia's economic exploitation of a

[1] For a further exploration of this thesis see, for example, the book by W. G. Krivitsky, *I Was Stalin's Agent*, London, 1939.

[2] See, for example, Z. Brzezinski, *The Soviet Bloc*, Praeger, 1962, pp. 124–8.

fraternal Socialist state, should be dubbed a 'Fascist', and Yugo-slavia expelled from the Cominform, in 1948.

A further implication of the 'Socialism in One Country' thesis involves the notion of a world divided into two hostile camps, the one of Socialism, the other of Capitalism and Imperialism. To this theory, initially propounded by Lenin, Stalin added something of Russia's traditional fear and suspicion of the Western world. Until shortly before his death he held war between the two camps to be inevitable and felt that only by skilful diplomacy to ward off the creation of an effective anti-Soviet coalition could it be postponed. To this end Stalin championed 'collective security' and 'disarma-ment' and the establishment of 'peace fronts' abroad, and sought to exploit any conflict within the opposing camps.

Not even during the wartime coalition was Stalin to relax his suspicion of the capitalist world. For example, the Allied delay in opening up a second front in France was seen as resulting not from strategic necessity but from an Anglo–American desire to see Russia bled white. After the war this attitude reached its logical expression in Zhdanov's speech at the founding convention of the Cominform in 1947, designed to keep the Soviet Communist Party closely in touch with the parties of Eastern Europe, France and Italy. 'The more the war recedes into the past', Zhdanov said, 'the more distinct become two major trends in post-war inter-national policy, corresponding to the tradition of the political forces operating on the international arena into two major camps, the imperialist and anti-democratic camp on the one hand and the anti-imperialist and democratic camp on the other.'[1] There fol-lowed Stalin's attempt to isolate Eastern Europe politically, mili-tarily and economically. Little wonder, then, that Western politicians talked of an 'Iron Curtain' between East and West!

But Stalin did not underestimate the strength or determination of Russia's presumed enemy and wished to give the West no undue cause for armed intervention. He acted, therefore, with circum-spection – at any rate in Europe. Territorial gains were made only

[1] *For a Lasting Peace, for a People's Democracy* (Belgrade), No. 1 (10 November 1947).

when the West was in no position effectively to oppose them. When her probes, as for example the Berlin blockade, met determined resistance, Russia was prepared to retreat. Even when armed hostilities were involved, as in Korea, the Russians fought by proxy. But it was not until one year before his death that Stalin in his 'Economic Problems of Socialism' revised his expectation of war between the two camps. He continued to hold, however, that some kind of confrontation with the West was inevitable in the long run.

But Stalin's tendency to see the world in terms of a two-camp image blinded him to the realities of what has come to be termed the 'third world'. To Stalin the new countries of the Middle East and Asia were mere appendages of the West. Thus, instead of wooing leaders like Nehru, Nasser and Sukarno, he castigated them as 'imperialist lackeys' and encouraged Communists to join with militant nationalists in Asia and the Middle East in proclaiming a common struggle against 'colonialism' and 'colonialist stooges'. True, Russian-backed militants scored notable successes in Indochina, but insurrections elsewhere were less effective and merely alienated the new governments.

Like Lenin, Stalin set the tone for Soviet foreign policy. But whilst Lenin had reluctantly to drop much of its revolutionary content, Stalin, though a Georgian, seemed eager to be cast in the role of a Great Russian nationalist. As early as 1931 he was speaking bitterly of the 'beatings' suffered by Russia in the past, and during the Second World War he drew heavily on patriotic feelings to produce the requisite fighting spirit. The Germans were portrayed as being uniformly evil, and the Russians were entreated to fight them not so much in the interests of Socialism as for the preservation of the motherland. The recovery by 1945 of territory Russia had lost to Japan in 1905 and to Western Europe in 1918 was treated by Stalin as Russia's rightful due. On the restoration, for example, of the Chinese concessions lost as a result of the Russo-Japanese war he claimed: 'For forty years we men of the older generation have waited for this'.[1]

[1] Article in *Bolshevik*, No. 16, August 1945, p. 2.

True, Lenin had also not hesitated to draw on patriotic sentiment to defeat the interventionists, but there is nothing in the Leninist period to compare with the exaggerated claims in the press during and after the Second World War relating to the Russian genius. Russians were credited with the invention of the lightning conductor, the electric motor, the electric telegraph, radio, the tank, penicillin, and so forth.

Stalin's foreign policy was also closely bound up with his internal struggle to enhance his power and reputation. The doctrine of 'capitalist encirclement' probably owed as much to Stalin's domestic ambitions and circumstances as to international reality. And because he believed that his domestic position could be affected by the fortunes of his Communist opponents abroad, his domestic purges were generally followed by an equally thoroughgoing purge throughout the Comintern. The purge first of Left then of Right Opposition elements in the 1920s had repercussions in every Communist Party. In the 1930s the Russian secret police was active in Spain during the Spanish Civil War, as George Orwell and Arthur Koestler testify, and 'unreliable' German Communist leaders in exile would sometimes be sent on missions to Germany after Stalin's agents had given the Gestapo ample warning.[1] Indeed, the purges of the late 1940s and early 1950s were carried to all the countries under Soviet control.

At the same time, with such complete mastery of both Party and government apparatus, Stalin was able to pursue policies, however unpopular, deemed to be in Russia's interest. A pact with Nazi Germany was possible precisely because he had eliminated those Jews, Poles and German refugees, Old Bolsheviks and military men who might oppose it.

(c) Stalin's Successors

With the death of Stalin the autocracy collapsed and with it the government's ability to formulate and execute policy with the minimum of domestic checks. Once more the USSR was managed by an oligarchy, and by now (1968) the Politburo has resumed the

[1] J. Valtin (pseud.), Out of the Night, London, 1940.

role of central decision-maker. But for some time after 1953 there was some confusion as to where ultimate political power resided, since the Party leaders were frequently at odds with each other, and the administrative machine under Prime Minister Malenkov was beginning to act with an almost unprecedented degree of autonomy. But by combining with Malenkov's many opponents in the party Nikita Khrushchev, who had been nominated First Secretary of the Party on the adoption of 'collective leadership' in September 1953, was able in the spring of 1955 to oust the independent-minded Prime Minister together with Malenkov's nominees in the bureaucracy. But although these measures rendered the new government of Marshal Bulganin far more amenable to Party control, powerful men in the administrative machine were able to frustrate certain Party directives. The most influential were the Foreign Minister, Molotov, and Shepilov, his successor. Their actions explain to some extent the apparent inconsistencies in Soviet foreign policy from 1955 until the summer of 1957, when they were removed from political office.

To Molotov, Stalin's 'two-camp image' was still substantially valid, and he could not share the revised international assessments of men like Khrushchev. He tried, therefore, to obstruct the implementation of a rapprochement with Yugoslavia and the withdrawal of Soviet troops from Austria in 1955. He opposed Russia's tolerance of political and ideological deviations in Eastern Europe, viewed the 'Geneva spirit' as a capitulation to the West, and saw little point in either economic aid to Asia and the Middle East or the resumption of diplomatic relations with Japan. Khrushchev's performance at the 20th Congress of the Soviet Communist Party was, of course, entirely anathema. He held Khrushchev's heresies – the attack on Stalin, the revisions of established doctrines on war, revolution, and peaceful coexistence, and the visions of a 'Socialist commonwealth' – responsible for the turmoil in Poland and Hungary in October and November 1956. In the aftermath of those events, Shepilov, who replaced Molotov in June 1956, found it politic to criticize the Khrushchev line and in a report to the Supreme Soviet on 5 February 1957 suggested, among other things, that the Soviet Union should try to extricate itself from its financial and military commitments to the Middle East.

In June 1957 anti-Khrushchev forces in the government sought to combine with the First Secretary's opponents in the Party Praesidium to oust him. A special meeting of the Praesidium was called, and Khrushchev was in fact outvoted. But he refused to admit defeat and insisted on having his case referred to the Central Committee, which had in the past acted as arbiter in such disputes. This was a body on which Khrushchev felt he could rely. It had elected him First Secretary; acclaimed his agricultural programme, including the 'virgin lands' scheme, to which Malenkov was opposed; demoted Malenkov and reprimanded Molotov for his 'reactionary' outlook and 'obstructionism'. By the end of an eight-day Central Committee plenum, Khrushchev had indeed triumphed. Molotov, Malenkov, and Kaganovich were removed from the Praesidium, and Shepilov and other supporters of the so-called 'anti-Party group' were demoted. The governmental apparatus came under Party control. Four months later Zhukov, who had put army planes at the disposal of Khrushchev's supporters for the crucial Central Committee vote, was accused of harbouring 'Bonapartist ambitions', dismissed as Minister of War, and removed from the Central Committee, with the complicity of Khrushchev. By mid-1958 Bulganin had been ousted from the premiership and Khrushchev combined the leading state and Party posts.[1]

From then on until his dismissal, the vacillations in Soviet foreign policy would appear to stem in no small measure from hesitations in Khrushchev's own thinking. On the other hand, his tendency to ignore the counsel of such articulate and relatively cohesive interest groups as the army, the secret police and the technocracy contributed to their rise in political awareness, and undermined his own power in the process. For instance, the security police, which he had tried to render politically harmless,

[1] The best detailed account of the 'anti-Party group' affair is Roger Pethybridge's *A Key to Soviet Politics*, Allen & Unwin, 1962.

was by the middle of 1964 successfully challenging certain aspects of his foreign policy. It is almost certain, for example, that the arrest of the American Professor Barghoorn, the roughing-up of three Western attachés who had been given permission to travel to the Soviet Far East and a mustard-gas attack on a West German diplomat were engineered by the K.G.B. to embarrass the Soviet leader.

Since Khrushchev had risen in the Party by posing as an expert on economic matters, in particular agriculture, he sought to employ foreign policy largely in the service of domestic economic advance, and as a means of making good his frequent boast that by 1970 or so the total economic output of the Soviet Union would equal that of the United States. This policy seemed to call for the strengthening of economic ties with Eastern Europe (though on a fairer basis than before), and in 1962 he suggested, but to no avail, the economic integration of the area through COMECON – the recently revived Communist economic pact.[1] It called, too, for some *détente* with the West to justify a transfer of resources from arms to industry and agriculture, and to stimulate East–West trade. On the other hand, Khrushchev was aware that such a policy would alienate the 'hawks' both at home and abroad, in particular in China.

In the event he was unable to pursue an East–West *détente* without interruption. In the first place, he had periodically to satisfy his 'hard-line' critics. Secondly, for reasons of ideology and Soviet prestige he was obliged to give some support to 'national liberation movements', whose targets were often regimes sympathetic to the West. Thirdly, like his predecessors, he was loth to by-pass an opportunity of extending Russian influence where there was little risk of direct conflict with the West. Moreover, Russia's space triumphs and development of intercontinental missiles in the years after 1957 seemed, for a time, to have increased her potential for scoring at the expense of the West. Fourthly, there were external events beyond Russia's control which sometimes neces-

[1] G. Ionescu's *No Reluctant Ally*, Ampersand, 1965, provides a short but reliable analysis of the failure of Khrushchev's proposal.

sitated actions which could only raise the level of East–West tension.

The decision to crush the Hungarian government in November 1956 is a case in point. After much deliberation it was decided that the suppression of the Nagy regime which had opted for neutrality and the multi-party system had less grave implications for Soviet policy than Russian acquiescence in the situation. Such a decision was, of course, facilitated by another external event–the Anglo-French intervention in Egypt.

The establishment of the Berlin wall in August 1961 was, again, largely a defensive reaction to an increasingly untenable situation. The East German party leader, Walter Ulbricht, collectivized about half of East Germany's agriculture early in 1960. In protest many farmers had killed their cattle and burned their crops–actions contributing to a food shortage and the reimposition of rationing in the towns. Discontent mounted, and refugees flooded into West Berlin and thence to West Germany. West Germany could add these able-bodied newcomers to its labour force, while by the middle of 1961 nearly a third of the East Germans were of pensionable age. The construction of a wall between East and West Berlin seemed to be a logical, if brutal, method of stemming the flow and enabling the East German economy to advance.

The decision to station missiles in Cuba in October 1962, though in all probability a probe to see how far the United States would react and what it might be prepared to trade for the withdrawal of the missiles, might also conceivably have been prompted by external events. After the Bay of Pigs invasion, Russia constantly feared an attack on her Latin American ally. During this period, too, Russia had been made aware that in the missile race she did not possess the strategic advantage hitherto assumed by East and West alike. Khrushchev might well have calculated, therefore, that his missiles could both protect his ally and narrow the missile gap.[1]

[1] For a further exploration of this view see the chapter by Malcolm Mackintosh in *Détente*, edited by E. L. Dulles and R. D. Crane, Praeger, 1965.

But although Khrushchev's policy sometimes put East–West relations under severe strain, towards the end of his office, as China's attitude became more hostile, Khrushchev seemed to be working for a *détente* at all costs, preparing, indeed, for a 'showdown' with opponents of this policy. Assistance to insurgents in Laos and Vietnam was considerably reduced; American action in destroying the North Vietnamese fleet in the Gulf of Tonkin in 1964 met only routine condemnation; and Western difficulties over Cyprus were not overly exploited. Within the last few months of Khrushchev's career he sent his nephew, Adzhubei, to the Vatican and was negotiating a visit to Russia's arch-enemy in Europe–West Germany. This visit was, however, not to occur. The idea was dropped, together with its sponsor, in October 1964 when both Praesidium and Central Committee voted against his continuation in office.

Though many had misgivings about the secrecy surrounding Khrushchev's fall, the fact that the First Secretary was toppled at all, and with non-lethal consequences to himself or his supporters, shows the extent of the changes since Stalin. Khrushchev had tried to rule, like Lenin, by persuasion, but finally his colleagues could no longer acquiesce in his policies or methods. He had alienated the army by demoting Zhukov and by interfering in military affairs. For, in order to economize and increase the labour supply, he had reduced the army in size to what its leaders regarded as dangerously low proportions, exposing Russia's eastern and western flanks, and had concentrated on the production of nuclear weaponry, which the military thought to be largely irrelevant to Russia's needs. He had antagonized the bureaucracy by his ill-considered agricultural and industrial schemes and the extension of Party control. He had annoyed the upper echelons of the Party by making important commitments without adequate consultation beforehand. There was the decision to send MIG fighters to India at the time of the Sino–Indian border war, the award of the highly prized title of 'Hero of the Soviet Union' to President Nasser, and Khrushchev's initiatives in respect of West Germany.

Among other charges against him, many relate to his foreign

policy. His threat to send rockets at the time of the Suez crisis in 1956, his forecast of Russia's early economic parity with the United States, and his boast (subsequently denied) that Russia had built a 'doomsday machine' of 50 megatons were mere 'phrase-mongering'. His behaviour towards the Polish First Secretary, Gomulka, in 1956 and towards the Chinese representatives who came to Moscow in 1963 for ideological talks was as 'immoderate and boorish' as his language at the Paris 'summit' conference of 1960 and his 'shoe-banging' at the United Nations in the same year. His insistence on a Communist 'summit' formally to exclude China from the Communist movement was thought to be over-hasty.[1]

Though more tentative and less theatrical, Russia's foreign policy since Khrushchev's dismissal shows evidence of a continuing inner debate. As in Washington there are 'hawks' and 'doves', 'ideologues' and 'pragmatists'. None of the many competing forces can have been wholly satisfied. On the one hand, East–West trade has grown, political and cultural contacts have been intensified and there has been some co-operation in the field of arms control. On the other hand, Russia's qualified support for 'national liberation movements' has tended to complicate her policy of 'peaceful coexistence' with the West. In particular, aid to North Vietnam and to militant Arab nationalists both before and after the Middle-Eastern war of June 1967 have reduced the tempo of *détente*. Attempts to weaken Western positions throughout the world continue and the Soviet military budget for 1967 was a record figure. But the outcome of Russia's debate seems to depend increasingly on such external factors as the growth of polycentrism in both Communist and Western alliance systems and the changing attitudes of the developing countries, China and the United States.

External considerations

If the intervention and blockade of Russia shortly after the Revolution substantially affected the Soviet outlook on the world,

[1] For a further commentary on the reasons for Khrushchev's fall see Mark Frankland's *Khrushchev*, Penguin, 1966.

the declared aims and activities of the Soviet leaders affected, in turn, the response of the Powers towards the Soviet Union. It was, for example, opposition to Russia's intention to quit the war which initially occasioned the intervention, and her default on her debts, together with the promotion of revolutionary activity in Europe and the Middle East, that led to a prolongation of that intervention, half-hearted though it was.

Revision of Russia's foreign political perspectives came in 1921 after the withdrawal of most foreign troops and the ebbing of the revolutionary tide in Europe and Asia. The new state, it was felt, would have to coexist with ideological opponents for a period longer than originally anticipated, but the expectation of hostilities remained. The notion that the period of coexistence could only be an intermittently peaceful affair was to survive the Leninist era partly because of the exigencies of Stalinism but partly, too, because of Russia's international experience even after the intervention.

Russia had had to endure the hostility of the *Cordon sanitaire* after France had given more than token assistance to the Polish attack in 1920. Her search for economic contacts had not met a satisfactory response, save from Germany and Britain, and she had had to build up her economy with comparatively little assistance from foreign capital. In the 1930s there was Hitler's deliberate rejection of the 'Rapallo spirit' and the tacit or explicit support of the *Führer* by some of Russia's neighbours. There was also the fact that no serious attempts had been made by the League of Nations to deter either Hitler or the Japanese, both of whom had designs on Soviet territory, from further conquest. Sanctions against Italy in 1935 had been neither universal nor comprehensive, and the Western Powers had failed to counterbalance the Italians and the Germans who had given material assistance to the nationalists during the Spanish Civil War. Russia had received no invitation to Munich in 1938, despite her interest in the fate of Czechoslovakia, and, understandably enough, the Russians took Britain's action in sending a comparatively junior Foreign Office official, William Strang (now Lord Strang), to negotiate for Britain in August 1939 as indicating that Britain was cool towards an alliance against Germany.

Yet even if there were some grounds for Russia's sense of 'alienation', Stalin's notion of 'capitalist encirclement' was almost certainly an exaggeration. Not every non-Communist country was basically antagonistic; many, indeed, had gone out of their way to be friendly. Turkey, Persia, and Afghanistan were well disposed towards the Soviet Union up to the Second World War, and Germany up until 1934. France was instrumental in getting Russia into the League of Nations, once the Soviet Union had dropped her opposition to the organization, and together with Czechoslovakia maintained cordial relations with Russia after their joint agreements in 1935.

If some apprehension of Russia's intentions remained, her leaders are partly to blame. Russia's conquest of Outer Mongolia in 1921 and her subversion of other Chinese border areas in the 1920s and '30s looked much like old-fashioned imperialism, and the continued existence of the Comintern, which had attempted to interfere in Chinese and British politics and had promoted revolutionary activity in Germany, Bulgaria and Estonia in the early '20s, could not but leave a residue of suspicion in the outside world. Moreover, many Socialists were unable to forgive Stalin's policies towards them in the early '30s, and there was also wide-spread revulsion at his internal policies, especially during the period of the Great Purges.

But from Stalin's viewpoint the decision in 1939 to make a pact of non-aggression with Germany was a rational response to an increasingly threatening international situation. Hitler's designs on Eastern Europe and Russia were well known. He had already re-armed Germany, re-occupied the Rhineland, seized Austria, and dismembered Czechoslovakia, and was about to destroy Poland. It seemed that only a temporary accord with Germany could stay Hitler's eastward advance, and the best short-run tactic appeared to be the division of Europe into spheres of influence.

Russia's subsequent annexation of the western Ukraine and western Byelorussia, the attempt to turn Finland into a client state, the incorporation into the USSR of the Balkan states, and the seizure from Rumania of Bessarabia and northern Bukovina must be seen partly in terms of Russia's strategic necessity. Likewise, her acquisitions from Germany, Czechoslovakia, Japan and China after the war, her territorial claims on Turkey, her pressures on Iran, Greece and Berlin, and the military, political and economic subordination of Eastern Europe have also in part a defensive rationale. For Stalin felt the need for added security against any potential threat from a revived Germany and Japan, and feared that his former allies might take advantage of Russia's exhaustion at the end of the war to try to destroy his regime. Characteristically, he interpreted America's sudden cancellation after the war of lend-lease and the Western Powers' insistence on 'free elections' in Eastern Europe as acts with hostile intent.

But although external considerations are in part responsible for Russia's expansionism during and after the Second World War, there were also other factors. Firstly, Stalin regarded the enlargement of Russia's territory and the right to intervene politically in her 'sphere of influence' as having some basis in the wartime agreements of the Allies and as being in any case a just reward for economic devastation and the sacrifice of some twenty million lives. Secondly, Stalin needed control of the economic resources of neighbouring areas to speed Russia's economic reconstruction. The time, moreover, seemed opportune. There was widespread sympathy for the Russians and their Communist supporters who had played a heroic role after 1941, and Stalin calculated that in view of the strategic position of the Red Army in Eastern Europe, Russia would experience little difficulty in successfully pressing some of her claims. He had no reason to believe that Russia's dictates would be resisted by Communists in the area so long as they could be persuaded that Russia would help advance the cause of Socialism.

But fear of precipitating a Western attack caused Russia at first to move cautiously in neighbouring territory. Communists in Bulgaria in 1944, Greece, Yugoslavia and Albania in 1945, were discouraged from establishing one-party rule, and for a time

Russian influence in Eastern Europe was exercised discreetly. When pressed to withdraw troops from Iran in 1946 she did so, and abandoned the blockade of Berlin in 1948 when the Western Powers stood firm. Yet by the time of the establishment of the Cominform in September 1947 the Russians felt sufficiently confident to establish their nominees in the security and defence ministries of most of the Eastern European states. By March 1948, when the Communist Party seized sole power in Czechoslovakia, Stalin was no longer disguising his mastery of the area.

But his policies had brought about the danger he had tried to avert – the consolidation of the West into an anti-Soviet coalition. The Americans were to re-establish a military presence in Europe within three years of the war. The Truman Doctrine of 1947 assisted Greek and Turkish resistance to Soviet and Communist pressures. In 1948 Marshall Aid, rejected by the Communist countries, began to counteract the appeal of Communism and helped stabilize Western Europe. In 1949 NATO was created, and three years later Yugoslavia, an independent state under Communist Party rule, combined with Greece and Turkey, both members of NATO, to form the Balkan Pact. Wherever the Soviet Union sought to undermine some of the newly independent countries by sanctioning insurrection and civil war the Western powers offered protection and assistance.

Hence, by the time of Stalin's death Russia's posited enemy of 1945 had become a very real enemy, partly because of Russia's own actions. By dismantling much of the foreign political edifice on which much of post-war Stalinism had been based, the new leaders in the Kremlin were tacitly admitting the dubious wisdom of much of Stalin's policies. Their first task was to take stock of the implications of recent technological advances, firstly as they related to economic development and secondly as they affected military matters.

By 1953 it was already clear that the introduction of new devices into industry and agriculture was widening the gap between the 'haves' and the 'have-nots'. Naturally the better-developed countries had more capital available to invest in these new techniques, and their application often reduced the need of the developed countries for the raw materials produced in the developing areas. With the mass production, for example, of synthetic fibres there was less demand for raw cotton or wool, and hence the prices of these commodities fell.

The political effect was two-fold. Firstly, in the developed, mainly Western capitalist, countries, which took best advantage of these technological innovations, standards of living began rapidly to rise. And it was not only the owners and controllers of capital who were enriched. Increasingly the classical Marxist notion that in developed societies more and more owners of capital would be driven into the working class was at variance with the facts. Such developments also called in question one of Lenin's tenets – that capitalism needs imperial conquests to survive. For the developed countries were never as prosperous as when they began divesting themselves of their colonies, and increasing their trade with other developed countries. Hence the prospect of violent class conflicts and revolution in the developed areas grew increasingly remote. If Communism were to survive in the West, it would have to be reinterpreted to fit in with changing conditions.

But if the developed countries seemed a poor field for revolutionary advance, the same could not be said of the newly independent countries. Here the problems of economic backwardness, technological inferiority, political and ethnical diversity and the general desire to be rid of economic and other obligations to the former imperial powers would provide a fertile field for Soviet diplomatic and economic penetration. Moreover, giving greater attention to the needs and aspirations of the 'have nots' in Asia and the Middle East seemed to be in the logic of developments in thermonuclear weaponry, to whose employment the militarily superior Western alliance was officially committed in the event of a Soviet thrust in Europe.

Considerations such as these led the Russians to retreat from their support of insurgency in the Third World and to return to the policy advocated by Lenin of embracing the non-Communist nationalist leaders as common fighters in the struggle against imperialism. Hence countries formerly regarded as imperialist appendages were now to be given Soviet financial and sometimes military assistance, encouraged to trade with the Soviet Union, to exchange visits of leading figures in politics, science and the arts, and send their talented youngsters to be trained in the USSR. The aim of these measures was to wean these new countries away from Western influence and increase their dependence on the Soviet economy. Ultimately, of course, the Russians hoped that Soviet generosity, economic success and the supposed relevance of the Soviet economic model would draw the developing countries in support of the Communist cause. The creation of a proletariat in the wake of industrialization was supposed to hasten this process. 'Peaceful co-existence', which was the slogan under which this new policy was launched, now came to imply a further attenuation of the revolutionary process and Russia's reliance on economic rather than military means in bringing about ultimate change. It envisaged no longer a mere interlude between wars, but a long-term, peaceful, though dialectical, transition to Communism.

Developments in the Third World

From January 1954 Russian economic and military assistance to selected developing countries began to mount and in the first ten years or so of the programme India, Indonesia, Egypt, Algeria and Ghana were the main beneficiaries. At the same time the Russians have often been willing to accept repayments in the form of the traditional exports of the recipients–natural rubber, raw cotton, wool, coffee, cocoa beans, sugar and so on–even if these are difficult to absorb into the Soviet economy. But their aid programme has suffered from certain disadvantages. Firstly, compared with the Western Powers, the Russians have relatively few technicians familiar with local languages, customs, and culture. In Guinea, for example, where Russian technicians faced acute language difficulties, President Sekou Touré has sought the return of French assistance, hastily withdrawn on Guinea's refusal to join the French–African community. Secondly, the Russians have greater difficulty than the Western powers in fulfilling their promises of aid when there are competing claims on their resources from other sectors of the economy. Thirdly, although Russian interest rates are comparatively low, the quality and prices of Russian goods are often such as to negate the economic effects of lower interest charges.

The availability of alternative sources of assistance from the West, and in some cases from China, has been among the many factors enabling many of the developing countries to resist Russian attempts to curb their freedom of action. True, some of Russia's protégés tend to preserve an anti-Western posture and a commitment to Socialism, but generally they try to maintain some of their ties with the West and insist on indigenous forms of Socialism– Arab, African or Asian. Indeed, all but a few, including some of the biggest recipients of Soviet aid, have outlawed the Communist Party, and, but for Cuba, no Communist party has seized control in the developing countries since the Soviet economic aid programme was launched. It was the Third World's strenuous opposition to Khrushchev's proposed changes in the Secretary-Generalship of the United Nations in 1960 which revealed to the Russians, perhaps for the first time, the limited political effectiveness of their aid programme. With the political demise of nationalist leaders like Ben Bella, Nkrumah and Sukarno, upon whom the Russians had set great hopes, and the attempt of some of Russia's recipients to involve her more deeply than she thought fit in risky military commitments, Russia's disillusionment began to grow.

In late 1961 Russia's disenchantment led to a cut-back in the aid programme, but the political and economic activity of Russia's rivals in the area forced them to raise their aid bill again in mid-1963. The main complicating factor, then, as now, was China which, by presenting herself as belonging racially and economically to the Third World and branding the USSR an 'accomplice of imperialism', has been trying to undercut the influence of Russia and win the leadership of the world's revolutionary forces. This poses a serious dilemma for Soviet foreign policy. It can either seek to rival China in militancy, thereby risking confrontation with the West and alienating non-revolutionary opinion in the Third

World, or leave the militant phraseology to the Chinese, in which case Russia runs the risk of losing altogether its position as world revolutionary leader.

The dilemma is by no means resolved. At times–as befits those skilled in dialectics–Russia tries to act both roles simultaneously. At other times, as in Khrushchev's last year, she has appeared to be on the verge of abandoning revolution altogether. This, after all, was the implication of Khrushchev's message of 21 December 1963 denouncing local conflicts though admittedly not 'national liberations wars'. Since his dismissal, and amid growing hopes of a Communist victory in Vietnam, the Russian leaders have attempted to salvage something of their diminishing prestige amongst the revolutionary forces by keeping up a stream of relatively militant verbiage, especially against the United States, and by supporting such radical militants as the Vietcong and the leftward-looking government of Syria headed by Prime Minister Zeayen.

But in case it should be thought that Soviet policy in Vietnam and the Middle East indicated a resolution of the dilemma in favour of militancy it is as well to bear in mind Russia's use of the 'hot line' and the call for an unconditional cease fire in the UN debate during the Arab–Israeli war, and Kosygin's 'summit' with President Johnson after it.[1] Nor have the Third World moderates been forgotten. Indeed, the rift with China has led the Soviet Union into strengthening its ties with India, Pakistan and Japan and in trying to forge links with such countries as Malaysia and the Philippines.

The Western alliance

Russia's policy towards the developed countries and towards the Western alliance in particular has been influenced by conflicting sets of factors. On the one hand, because of the West's nuclear superiority, its resistance to Soviet probes, and the political and

[1] For a further survey of the Russian dilemmas in respect of the developing countries see, for example, Uri Ra'anan's 'Tactics in the Third World' in *Survey*, October 1965, and Richard Lowenthal's 'Russia: the One-Party System and the Third World' in *Survey*, January 1966.

social consequences of the economic growth of Western Europe and North America, already outlined, Russia can hope to achieve little more than minor foreign policy changes within the Western alliance. On the other hand, the fragmentation of NATO could have political consequences adverse to Russia, particularly if it strengthened those elements in West Germany who want an active policy in support of German reunification, her return to pre-war frontiers and control of nuclear weapons. Moreover, because of the strains at present burdening her economy, Russia needs a political climate conducive to a reduction in the military budget and long-term credits and technical expertise from the West—ambitions which might be jeopardized were there to be a marked increase in East–West tension. Hence there are limits to the degree to which Russia can afford to intrigue against the West.

These conflicting needs have resulted in policies which the psychologist William Sargent has described, mistakenly in the present writer's view, as 'Pavlovian' in inspiration. On the one hand, there have been such acts as the return in 1955 of the Porkkala naval base to Finland and the withdrawal of Soviet troops from Austria or the partial nuclear test ban treaty of August 1963, all of which contributed to a lowering of tension. On the other hand, there have been such measures as the break-up of the Paris 'summit' in 1960, the creation of the Berlin wall, and the introduction of missiles into Cuba in 1962, which have heightened East–West tension and consolidated Western opposition. Some of these apparently provocative acts have, as was argued earlier, stemmed in part from actions beyond Russia's control. Others, however, result from the basic ambivalence of Russia's position, in particular her need to score against the West but without provoking the West too far.

A major tactic in Russia's policy *vis-à-vis* the West has been to frustrate any attempt at Western military or economic integration. Her chief device in this respect is an appeal to a residual nationalism in Western Europe. Anti-American sentiment in the area is exploited, and many of Russia's proposals—the idea of a European security conference, for example—are designed to foster the notion that America is in some sense an intruder in European affairs. At the moment General de Gaulle is held up as a shining example of a great European because of his country's withdrawal from NATO's integrated military command and French criticism of the American position on Vietnam. Correspondingly, Harold Wilson is denigrated as an American stooge, because London appears to share Washington's view on many foreign policy issues. At various times Russia has sought to play off one Western European country against another and to exploit already existing contradictions, as for example between Greece and Turkey over Cyprus and between Britain and France over Britain's proposed membership of the European Economic Community. At the same time, Russia encourages them all to keep an especially watchful eye on West Germany, whose entry into NATO in 1955 she tried strenuously but unsuccessfully to block.[1] The Warsaw Pact was, in fact, a stunted offspring of these Russian endeavours at that time.

A further Soviet ambition has been to obtain from the West recognition of the *status quo* in Europe, in particular the division of Germany and Poland's control of the Oder–Neisse territories. To this end she has advocated disengagement and the signing of a peace treaty with East Germany and has called repeatedly for a non-aggression pact between NATO and the Warsaw Treaty Organization.

But Russia's outlook on the developed as well as the developing world has been influenced by polycentrist tendencies within what used to be called the 'Communist Bloc'. As the problem of China, with her territorial claims, political and ideological ambitions, become more difficult to cope with, the Russians tend to think increasingly of short-term political accommodations with the Western Powers, and in particular the United States. Such arrangements are made easier by the fact that the United States and her allies are prepared, despite the Vietnam War and the Middle Eastern crises, to move towards 'peaceful engagement' with the Soviet Union and her supporters.

[1] Thomas Barman's 'A diplomatic correspondent looks back' published in *The Listener*, 5 January 1967, traces the extent of Russia's residual anti-Germanism.

The 'Communist World'

Although the intensification of the Sino–Soviet dispute since 1960 has in turn contributed in no small measure to the fragmentation of the 'Communist World', there had until recently been limits on the disintegration of the former Communist monolith.[1] Firstly, the memory of Soviet military action in East Berlin in 1953 and again in Hungary in 1956 and the continuing presence of Soviet troops in Hungary, Poland and East Germany had served to discourage popular attempts at overthrowing Communist regimes. In any case, the promise of Russian 'protection' against any manifestation of 'West German revanchism' had made tolerable the Soviet alliance, at least in the northern tier of the Warsaw Pact–Poland, Czechoslovakia and East Germany. And there is a general feeling that Russia still has an indispensable role to play in the economic development of her Communist neighbours. Albania alone of the Communist countries has succeeded in relinquishing the Soviet economic tie, but this is dependent on Chinese aid and goodwill–which might not always be forthcoming.

So far as Communist governments were concerned, the tie with Russia was becoming generally less onerous and more beneficial. In the mid-fifties the Russians had shown themselves ready to assist Yugoslavia and Poland in developing an independent Socialist road (so long as the path followed was within certain fairly well-defined political limits) and there was little logical reason for other Communist states not to do likewise. However, there were limits to independent action, set in part by the fact that the Russians were still prepared to employ economic and other pressures against policies of which they did not approve–as Albania found to her cost in 1960–and in part by fear of the internal consequences of a rapid shift in political and economic policies. Their leaders realized, moreover, that countries under Communist Party rule still belonged, as it were, to the same species and had certain interests in common–for example, the preservation of the one-party system.

[1] The course and consequences of the Sino–Soviet dispute are traced in greater detail in the following chapter of this book.

On the other hand, there are now serious conflicts of purpose and intention between Russia and China, and these differences enable the Communist countries to raise their price for the support of one or other disputant. The quarrel has also provided an opportunity for an ertswhile faithful supporter of the Soviet Union–Rumania–to make a successful bid for economic and political independence and to oppose any attempt by the Russians to make her put bloc interests before national interests. And now Czechoslovakia is seeking to construct a much more liberal form of Communism. Already opposition to Russian policies–the demotion of Khrushchev, the insistence on a Communist 'summit' to discuss the question of China, the imprisonment of the two Soviet writers, Sinyavsky and Daniel, and so forth–has mounted even amongst formerly pro-Soviet Communist parties, and the Chinese have their break-away Communist groups in virtually every country–including those of the Soviet bloc. The effect has been to weaken Soviet power within what used to be called the 'World Communist Movement' and to create a crisis of self-examination among Communists throughout the world. It may be that as the Communist Movement abandons the Soviet Union as its primary source of inspiration, the Soviet Union will finally abandon it. For already, as a thermonuclear Power with global responsibilities transcending ideological allegiances, it must at times be sorely tempted to forego its Communist mission. But, as we have seen, ideologies are not so easily jettisoned. For some time to come, therefore, we may expect the continuation of the ambivalence in Soviet foreign policy that stems from its awareness of its success as a world Power and its failure to attain all its ideological purposes.

BIBLIOGRAPHY

BRZEZINSKI, ZBIGNIEW K. *The Soviet Bloc: Unity and Conflict.* Rev. ed. Cambridge, Mass.: Harvard University Press, 1967. (Paperback ed.: Praeger.)

——— and HUNTINGDON, SAMUEL P. *Political Power: USA/USSR.* New York: Viking, 1964. (Paperback ed.: Viking.)

DEUTSCHER, ISAAC. *Stalin: A Political Biography.* 2d ed. New York: Oxford University Press, 1967. (Paperback ed.: Oxford.)

FRANKLAND, MARK. *Khrushchev.* New York: Stein & Day, 1967.

HULICKA, KAREL, and HULICKA, IRENE M. *Soviet Institutions, the Individual and Society.* Boston: Christopher, 1967.

KENNAN, GEORGE F. *Russia and the West Under Lenin and Stalin.* Boston: Little, Brown, 1961. (Paperback ed.: New American Library.)

KOLKOWITZ, R. *The Soviet Military and the Communist Party.* Princeton, N.J.: Princeton University Press, 1967.

LEDERER, IVO J. (ed.). *Russian Foreign Policy: Essays in Historical Perspective.* New Haven: Yale University Press, 1962. (Paperback ed.: Yale.)

MACKINTOSH, J. M. *Strategy and Tactics of Soviet Foreign Policy.* New York: Oxford University Press, 1962.

PETHYBRIDGE, ROGER. *A Key to Soviet Politics: The Crisis of the Anti-Party Group.* New York: Frederick A. Praeger, 1962.

SHUB, DAVID. *Lenin.* Baltimore: Penguin Books, 1968. (Original paperback.)

SHULMAN, MARSHALL D. *Beyond the Cold War.* New Haven: Yale University Press, 1966. (Paperback ed.: Yale.)

STERN, G. *Fifty Years of Communism.* London: Ampersand, 1967.

TUCKER, ROBERT C. *The Soviet Political Mind: Studies in Stalinism and Post-Stalin Change.* New York: Frederick A. Praeger, 1963. (Paperback ed.: Praeger.)

4·THE FOREIGN POLICY OF CHINA

Coral Bell

Scrutiny of the processes through which foreign policy evolves is an uncertain enough enterprise even in the open and familiar societies of the West. In the case of a society like China, where actual decision-making is curtained-off from direct investigation by every sort of obscurity, the evidence available is necessarily even more fragmentary and ambiguous. The effort at interpretation cannot be abandoned, for China is a formidable fact, and hypotheses about the present nature and possible future drives of its foreign policy are necessary to an analysis of world politics. But the observer is in no position to offer certainties, only a tentative assessment subject to modification as further evidence comes in.

With this reservation always in mind, one may nevertheless say that contemporary Chinese foreign policy seems to grow out of the past of the country itself and that of its leaders with a visible and direct logic. When Mao Tse-tung and his lieutenants proclaimed the People's Republic in 1949 a good deal was already discernible about the objectives and methods of the new government. As adherents of Marxism–Leninism, the Chinese leaders shared a theoretical proletarian internationalism. As members of the international Communist movement since the early 1920s, they had the memories of twenty-eight years' somewhat ambivalent experience of advice and guidance from the Russians. As men who had spent most of their adult lives in revolutionary guerrilla campaigning, they defined the world in concepts and maxims derived from that experience. As victors in the Chinese civil war, they had inevitably an impatience to dispose of the remnants of the enemy force, and a suspicious resentment of its main source of strength, the USA. Above all, as Chinese they were heirs to the long centuries when the Chinese Empire was, in Chinese eyes, co-extensive with civilization, and to the single abrasive century in which that Chinese view of the world was shattered.

All these elements may be seen in the subsequent conduct of policy by the new regime. What was most apparent in the initial phase was the theoretical proletarian internationalism, made formal in the Sino–Soviet Alliance of February 1950. The basic apparent premise of Chinese policy in this period, which lasted perhaps to 1959, may be called the assumption of the United Bloc: that is, of a natural solidarity of diplomatic interest with other Communist powers, especially Russia. Such a solidarity had been proclaimed earlier, in the well-known phrases of Mao Tse-tung's essay *On the People's Democratic Dictatorship*, in which he enunciated what has since been known as the 'lean-to-one-side' principle as the basis of China's foreign relations. The policy of the new China, he said, would be 'to unite in a common struggle with those nations of the world who treat us on a basis of equality, and the peoples of all countries. This is to ally with the Soviet Union, to ally with the new democratic countries of Europe, and to ally with the proletariat and masses of the people in all countries.' This, he went on, might bring the accusation of 'leaning to one side', but the forty years' experience of Sun Yat-sen and the twenty-eight years' experience of the Communist Party had convinced them that in order to win victory and consolidate victory, they must lean to one side. 'One either leans to the side of imperialism or the side of socialism. *Neutrality is a camouflage and a third road does not exist.*'[1]

This vision of the world as resolving itself inexorably into just two camps had, of course, some implication for the future of China's relationship with those Powers who chose to regard themselves as non-aligned, and had also perhaps some consequences in the way of time-lags and general intellectual uneasiness when the Chinese leaders found they must make policy decisions in a world

[1] For the text, see *A Documentary History of Chinese Communism*, ed. Brandt, Schwartz & Fairbank, Harvard University Press, 1952, pp. 449–61. The official 1961 edition of Mao's works, published by the Foreign Languages Press in Peking, has a revised version of this essay.

that did not conform very adequately to the theory. However, in the first eight months or so, up to the outbreak of the Korean War, the gap between vision and reality scarcely hinted at its presence, and the Sino–Soviet Treaty[1] appeared to promise a highly collaborative future. It envisaged a mutual defence alliance of thirty years' duration and provided among other things for the transfer to China in due course of the Chinese Eastern Railway and the base of Port Arthur, and the grant by Russia to China of financial credits, originally of $300,000,000 value. (Other credits were provided later.) Military co-operation between the two Powers was rapidly established. Numerous Soviet military advisers were engaged from 1950 to about 1959 in modernizing the organization, training and equipment of the Chinese armed forces. The supply of actual military equipment appears to have been very considerable up to 1959–60, as was the supply of economic and industrial experts and equipment and blueprints.

The Chinese Eastern Railway was actually transferred to China in 1952, though the last Russian soldiers were not removed from Port Arthur until 1954, when a supplementary agreement was reached, under which Russia agreed to evacuate its forces from the jointly-used naval base there, and transfer the installations without compensation to the Chinese government. The Russians also agreed on this occasion to transfer to China the Russian share in four Sino–Soviet mixed companies which dealt with the mining of non-ferrous and rare metals in Sinkiang, oil procurement and refining, the building and repair of ships in Dairen, and the organization and operation of civil air transport. These assets were not free gifts. China was required to pay for them over a number of years by exports.

Since the schism between China and Russia became overt in 1962, it has become the convention in China to maintain that the alliance was never of any use to the Chinese. Chen Yi has said in so many words, 'Soviet protection means nothing to us', and has implied quite strongly that the economic aid was not of much help

[1] Published in R.I.I.A., *Documents on International Affairs* for 1949–50, London, O.U.P., p. 541.

either. There were good enough reasons, which will be explored later, for the Chinese to be disappointed with the measure of aid extended by Russia, but for all that it was quite substantial. Between 1949 and 1959 the Chinese probably received in all the equivalent of $2,200 million in loans from Russia, about a quarter of this being military credits. In addition they got technical assistance in the form of about 10,000 Russian experts of various sorts. According to Mr. Suslov, Russian aid helped create 25 per cent of China's power resources, all her synthetic rubber, 70 per cent of her tin output, a large part of her capacity in iron and steel making and coal mining and tractor and lorry building. That is to say, much of her industrial base. Even when the alliance was beginning to decline, after 1957, the Russians continued some aid deliveries. The experts were not withdrawn until 1960.[1]

Thus one can in general say, as the Russians do say, that the existence of the alliance was a major factor–perhaps *the* major factor–in the growth of China towards the economic strength necessary to establish her claims as potentially one of the dominant Powers. However, the clearest and most crucial of the advantages of the alliance to China was that it brought the country under the umbrella of the atomic stalemate. This was of vital importance, by any estimate, in the successive disputes between the U.S.A. and China between 1950 and 1962. As Mr. Dulles once said, the issues of Korea in 1953 (and probably in early 1951), Indo-China in 1954, and Formosa in late 1954–early 1955 (and he might have added the Taiwan Straits crisis in 1958), all entailed an approach to the brink of war. In the great debates within the American administration which resulted in each case in a decision against taking risks that might lead to general war with China, many issues were important, but the possibility of certain modes of attack proving the *casus foederis* for the Sino–Soviet alliance, and possibly precipitating general war, was probably the most important. If the alliance had not been concluded, and if therefore this

[1] See I. F. H. Wilson, 'The Sino–Soviet Dispute and the Internal Affairs of China', in J. D. B. Miller and T. H. Rigby, *The Disintegrating Monolith*, Canberra, A.N.U., 1965, for a more detailed account of the economic aspect of the alliance.

risk had looked less formidable or had been non-existent at these dates, the whole climate of opinion in which the issues were argued in Washington would have been different. This was a particularly important consideration affecting the influence that the European allies of the United States brought to bear on American policy in each instance. No doubt the Europeans have had other good and sufficient reasons for being averse to an American war with China (even if they did not intend to take much part in such a war), but the violence of their reactions in each approach to the 'brink' with China up to 1962 was undoubtedly largely due to the apprehension that any major military clash between the U.S. and China, in which atomic weapons were used, might precipitate Armageddon. Since 1962 it has been argued that risks *vis-à-vis* China have probably been 'de-coupled' from risks *vis-à-vis* Russia, and this has been one of the factors in the comparative mildness of European reaction to escalation in Vietnam, but it does not diminish the importance of the Russian alliance to China's earlier security.

Aside from this particular variety of military protection, the Chinese also received, as was mentioned, conventional military backing and aid in the building up and equipment of their armed forces. In this field they were originally extremely dependent on Russia, and by most normal standards of judgment hardly in a position to do without the alliance, so long as there existed the possibility of their coming into conflict with a Western Power. One must admit that this possibility not only still exists, but probably bulks a good deal larger in Chinese eyes than it does in Western ones, since they have among their background mental furniture not only the general Marxist conviction of the inherent hostility of the capitalist world, but a wary Chinese memory of the encroachingness of Europeans, and resentments specifically against America.

Considering the magnitude of the benefits received, it must seem astounding that the alliance which provided them was allowed to begin cracking only seven years after it had been concluded, and that so much of the dynamics of the cracking process came from the side of the beneficiary, China. There is no doubt, on any reasonable assessment, that the major advantages of the alliance were on the Chinese side. The motivating forces at various stages of the schism will be looked at presently, but one factor which may be noted in passing is that Chinese governments have not had much historical experience of alliance, and have therefore perhaps no adequate understanding of the limits of what is to be expected from an ally. By average standards of diplomatic practice Russia was in many respects a very useful ally to China in the period 1950–9. But reckoned against expectations based on an assumption of proletarian brotherhood, her performance, whether measured in aid, in diplomatic backing, or in military assistance, was bound to seem bleakly disappointing, probably as early as 1953 when the costs of the Korean War were being apportioned.

Neighbours in Asia

Before attempting an examination of Chinese policy after the great divide, it is useful to look at its other diplomatic activities in the period of the United Bloc. This is the time of China's major international successes, mostly won by Mr. Chou En-lai in the years 1954–7. The dominant drives of his diplomacy were directed firstly towards securing China's position and borderlands in Asia, secondly towards establishing connections with Third World Powers, particularly in Asia, and thirdly towards obtaining acceptance of China's claim to operate as one of the Powers of the central balance.

The first of these objectives, securing China's position and borders in Asia, may be seen in the assertion of sovereignty in Tibet, the intervention in Korea in late 1950 when the fighting approached the Yalu, and the claim to a voice in the disposition of Indo-China at the Geneva conference of 1954. The assertion of sovereignty over Tibet belongs to a field of decision which can be represented as domestic rather than foreign policy, in the sense that all Chinese governments for the past few centuries have laid claim to Tibet, but it was to prove a main determinant of Chinese foreign policy in the area of relations with the Indian subcontinent, and warrants analysis also as an indicator of the attitude of the new regime to the acquisitions of the Chinese Empire. Between the fall of the Manchu Empire in 1911 and the Communist accession to power in 1949, Chinese control in Tibet was so slight that the Tibetans may be said to have established *de facto* autonomy. Undoubtedly the British 'forward policy' under Lord Curzon, and the expedition of 1903, had conduced towards the transformation of Tibet from an appanage of the Chinese Empire to a quasi-autonomous state providing a protective buffer for the northern frontiers of India. The Chinese army was sent into Tibet in October 1950, and various aspects of its policy made it clear that the government in Peking now intended full sovereign control rather than a formal suzerainty. The Indian government, as heir-apparent to the sphere of influence and the material assets in Tibet acquired by the British raj, had to decide how far it should interest itself in combating this extension to its borders of the direct military power of Peking. At first Mr. Nehru appeared inclined to resist it, but an Indian note of protest against the Chinese invasion evoked a curt and hostile answer, and there appears to have been a decision in Delhi against pursuing the argument further. Neither the Indian government nor anyone else effectively supported the Tibetans when they protested to the UN. Strategically Tibet is not of importance except to China, India and perhaps Russia, so that once it was clear that the Indians were not prepared to make an issue of the question at this time, it was unlikely that anyone else would. Subsequently Delhi confirmed its acquiescence in the Chinese assumption of direct control by various measures, such as renaming the India Mission in Lhasa a Consulate-General, and by signing in 1954 an agreement on 'Trade and Intercourse between the Tibet Region of China and India'. Perhaps the most important part of this treaty to China was the title, explicity recognizing Tibet as part of the metropolitan territory of China, and under complete Chinese sovereignty. The substance of the treaty also represented a full concession of the Chinese claims. India agreed to withdraw the small military groups it had maintained, to hand over as a gift the postal, telegraphic and telephone communications set up originally by the British, and to sell twelve rest homes maintained for travellers.

It is often argued that all this merely restored to China its historical rights in Tibet, and represented a reversion to the *status quo ante* 1911, or 1903. Against this view, one may point out that though Tibet certainly lay within the imperial 'claim line' of the Chinese Empire, as Ireland did within the imperial 'claim line' of Britain for about an equal number of centuries, the Tibetans, like the Irish, had asserted their independence, and had maintained it, in the Tibetan case, for thirty-eight years more or less successfully. The parallels between Tibet's situation *vis-à-vis* China and Ireland's *vis-à-vis* England are quite close in a number of fields: the differences in religion, social organization and level of economic development, the cultural cross-influences, and the strategic importance of the weaker to the stronger. The traditional Chinese imperial view has been that territory once won for civilization (that is, for the Chinese Empire) must not be relinquished, even when circumstances require postponing its actual reclaim. It is a view that potentially has application elsewhere than Tibet. The imposition of full and ideologically-oriented control over the Tibetans involved in the succeeding years a level of 'pacification' and 'democratic reform' that have kept the Chinese army in Tibet in considerable strength, fighting a guerrilla war, and that induced the Chinese to build a military road between Tibet and Sinkiang (where also local armed resistance was endemic) across territory claimed by India, the Aksai Chin, and thus made inevitable friction along the whole line of the Himalayas.[1]

In the post-1954 phase of Chinese diplomacy, the Tibet Treaty also provided a sort of windfall or bonus in what were called the *panch shila*, or Five Principles of Co-existence. They appeared in the preamble of the treaty, and were later used by Mr. Chou En-lai very successfully as a sort of substitute for a non-aggression pact, a useful technique which created a glow of reassurance all round

[1] For the further development of Chinese–Indian relations see the chapter on India.

without actually providing for anything very enforceable. The Five Principles were (1) Mutual respect for each other's territorial integrity and sovereignty; (2) Mutual non-aggression; (3) Mutual non-interference in each other's internal affairs; (4) Equality and mutual benefit; (5) Peaceful co-existence. Mr. Chou's dexterity in the use of these hopeful platitudes at the Bandung period and later was rather a *tour de force*. Whatever his later failures, at his best period he was perhaps the most notable diplomatic conjurer since Bismarck. It is not every diplomatist who can induce a neighbour (however green) to ratify with a treaty a marked deterioration in his own strategic situation (which the Chinese move into Tibet was to prove to India), and at the same time to hand over an assortment of assets without *quid pro quo*, provide a useful international acknowledgment of a contested and dubious title to the territory concerned, and endorse a set of copybook phrases which many guileless persons will mistake for one's foreign policy, all without obtaining in return even a clarification of contested border points. In its way the Tibet Treaty was a masterstroke of Chinese diplomacy.

The next instance of Chinese concern to make good its borderlands was the intervention in the war with Korea when the fighting began to approach its frontier at the Yalu in November 1950. The Korean War appears to have been one of the causes of dissension between China and Russia: the Chinese have recently indicated that they incurred about $700,000,000 in debts to the Russians because of their involvement in it.[1] They would be entitled to add that one of the side-effects of the war, the American neutralization of Taiwan, postponed to the indefinite future China's prospects of completing the victory in the civil war and mopping up the remnants of the Kuomintang army and government on Taiwan, by putting the latter under the protection of the US Seventh Fleet. Moreover the war deflected the main force of US hostility *vis-à-vis* the Communist world from Russia to China, a development whose total results are still unpredictable. Until June 1950 there were good prospects that the American government would

[1] See an interview given by Chen Yi, *Evening Standard*, 31 May 1966.

quite soon reconcile itself to the change of regime in China, extend recognition, cease to block Peking's entry to the United Nations, and in general move to a wary but not necessarily hostile co-existence with this new force in Asia and the Pacific. The Korean War ended these possibilities for a period which has now lasted almost twenty years, and may yet be prolonged. Undoubtedly it might be considered the major early disaster of China's foreign relations and if, as some of the evidence appears to suggest, the Chinese were not consulted or even forewarned about the initial North Korean drive south, they had good reason to feel embittered at the policy-decisions concerned.

Given that there is no reason to regard the initiation of the war as a measure of Chinese policy, we may ask what factors induced the Chinese leaders to take the dangerous decision for intervention, when it meant encountering a Western army at so early a stage of national consolidation. The answer is probably a special sensitivity about Korea as an invasion path and because of its proximity to the vital industrial area of Manchuria, as well as particular apprehensions at the time about the possible American role in support of the counter-revolutionary army and government of Chiang Kai-shek. These apprehensions were lent some colour by the policy-urgings of General MacArthur during this period. An attempt was made by some Western leaders (especially Ernest Bevin) to convey to Peking via the Indian Ambassador there (who was at the time very much *persona grata*) that no incursion into Chinese territories need be feared, but it is hardly surprising that this effort at reassurance was unsuccessful.

The Korean intervention, though on balance diplomatically disadvantageous to China, provided it with some benefits, aside from the obvious one of a buffer-state to protect a vulnerable sector of the frontier. Successful resistance to a Western army and, more important, a demonstrated ability to survive under concentrated Western air-power offered lessons which Chinese army leaders were not slow to absorb and expound to others, and the war in its later stages undoubtedly contributed to that 'polarizing' of opinion between the West and the Third World which was the basis for most Chinese diplomatic successes over the succeeding nine years.

So also did the next major episode in Chinese foreign policy, a successful bid for a voice in the settlement of the Indo-China war. Only three months after the Korean armistice was concluded in July 1953, the military situation in North Vietnam began to move into the phase that was to culminate in the French decision to quit. The French high command resolved to challenge General Giap to a conventional battle which it was hoped would destroy his resources and morale, and accordingly began in November 1953 to fortify the armed camp at Dien Bien Phu, in the midst of mountainous country long held by the Viet Minh. One may regard as an instance of Chinese luck the concatenation of events which consequently provided China with a mode of entry to the Vietnam situation. The French choice fell on a site which was within fairly easy supply distance of southern China, the end of the fighting in Korea had made military supplies available, and the political circumstances were so arranged, mostly by Western leaders, as to provide Ho Chi Minh with irresistible reasons for acquiescing in a dependence on China which Vietnamese nationalism had earnestly sought to avoid. The Western leaders in Berlin in January 1954 had arranged a conference which was to discuss Korea and Indo-China, thus providing the Vietnamese general, Giap, with three months' notice to make the point at Dien Bien Phu of the military ascendancy of the Viet Minh–three months in which he could look only to China for the artillery and other heavy equipment with which to reduce the French camp. The military operation was judiciously mounted: the French resistance actually ended the very day the conference opened. It was as if the West first offered Ho a lever to secure his political objectives, and then carefully arranged that he must turn to China for the little extra power he needed for his elbow. The process whereby the Vietnamese, historically perhaps the most anti-Chinese of all the peoples of South-East Asia, have come to find themselves, in effect, the military proxies of China in its hostilities with the United States, begins with this disastrous episode.

The Vietnam involvement has since then operated as a sort of ladder for China in its determined climb to a place among the dominant Powers, the 'top table' of the world's debate. China's first solid experience of dealing jointly with the other Powers of the central balance as an equal was during the three-month-long negotiations at Geneva on Indo-China. Mr. Chou En-lai's first marked success in the 'personal tour' style of diplomacy was his visit to India and Burma during the interval of the Conference. This was at a time when the polarizing of Asian opinion against the West in the diplomatic field, which has been mentioned as one of the side-effects of the Korean War, had become especially acute, because of a rise in expectation that America might be about to intervene in Indo-China. It was also this Vietnam crisis which dominated the Colombo Powers Conference (India, Indonesia, Pakistan, Burma, Ceylon) in April–May 1954, which eventuated in the decision to hold the Bandung Conference in Indonesia in 1955. That meeting in turn was not only the scene of Mr. Chou's greatest success *vis-à-vis* Afro-Asian opinion, but offered a first approximation to what later became the most vital element in Chinese foreign policy generally, the theory of the revolutionary 'countryside of the world'. Of course, it may be argued that these developments might well have occurred without the initial Vietnam involvement of 1953–4, but as a sequence of events they did undoubtedly stem from it.

Chinese foreign policy has been a curious mixture of the pragmatic and the ideological, with Mr. Chou usually assumed to be responsible for the pragmatism and Messrs. Liu Shao-chi, Teng Hsiao-ping and Lin Piao for the ideology, within the general framework of the 'thought of Mao Tse-tung'. The pragmatic strand is demonstrated by, for instance, the continued Chinese tolerance until 1967 of Hong Kong,[1] despite its incompatibility

[1] To speak of pragmatism in connection with Chinese acceptance of the situation of Hong Kong means no more than that, up to 1967, the government in Peking felt that the balance of practical advantage *for the time being* lay in leaving the situation mostly undisturbed. Obviously at any time it was possible for them to revise this judgment and events from May 1967 seemed to indicate that in

with revolutionary anti-imperialism, for the practical advantages it offers as a supplier of foreign currency. Mr. Chou's relations during the period 1954–9 with the leaders of the Third World–Nehru, Sukarno, U Nu, Nasser and others–is also a good example of it, the cultivation of useful diplomatic friendships taking precedence at this time over the waving of ideological banners. Possibly as the tensions within the Chinese leadership grew after 1962 with the prospective need for providing for the succession to Mao and with the obsessive fear of 'revisionism' in China itself, this early tactical flexibility of Mr. Chou made him personally vulnerable, and necessitated the more rigidly ideological diplomacy of the period after 1963, despite its demonstrated tendency to tactical failure.

In some instances of policy-decision, pragmatism and ideological preconceptions conduced in the same direction, as in Vietnam. In others, such as the early stages of the schism with Russia, many analysts have held that these two sets of preoccupations were in conflict, and that the ideological drives proved stronger than the practical advantages of continued good relations with Russia. This is a tenable position, yet one may also argue that from a Chinese-eye view, the practical disadvantages of quarrelling with Russia looked on balance less damaging than the 'opportunity-costs' of remaining on good terms. This is a view which enables one to see a reasonable logic in the timing of the schism.

The Great Schism

One might say that the seeds of dissension between the USSR and the Chinese People's Republic were sown in the encounters between the Chinese Empire and the Russian Empire from the sixteenth century on: that they germinated in the twenty-eight years of rather doubtful help and advice that the Chinese Communist leadership received from Russia before its accession to power, and that therefore when the first frail-seeming shoots of

conditions of domestic political tension a source of foreign exchange, no matter how useful, could not necessarily count on remaining sacrosanct.

visible difference showed above ground to outside observers in 1958, these constituted tokens of a strong and multiple-rooted development underground which could readily produce an impassible thicket by 1962. There are many points at which one might begin the examination of this process, but perhaps the most convenient for our purposes is the Soviet revision of the Leninist doctrine concerning war, first promulgated by Malenkov in 1954, and elaborated by Khrushchev in 1956. The essence of the change was recognition that the existence of nuclear weapons had lessened the acceptability of risks of general war as a midwife of revolution. Many people assume that because the Chinese scornfully call the Russians 'revisionists' this means that they, the Chinese, altogether reject this variant of Leninist doctrine and continue to believe in the inevitability of central war, and even to welcome the idea. This is by no means an accurate statement of the Chinese position, though it has been given currency by the Russians. Actually what the Chinese do is accept the transforming impact of nuclear weapons on the readiness of states to make war, but draw a different maxim for policy from it. They take the nuclear stalemate more seriously, in a way, than anyone else, saying, in effect: 'The camp of socialism and peace is so strong (with its nuclear weapons) that the reactionaries are deterred: they dare not unleash nuclear war and therefore "wars of national liberation" can and should be militantly pursued'. They accuse the Russians of being cowards who are so scared of nuclear war that they will not give any proper fraternal assistance to the revolution-aries in wars of national liberation. That is, they are much more *optimistic* than the Russians: they believe much more in the reality of the Communist nuclear advantage, and hold therefore that the Communist camp can afford to risk a quite determined erosion of Western positions by guerrilla and political means under its protective cover.[1] The Russians (who, of course, know a great

[1] A more detailed study of Chinese attitudes concerning nuclear weapons is to be found in Morton Halperin, *China and the Bomb*, Pall Mall, London, 1965, and in Alice Langley Hsieh, *Communist China and the Nuclear Force*, Rand, Los Angeles, 1965, to both of whom the author acknowledges a large debt.

deal more than the Chinese about the details of the actual nuclear balance between themselves and the Americans) behave on the whole as if they were adherents of the Western doctrine called 'the delicate balance of terror': that is, that the nuclear stalemate will probably deter the other side, but is a fairly fragile arrangement, delicate enough to inhibit sensible people from doing anything that may disturb it. Around these two viewpoints the essential Russo–Chinese argument developed progressively from late 1957. It was first indicated in November 1957, at the international Communist conference in Moscow for the fortieth anniversary of the 1917 revolution. On the surface this was quite a harmonious occasion, but Mao Tse-tung made some statements which were incompatible with the Russian position, if taken literally, and which the Russians and others have been publicly reproaching him with ever since the schism became overt. These statements included the slogan that the east wind was prevailing over the west wind (i.e. that the balance of power had shifted decisively in favour of the Communist world) and that, if the worst came to the worst, and the imperialists plunged the world into nuclear war, and 'even if half mankind were killed', nevertheless only imperialism would vanish, while the survivors of the battle would build themselves a brilliant future in a socialist society. This, of course, was the *old* Russian position which Malenkov had prematurely cast doubt on in 1954, and Khrushchev had modified only in 1956, but it has been used by the Russians since 1962 to illustrate Mao's alleged nuclear recklessness.

However, 1957 was in one way, despite this November speech, a high point in Sino–Soviet good relations, for just after the Russians had launched their first satellite in October 1957 *they signed an agreement to help China in atomic development*. This agreement remained in force less than two years: it was unilaterally denounced by the Russians, according to the Chinese, in June 1959, about the time of Mr. Khrushchev's journey to America. The Chinese call Mr. Khrushchev's denunciation of the agreement 'a gift to President Eisenhower'.

THE FOREIGN POLICY OF CHINA

The Chinese optimism about the east wind prevailing over the west wind, and about the scope for militancy provided by the nuclear stalemate, issued in a dispute with Russia over diplomatic strategy only eight months after the 1957 agreement. In July 1958 there occurred the *coup* in Iraq, under the leadership of Brigadier Kassem, which overthrew the old-line nationalists led by Nuri Es-said, disposed bloodily of him and many of the dynasty, and was believed at one stage to be the signal for general turmoil and a leftist take-over through a large area of the Middle East. An American landing in Lebanon and a British one in Jordan were mounted to preclude this. At that time there appears to have been a major dispute between Mao Tse-tung and Khrushchev about the handling, diplomatically, of these events. Mr. Khrushchev was summoned urgently to Peking in the middle of the crisis. A few weeks later, in August–September 1958, China began to mount what looked like a serious offensive, bidding for Quemoy and Matsu. Again Peking's view of what should be done was apparently frustrated by Mr. Khrushchev's caution. He seems to have refused to back China with the air-power essential for any confrontation with the US Seventh Fleet, though he did send a letter to the US, warning that a nuclear attack on mainland China would precipitate general war.

The Russians still claim that their power of nuclear strike protected China in this 1958 Taiwan Straits crisis, but the Chinese interpretation of the incident appears to imply that the Russians refused support until it was clear that they would not be involved in war: 'The Soviet leaders expressed their support for China on 7 and 19 September respectively. Although at that time the situa-in the Taiwan Straits was tense, there was no possibility that a nuclear war would break out and no need for the Soviet Union to support China with its nuclear weapons. *It was only when they were clear that this was the situation that the Soviet leaders expressed their support for China.*'[1]

The 1958 Quemoy and Matsu crisis offered a very good illustration, if one were needed for the Chinese, of the importance of

[1] *Peking Review*, 6 September 1963.

nuclear weapons under their own control. For the Russians it illustrated the dangers of a potentially-nuclear ally with urgent ambitions to remake the world power structure. So that by early 1959 relations were already bad, and in 1959 Mr. Khrushchev chose to go off and visit the enemy: that is, to tour America and confer with President Eisenhower at Camp David. One could perhaps regard the middle of 1959 (the Russian repudiation of the atomic agreement) as the point at which the parting of the ways began to seem permanent to both China and Russia.

In 1960 there was a good deal of undercover manoeuvring, including perhaps an effort by Peking to turn the Russian party against Khrushchev, and some border friction in Sinkiang. There was another summit meeting of Communist Parties in Moscow in December 1960. Retrospectively this must be seen as an effort by Mr. Khrushchev to rally the world's Communist Parties behind the Soviet Union, and at the time he seemed largely to succeed, marshalling overwhelming support for the Russian line. But the Chinese, though defeated, were not convinced that their defeat was permanent: the Chinese delegate at Moscow, Teng Hsiao-ping (regarded until the convulsions of 1966 as in the line of succession to Mao), proclaimed China's right to form a 'fraction' within the world Communist movement, and to work at converting other Communist Parties to its own view.

From the Chinese point of view the Cuba crisis of October 1962 offered an ideal moment for Mao Tse-tung to make the quarrel with the Russians official, an issue in which he could represent Khrushchev as both an 'adventurist' and a 'capitulationist' (the first for putting the missiles *in*, the second for backing down and taking them *out* at America's behest). The Soviet Union's main claim to determine diplomatic strategy for the Communist Bloc was the claim that it (or Mr. Khrushchev) was not only cautious but successful. On this instance Mao could claim that Khrushchev was reckless (not cautious), in that he brought the world to the nuclear brink, and that moreover his policy failed; since the American imperialists were allowed to get away with dictating their ultimatum about the rockets. The fact that tactically speaking this was a well-judged point to make the quarrel open is shown in considerable Chinese success in the following two or three years in the ideological competition with the Soviet Union.

If there had been any hope of a reconciliation after 1962, the nuclear test ban treaty of July 1963 would have dispelled it. For the treaty rested, as the Chinese have since proclaimed, on a Russian assumption of a similarity of interests with America (and Britain) as against the rest of the world, including China. China's reaction was therefore fierce: the treaty was called 'a dirty fraud', the Russian leaders 'freaks and monsters', and Mr. Khrushchev himself 'Russia's shame'. In reply, the Russians accused China of 'connivance with those who advocate world thermo-nuclear war' and compared Mao with Dr. Adenauer, than which Communist reproaches could hardly be stronger.

Looking back over the schism as a whole, it may seem that the alliance apparently foundered on rocks which other alliances of less moment have survived: a difference in assessment of the balance of power, an asymmetry of diplomatic interests, conflicting interpretations of dogma. Possibly the doctrinal element was responsible: apostates and heretics evoke much more hatred than mere infidels. But in the later stages it became apparent that the historic grievances of China as a state were a crucial element even in this most ideologically-oriented of her diplomatic relations. It is not only that the heirs of the old Chinese Empire have some debts to claim from the heirs of the old Czarist Empire, but that the status of a protégé of the U.S.S.R. in world politics, and confinement to second fiddle in the Communist orchestra, were always deeply incompatible with the Chinese view of China's place in the world.

The Central Land

This is, in fact, an influence on decision-making which must be understood in order to make sense not only of China's relations with Russia, but its relations with the states round the periphery of China, and the central drive of its foreign policy. It is the five-eighths of the iceberg which lies beneath the surface and makes it

THE FOREIGN POLICY OF CHINA

formidable. The traditional and immemorial Chinese concept of China as the 'Central Land', the central and light-bearing civilization of the world, carries in itself overtones about the status of outsiders. The Chinese world-picture was never that of a system of equal sovereign states: it was of the Chinese area of civilization surrounded by a penumbra of near-by barbarian kingdoms, such as Burma, which paid due tribute, and more distant barbarian kingdoms whose first envoys, such as Lord McCartney in 1793, were originally assumed also to represent tribute-bearing missions, and were expected to perform the nine ritual prostrations in token of this role. The tributary system was by no means simply a picturesque charade of no political significance, as is sometimes alleged. It stemmed directly from Confucian doctrine:

> The Confucian view of the foreigner depends partly on the stress given to the unique nature of the earthly authority delegated to the Son of Heaven. Such authority *precludes the need for or the legality of other political units, and compromises a temporal power over all members of the civilized world*. . . . Thus once a barbarian people has shown itself sufficiently well educated to appreciate the benefits of Chinese authority, it qualifies to become a full member of the Empire. . . . Subject peoples can acknowledge his [the Emperor's] authority by the payment of material tribute, whose presence at court serves to enhance the Emperor's majesty and *to demonstrate the universal acceptance of his title to power*.[1]

The present leaders of China are not Confucianists, but they were children of the most historically-minded and traditionalist of cultures, and there are a considerable number of parallels between Confucian and Maoist doctrine, most relevantly in the notion of a duty to educate the peoples in wisdom and virtue, now epitomized in 'the thought of Mao Tse-tung'. Mao himself produces in many of his writings and interviews the impression of a man profoundly influenced by his own concept of historical justice. As to what that

[1] Michael Loewe, *Imperial China*, Allen & Unwin, London, 1966, pp. 248–9. Italics added.

concept may be, there was some evidence in an interview he gave in July 1964 to a visiting delegation of Japanese socialists:

There are too many places occupied by the Soviet Union. In accordance with the Yalta agreement the Soviet Union, under the pretext of assuring the independence of Mongolia, actually placed the country under its domination. In 1954 when Khrushchev and Bulganin came to China we took up this question, but they refused to talk to us. The Russians took everything they could. . . . The Soviet Union has an area of 22 million square kilometres and its population is only 220 million. *It is about time to put an end to this allotment.* . . . About a hundred years ago the area to the east of Lake Baikal became Russian territory, and since then Vladivostok, Khabarovsk, Kamchatka and other areas have been Soviet territory. *We have not yet presented our account for this list.*[1]

Chou En-lai also talked to the same delegation:

The USSR is holding a large amount of territory which was taken from others since the Czarist period, and it is logical and justifiable for newly-independent countries to claim their former territories. At the interview with Premier Khrushchev in January 1957 I requested that the USSR make proper arrangements for the territorial issues covering *Japan, China, the Middle East and Eastern European countries including Finland*. I could not get a satisfactory answer from him then but the announcement of the issue was kept secret because the Sino–Soviet dispute was not public at that time.[2]

If the Chinese were, as this implies, already in 1954 and 1957 suggesting that the Russians give back their ill-gotten gains of the past few centuries, it is not surprising that they swiftly came to look like very inconvenient allies to Moscow. The Russians were naturally irked also at these 1964 statements by the Chinese leaders and denounced them editorially:

[1] Interview originally published in Tokyo, *Sekai Shuko*, 11 August 1964.
[2] Tokyo, *Asahi Shimbun*, August 1964.

The Chinese leaders no longer even attempt to camouflage their expansionist ambitions. ... We are faced with an openly expansionist programme with far-reaching intentions. ... They would like to deprive Mongolia of its independence and make it a Chinese province. It was precisely about this that the P.R.C. leaders offered to reach agreement with N. S. Khrushchev and other Soviet comrades during their visit to Peking in 1954. N. S. Khrushchev naturally refused to discuss the question. ... The true schemes of the Chinese leaders became obvious. They are permeated through and through with great-power chauvinism and hegemonism.[1]

There is some further evidence of a Chinese preoccupation with remaking the map of Asia, in a fashion closer to its eighteenth-century edition, in a book published in 1954, in Peking, entitled *A Brief History of Modern China*. This volume shows the area wrongfully wrested from Chinese sovereignty or suzerainty since 1840 as including Ladakh, Nepal, Sikkim, Bhutan, the North Eastern Frontier Area, Assam, the Andaman Islands (all now under Indian sovereignty or influence), Burma, Malaya, Singapore, Thailand and Indo-China, the Sulu Islands, the Ryukyus, Korea and Formosa, and the very large areas now held by the USSR: the whole of Eastern Turkestan, Kazakhstan, the area of Siberia west of the Amur River, the maritime provinces east of the Amur running down to Vladivostok, and the island of Sakhalin. This area of potential *irredenta* is so vast that it is difficult to take it all seriously as an object of intended reclaim, even though there are some elements in recent Chinese diplomacy, especially *vis-à-vis* India, which would support such a view. Aspirations of this size must seem as remote from immediate policy-making as those in Mussolini's Italy to re-create the Roman Empire, but one might note, thinking of the remoter future, firstly that sovereignty or suzerainty has been lost only for a century, a mere temporary setback to those accustomed to think in terms of the span of Chinese history, and secondly that China's potential strength relative to

[1] *Pravda*, 2 September 1964.

the Asian neighbours concerned is very formidable. Its comparative impotence at present, even round its own periphery, is a function of a still disadvantageous position *vis-à-vis* the two dominant Powers of the central balance, America and Russia, rather than of any *local* weakness in Asia. This is a point which becomes of importance when we consider the motives behind the strenuous Chinese drive for effective nuclear strike-power.

Before examining this aspect of policy, however, one may note a few additional influences deriving from China's historical experience of the area round her own periphery. There is firstly the fact that the north has been on the whole a sphere of vulnerability and danger, and the south a sphere of opportunity. Until the arrival of the West in Asia, the problem of its hard-to-defend northern frontier was the central preoccupation of Chinese defence policy. One of the solutions tried was the Great Wall of China, which at various times from the seventh to the seventeenth century was an important element in the Chinese security system. Like its later analogue, the Maginot line, it was not entirely successful at keeping out the traditional invaders, who in the Chinese case were the primitive but militarily formidable peoples of North-Central Asia, Mongols and Manchus.

The south, on the other hand, was geographically less open, was inhabited by peoples who did not pose any serious dangers, and was far more commercially promising. There were probably small colonies of overseas Chinese, chiefly merchants, settled in Sumatra, Java, and Malaya by the sixth century A.D. During the Ming dynasty, in the fifteenth century, there was a series of Chinese maritime expeditions to the Nan Yang—the south seas—and across the Indian Ocean, as far west as the Persian Gulf, the Red Sea and the east coast of Africa (from which they brought back a giraffe for the Emperor's zoo).[1] As C. P. Fitzgerald points out, China for a time enjoyed maritime supremacy in these waters. The fleet was based on Foochow in South China and was of a great size for those days, sixty-two vessels carrying about 37,000 men.

[1] C. P. Fitzgerald, *The Third China*, Cheshire, Melbourne, 1965, p. 5.

The forward base was in Malacca,[1] the straits being, then as now, of great strategic significance.

One of the relics of this Chinese *Drang nach Süden* in its commercial and individual phase is the presence in this part of the world of the communities of Overseas Chinese (most of whom, as someone has pointed out, are merely Over Land). These communities are now estimated in all at 12 or 13 million, the largest concentrations being in Malaya and Singapore, where they constitute about 40 per cent and 80 per cent of the populations respectively. They have had an oddly backhanded influence on China's relations with the countries concerned. The presence of the Chinese, their clannishness and commercial acumen, make them the targets of a sort of Asian variant of anti-semitism at the popular level, complete with all the attendant phenomena such as pogroms and discriminatory legislation. But unlike the Jews in Europe they have at hand a potentially powerful motherland. This means that they also readily take on the aspect of a fifth column or Trojan horse to the government under whose aegis they live. The sense of being under pressure from China which dominates the foreign policy of, for instance, Thailand, relates as much or more to the presence of the Chinese among the Thai as to the existence of China as a neighbour. This reaction has not much to do with Communism: it was just as marked in Thai attitudes in the century before 1949. The sense of being under pressure from the Han people is not paranoid fantasy: it reflects ethnic experience. It may result, as in the Thai case, in taking out strategic 'insurance' with an outside Power, in this case the United States. This in turn increases the incentive for Chinese 'psychological warfare', and the encouragement of a guerrilla campaign against the Thai government, if only in order to demonstrate that the installation of US protection attracts the lightning. The existence of the Overseas Chinese, on the whole, can thus be regarded as having constituted a problem rather than an asset for Chinese foreign policy, exacerbating among its neighbours, especially the Thai and the Malay peoples (including Indonesians and Filipinos), the fears and

[1] *Ibid.*

resentments which make a good many of them look for the re-assurance of a Western countervailing presence. That is not to say that these Overseas Chinese communities could not at some future date be useful to China. Two insurgent movements, that in Malaya and the C.C.O. in Borneo, have already been based upon them, and possibly others could be.

Nuclear weapons

On the whole, one should probably relate the Chinese drive for nuclear weapons primarily to the claim to a place among the dominant Powers of the central balance rather than to local military preoccupations in Asia. To quote a Chinese journal, 'A country which has fine delivery vehicles (long-range missiles and guided missiles) and a large quantity of nuclear bombs of great variety is a super-state, and only a super-state is qualified to lead the world and to control and direct those countries which do not have nuclear weapons or have only a small quantity of nuclear weapons without delivery vehicles'.[1]

Investment in almost any other form of military equipment (e.g. fighter aircraft, long-range artillery, tactical bombers, motor transport, naval vessels) would have been of more immediate relevance in local quarrels in Asia than nuclear weapons: it is only in the Chinese confrontation with the two dominant nuclear Powers that a nuclear-strike capacity of its own can have seemed a sufficiently vital necessity to warrant allocating the very substantial resources it absorbs, in competition with their other needs.

It may seem unconvincing to argue that so vague and indefinite a concept as that of becoming one of the dominant Powers of the central balance can account for the intensity of this Chinese drive. But one must remember the emotional force deriving from China's past experience: the two thousand years or more of being not only *a* dominant Power but *the* dominant Power in her own world, plus the century of eclipse and powerlessness. Of course, China might be held to have a claim for a place among the dominant Powers even without advanced weapons, on the simple

[1] *China Youth*, February 1963, quoted in Halperin, *op. cit.*

basis of size and population. But China's size has been even greater, geographically, and its population probably always as much in excess of Europe's as it is now, and these factors failed in the past to establish its claims, since they were not backed by efficient military power. Again one could say that with its enormous resources in manpower, China might more easily establish its claims on the basis of *conventional* as against nuclear military power. But the Chinese leaders have been faced by the fact, over the past 18 years, that even with their very large army (2½ million, the largest in Asia, with a 30-million militia) it is not feasible to venture far beyond China's own frontiers, lacking air and naval forces, and subject to the sanction of possible nuclear strike, either US or Russian. In general strategic theorizing it has often been argued that the possession of nuclear weapons has now become the necessary condition under which conventional weapons become effective. This was the strategic concept behind the Western conventional build-up in Europe after the Russian acquisition of nuclear weapons, and is one of the footnotes to the theory of nuclear stalemate to which, as previously noted, the Chinese have adhered.

The Chinese appear, to judge by a classified military publication obtained by US intelligence services,[1] to have believed since 1961 that they were not likely to receive Soviet assistance in case of nuclear war with America: that is, they have at least since then doubted the credibility of the Russian nuclear guarantee. On the other hand, they argue strongly against the likelihood of nuclear weapons being used in 'wars of national liberation', *either* by the Americans or to help the insurgents. They stress that the decisive factor in such hostilities is the local strength of the insurgents and their relations with the people on whom they are based. This might be regarded as a convenient rationalization for limiting their aid to Vietnam, but it is also an exemplification of the general theory that men not weapons are decisive, and it is blessed by a text

[1] *Bulletin of Activities of the General Political Department of the People's Liberation Army*, a publication apparently circulated at the level of regimental commander. See *China Quarterly*, April–June 1964.

from a Mao Tse-tung statement dated August 1945, 'Some of our comrades too, believe that the atomic bomb is all-powerful: that is a big mistake.... The theory that "weapons decide everything", the purely military viewpoint ... individualist thinking and the like ... these are bourgeois influences.'[1]

Some of the purges of high-ranking army officers in 1966 may have been related to their addiction to such a 'purely military viewpoint'. In the case of 'wars of national liberation' there is also the commonsense point of the character and locale of the fighting, in which mass-destruction weapons are likely to be equally damaging to insurgents and defenders. The Chinese do not say that nuclear weapons are *irrelevant* to such struggles: on the contrary, they argue that such weapons provide the cover of the nuclear stalemate, under which adequate fraternal aid to insurgents can be given by China (and should be, though they say it is not, given by Russia). Thus the Chinese government statement at the time of the first Chinese nuclear test:

> The mastering of the nuclear weapons by China is a great encouragement to the revolutionary peoples of the world in their struggles and a great contribution to the course of world peace.[2]

Contrasting their own attitude with that of the Russians, they allege that the Russian leaders 'hold that with the appearance of nuclear weapons the oppressed peoples and nations must abandon revolutionary wars and wars of national liberation'. The Russians have thus, according to Chinese arguments, become collaborators in an alleged US policy of 'nuclear blackmail'.[3]

The Chinese also reject the argument, which the Russians by the signature of the test-ban treaty and by the interest in an antiproliferation treaty have appeared to endorse, and which of course they share with the West, that the multiplication of nuclear forces is in itself a danger to the survival of the world:

---

[1] Though this statement is dated in the *Selected Works of Mao Tse-tung* (IV, 21–22) as though it were an initial reaction to atomic weapons, it has been suggested that it may have been written later; Halperin, *op. cit.*

[2] *Peking Review*, 16 October 1964.   [3] *Ibid.*, 15 August 1963.

With regard to preventing nuclear proliferation, the Chinese Government has always maintained that the arguments of the US imperialists must not be echoed, but that a class analysis must be made. Whether or not nuclear weapons help peace depends on who possesses them. It is detrimental to peace if they are in the hands of imperialist countries: it helps peace if they are in the hands of socialist countries. It must not be said undiscriminatingly that the danger of nuclear war increases along with the number of nuclear powers. . . . Nuclear weapons in the hands of a socialist country are always a means of defence against nuclear blackmail and nuclear war. . . . A fierce class-struggle is now going on in the world. In this struggle the greater the strength of our side, the better.[1]

Like some right-wing Westerners, the Chinese argue that Communist states have only been, and can only be, established by armed struggle: to renounce armed struggle is to renounce revolution. And they go on to argue that as well as being a betrayal of the people this would endanger peace by allowing the reactionaries to strengthen themselves. In other words, like Mr. Dulles, they reject 'appeasement', both on moral and on prudential grounds. The difference between what the Chinese leaders actually say and what the Russians *allege* that they say is in part a matter of spirit and emphasis, but on the whole one can probably agree that the Chinese are justified in accusing the Russians of deliberately misrepresenting Mao Tse-tung's position. However, one point on which the Russians could perhaps make a more convincing case than they at present do is their implication that the Chinese do not know what they are talking about and have misconstrued the existing balance of forces, since they do not have the detailed intelligence estimates. Mao's famous November 1957 remark, 'It is characteristic of the situation today, I believe, that the East wind is prevailing over the West wind. That is to say, the forces of socialism are overwhelmingly superior to the forces of imperialism', always was exceedingly optimistic. The Russians have said in semi-rebuttal:

[1] *Ibid.*

Of course we cannot now divulge such things as, for instance, the concrete results of the nuclear weapons tests we carried out in 1961–2. . . . The Chinese leaders cannot be unaware of the fact that obtaining really reliable information on Soviet nuclear and missile weapons is exactly what the military staffs of certain powers and aggressive military blocs dream of.[1]

The Russians unfortunately cannot push this line of attack very far without implying that their own strength has always been rather less than they had earlier claimed *vis-à-vis* the Americans.

Prospects

Over the next ten years China will presumably, at its present rate of development, move from nominal to reasonably effective nuclear power. It will have not only nuclear warheads, but adequate delivery vehicles, including rockets of sufficient range to interest the US in an A.B.M. system directed at China. Rockets of adequate range for American cities would also, of course, reach the cities of European Russia or of Western Europe. What are the prospects for Chinese foreign policy in that new era? Is it likely to mend its relations with either of the two dominant Powers of the central balance, the United States and the Soviet Union? How well is it likely to fare in its search for tactical allies in Europe or elsewhere? What are the long-term (or medium-term) powers of attraction of its brand of revolutionary doctrine?

Examining first China's relations with the United States, there are few reasons for optimism, but on the other hand the assumptions which are often made of early and cataclysmic general war do not appear justifiable. Even in ten years China is very unlikely to have attained an approach to nuclear parity with America, the only condition which might make the decision to risk general war look worth daring. There is more prudence and control on both sides in relations between the two countries than is usually assumed to be the case. There is also a regular channel of diplomatic communication, the meetings between the Chinese and American ambassadors in Warsaw, which the Chinese readily use,

[1] *Pravda*, 21 August 1963.

and which seem to serve fairly adequately the basic purposes served by formal diplomatic representation.[1] America appears to have opted for what is usually called the 'two Chinas' policy, but which might more accurately be called the 'China and Taiwan' policy, which will seek to preserve the separate government of Taiwan, but will not seriously regard it as the government of China. The government in Peking will not accept this separation of Taiwan as permanent, of course, but in fact Taiwan has been under a different government from that of the mainland of China for most of the past seventy years. Its re-integration need not necessarily seem urgent enough to justify a risk of nuclear war with so formidable a Power as America, especially as the chances of an ultimate political re-integration must seem promising to Peking. The other potential *casus belli*, the hostilities in Vietnam, also are rather less likely to expand into general war between China and America than is sometimes implied. There is no warrant in the Chinese theory of the war of national liberation for Chinese initiation of such a development, and the strategic advice apparently being tendered by Peking to Hanoi would appear on the contrary to conduce to reduction of the level of military action to that of regional guerrilla operations indefinitely extended. There are good military reasons for doubting the likelihood that any American invasion of North Vietnam would approach the Chinese frontier, as in the Korean case. American bombing attacks on Chinese targets may, unfortunately, be rather more likely, though there are strong political inhibitions in Washington against them. Given China's present military limitations, and the persistence of the schism with the Soviet Union, even this would be likely to produce expanded peripheral war, rather than central war.

[1] It is noteworthy that the Russians have recently accused the Chinese of using this channel to reach an agreement of sorts with the Americans about the conduct of the war in Vietnam. While the Russians undoubtedly published this material simply as a retort to the Chinese accusations against them of 'collaboration in American nuclear blackmail', it makes an interesting addition to the already considerable evidence that these meetings constitute effective communication, and have even resulted in a modification of policy-decisions on both sides.

Ought one, however, to assume that China will mend its quarrel with the Soviet Union? On present evidence this seems even less likely in the future than it has been in the past. In fact China might seem to the Russians, for the foreseeable future, even more dangerous as an ally than she is as a hostile rival. This is a matter of China's growing nuclear status and the mood of the present and prospective Chinese leadership. Even before China was within distance of an independent power of nuclear strike, she was from the Soviet point of view an awkward, risk-entailing ally, with an excessive tendency towards 'brinkmanship' *vis-à-vis* America. If the alliance were restored, *in a context in which China will be controlling her own nuclear weapons* (and China is certainly not going to give up such independent control), then the Soviet Union would potentially be exposed to hair-raising risks by the alliance. One has only to think of a re-run of the Quemoy–Matsu crisis in 1968 instead of 1958, with China thinking itself able perhaps to 'trigger' the Russian nuclear strike by using its own weapons first. The Soviet Union has the same problems *vis-à-vis* China as the United States might potentially have *vis-à-vis* the European nuclear strike powers, but at a much more dangerous level. Thus the Russians would now have good reasons for caginess about restoration of the alliance, even if China were ready to settle for anything less than total victory in the debate over diplomatic strategy, and of this there is no sign. The Soviet Union lost nothing economically and very little militarily by the break with China, and what it has lost in clear title to leadership of the Communist camp is far less serious than the risks it would take by sharing the control of strategy with China.

Since the Chinese leaders discarded the assumption of the 'United Bloc', perhaps in 1959, they have depicted the struggle for the world as essentially a three-cornered one: the true revolution, as incarnated in themselves, the camp of imperialist reaction, as led by the United States, and the corrupted revolution, or revisionists, under the leadership of Moscow. Chinese spokesmen have not hesitated to imply an actual military understanding between 'reactionaries' and 'revisionists': Chen Yi in an interview given to two journalists in 1966 asked, in the context of discussion of a possible American–Japanese attack on China, 'How can it be said that Russia would not aid America?'[1] Aside from these three competing camps, the Chinese see the world as consisting of the 'first intermediate zone', which is roughly the poor, developing world of Asia, Africa and Latin America, and the 'second intermediate zone', the rich, industrialized, bourgeois world of Europe and its fellow-travellers, and perhaps Japan. They have some hopes regarding this prosperous world of the 'second intermediate zone', especially with respect to Japan and dissident US allies like France. The theoretical rationale of these hopes is that, even though the countries concerned are dominated by a reactionary bourgeoisie, they are themselves suffering from the oppression of the leader of the imperialist camp, America, and therefore may be useful as tactical allies. Thus for instance a sympathetic interest in French nuclear development becomes logical. In fact the Chinese have found that nationalist resentments, even inside the Communist camp, as in Rumania, may be an extra weapon against both the present dominant Powers.

However, the main focus of Chinese revolutionary diplomacy is on the first intermediate zone or, as it has been more picturesquely called since 1962, 'the countryside of the world', for which the Chinese have developed a rather haunting line of theory. Though the name has only been in use since 1962–3, the roots of this theory are in the original Maoist concept of the revolutionary role of the peasantry, dating to before 1927. One can regard the whole theory as a transposition to the international scene of the political and strategic concepts by which Mao came to power in China. Long before the quarrel with Russia, as early at least as 1939, Mao had expressed the view that the revolution in *all* colonial and semi-colonial countries would follow the same laws of development as in China, and this idea was reiterated by Liu Shao-chi at a vital Peking policy conference just after the victory in China. It is a view which always contained the potential for a major theoretical conflict with Russia, because it rested on a fundamental difference

[1] *Evening Standard*, 3 May 1966.

of analysis, in Marxist terms, of what are called the 'main contradictions of the present period of history'. The Russians still maintain that the main contradiction is the power-struggle between themselves and America: the Chinese say that the main struggle is that to control these 'intermediate zones'.

The main contradiction of our time is the contradiction, *not between socialism and imperialism, but between the national liberation movement and imperialism* . . . the various types of contradictions in the contemporary world are concentrated in the vast areas of Asia, Africa and Latin America . . . the whole cause of the international proletarian revolution hinges on the outcome of the revolutionary struggles of the people of these areas, who constitute the overwhelming majority of the world's population.[1]

Thus from the Chinese point of view any militant revolutionary movement in the colonial or ex-colonial world is worth supporting, whether it embraces any genuine Communist element or not: indeed even if it represents atavistic reactionary tribalism, as in fact was the case with one of the African groups that Chinese funds helped.[2]

The objective character of the 'first wave' of the revolution is subordinate to the fact that it destroys established structures of authority: the party cadres will capture power in a 'second wave' revolution, just as the Communists did from the Nationalists in China. This doctrine, which ought perhaps to be called Maoism rather than Marxism, fits the contemporary phase of world politics rather tellingly, since the only countries of actual revolutionary or pre-revolutionary crisis at present are Third-World countries with subsistence peasantries not far above starvation level. In particular, countries that are formally independent (and thus have lost the anti-revolutionary protective forces and experience of the metropolitan Power), yet whose new nationalist

[1] *Peking Review*, 21 June 1963.
[2] See Colin Legum, 'Africa and China: Symbolism and Substance', in *Policies Towards China* (ed. A. M. Halpern), McGraw-Hill, 1966.

élites are not very competent in securing administrative order, or providing economic development or even military control, and where there are still, for instance, large Western investments (as in Latin America) or Western aid-schemes (as practically everywhere) which may serve as a focus of nationalist resentments, and be blamed for whatever goes wrong. The lapse of time between 'first wave' and 'second wave' may be considerable: in China's own case it was thirty-eight years from the victory of the nationalist élite in 1911 to that of Mao in 1949. Assuming the Chinese genuinely think that the maxims they derive from their own experience represent laws of social development for Third-World countries generally, they must logically expect 'second wave' revolutions in most of Asia and Africa. In some cases, as Vietnam, the 'first wave' and 'second wave' revolutions may be regarded as inextricably intermingled; in others they may be distant in time from each other.

It would be quite natural in view of this theory that the Chinese, or those they advise, should sometimes 'jump the gun' in a Third-World country where the nationalist élite has been less than economically successful, and where particular local circumstances could be interpreted as a 'second wave' impending. This is a point of some interest with regard to Chinese policy towards Indonesia. There was a great deal of Indonesian influence on the evolution of the 'countryside of the world' theory. In fact, it was at one time attributed to the Indonesian Communist leader, D. N. Aidit, and he in turn seems to have formulated it as a Marxist version of President Sukarno's doctrine of the 'new emerging forces'. The Sukarno version was enunciated at the Belgrade Conference of September 1961, and postulated a sort of revolutionary-nationalist international of ex-colonial countries, quite compatible with Islam or Buddhism or even Hinduism, since it did not impose any specific view of the nature of domestic society, and was far removed from the intellectual rigour and sophistication of Marxism. As reformulated by Aidit and the Chinese it acquired a 'class content' and a much sharper cutting edge. Its influence may be seen, along with the influence of some conflicts in military policy, in the important essay by Lin Piao, published in September 1965, called *Long Live the Victory of the People's War*.[1]

This doctrine provides the Chinese with a moral base in the demands of the poorest, for the world's non-white peasantry is certainly much poorer than the urban industrial proletariat, who are nowadays quite affluent even in Russia. The world peasantry may be construed as being exploited by the industrialized worker,

[1] Text in *Red Flag*, 3 September 1965. It is also reprinted in Samuel B. Griffith, *Peking and People's Wars*, Pall Mall, London, 1966.

Since Lin Piao appears to be Mao's chosen heir, and this essay represents an influential formulation of foreign and military policy, it seems justifiable to quote its salient ideas.

. . . 'Taking the entire globe, if North America and Western Europe can be called "the cities of the world", then Asia, Africa and Latin America constitute "the rural areas of the world". Since World War Two, the proletarian revolutionary movement has for various reasons been temporarily held back in the North American and West European capitalist countries, while the people's revolutionary movement in Asia, Africa and Latin America has been growing vigorously. In a sense, the contemporary world revolution also presents a picture of the encirclement of cities by the rural areas. In the final analysis, the whole cause of world revolution hinges on the revolutionary struggles of the Asian, African and Latin American peoples who make up the overwhelming majority of the world's population. The socialist countries should regard it as their internationalist duty to support the people's revolutionary struggles in Asia, Africa and Latin America.' . . .

. . . 'Ours is the epoch in which world capitalism and imperialism are heading for their doom and socialism and communism are marching to victory. Comrade Mao Tse-tung's theory of people's war not only is a product of the Chinese revolution, but has also the characteristics of our epoch. The new experience gained in the people's revolutionary struggles in various countries since World War Two has provided continuous evidence that Mao Tse-tung's thought is a common asset of the revolutionary people of the whole world. This is the great international significance of the thought of Mao Tse-tung.' . . .

. . . 'At present, the main battlefield of the fierce struggle between the people of the world on the one side and US imperialism and its lackeys on the other is the vast area of Asia, Africa and Latin America. In the world as a whole, this is the area where the people suffer worst from imperialist oppression and where imperialist rule is most vulnerable. Since World War Two, revolutionary storms have been rising in this area, and today they have become the most important force directly pounding US imperialism.' . . .

. . . 'US imperialism relies solely on its nuclear weapons to intimidate people.

in respect of terms of trade and general economic status, and it is certainly the most numerous group, about two-thirds of the world's population. The approximation of its position to that of Mao's armies in the Chinese civil war, surrounding and ultimately defeating the 'cities of the world'–the prosperous industrial countries–as the Chinese cities were surrounded and ultimately defeated by the insurgent countryside, has the dream-like vagueness of some of the most effective political myths.

At the time of launching of the 'great proletarian cultural revolution', about mid-1966, it was possible to argue that the Chinese had suffered a number of setbacks in their efforts to cultivate this revolutionary 'countryside of the world'. The failed *coup* in Indonesia in September 1965, the Chinese quarrel with Cuba, the resentments aroused in Africa by apparently tactless statements on Mr. Chou's part, the downfall of Dr. Nkrumah while he was actually visiting Peking, and the expulsion of various Chinese embassies from Africa were among the evidence that might be cited. The Chinese represented these episodes as mere short-term ebbs in the revolutionary process, and could do so with some colour of historical plausibility, yet taken together with the

---

But these weapons cannot save US imperialism from its doom. Nuclear weapons cannot be used lightly. US imperialism has been condemned by the people of the whole world for its towering crime of dropping two atom bombs on Japan. If it uses nuclear weapons again, it will become isolated in the extreme.' . . .

. . . 'The Khrushchev revisionists have come to the rescue of US imperialism just when it is most panic-stricken and helpless in its efforts to cope with people's war. Working hand in glove with the US imperialists, they are doing their utmost to spread all kinds of arguments against people's war and, wherever they can, they are scheming to undermine it by overt or covert means.' . . .

. . . 'The Khrushchev revisionists maintain that a single spark in any part of the globe may touch off a world nuclear conflagration and bring destruction to mankind. If this were true, our planet would have been destroyed time and time again.' . . .

. . . 'The essence of the general line of the Khrushchev revisionists is nothing other than the demand that all the oppressed peoples and nations and all the countries which have won independence should lay down their arms, and place themselves at the mercy of the US imperialists and their lackeys, who are armed to the teeth.' . . .

increasing American involvement in Vietnam they provided a sort of darkening and ambiguity of the international context for China.

The roots of the cultural revolution were undoubtedly in domestic and intra-party developments within China, but attitudes to and of the external world have had some impact on its manifestations. It must be seen as a reassertion of values associated with the Yenan guerrilla period against Soviet and bourgeois errors, and this insistence on a specifically Chinese experience as a guiding pattern for the world has sharpened the ever-present edge of chauvinism in China's relations with other states and doctrines. Until 1966 it was possible to maintain that the guiding operational tenet of Chinese foreign policy had been the Maoist maxim: 'Despise the enemy strategically; respect him tactically'. This was a development of a more directly military maxim, from the guerrilla war in China: 'Our strategy is to pit one against ten: our tactic is to pit ten against one'. Applied to foreign policy, it meant that Chinese decision-makers would not push events beyond the point at which the relevant balance of forces was favourable. Thus China accepted stalemate in Korea, climbed down over Quemoy–Matsu in 1958, and avoided any action in Indo-China likely to provoke an American strike against China itself, such as committing troops. It pulled back in the Himalayan area rather than dangerously extend its lines of communication, and restricted its aid to Pakistan to arms and intimidating gestures. This was the 'respect the enemy tactically' side of the maxim. China of course adhered equally clearly to the injunction 'despise the enemy strategically'. The best evidence of this was its willingness to pile up the strategic odds against itself to an awe-inspiring degree by quarrelling *simultaneously* with America, Russia and India, making no concessions to buy them off even for temporary strategic purposes, and adopting verbally a total intransigence.

This strategic boldness has to be 'read with' the tactical caution for the whole period since 1949. From 1966, however, the relation between the two seemed to be put somewhat out of kilter by the domestic stresses of the cultural revolution. The apparatus and system of values associated with conventional or traditional diplomacy could not co-exist very comfortably with the puritanism and xenophobia of the cultural revolution, as was demonstrated in the personal pressures to which foreign diplomats in Peking and Chinese diplomats abroad were subjected. Diplomatic immunity was described by a spokesman of the Foreign Ministry as a 'relic of bourgeois norms' and the unfortunate representatives of China in foreign capitals had appropriate modes of behaviour prescribed for them by Red Guard newspapers. The control of the Foreign Ministry came into dispute between moderates and zealots, and even the protection of Chou En-lai was inadequate to shield the Foreign Minister, Chen Yi, from political disfavour. The quasi-deification of Mao Tse-tung, and insistence on his universal status as a 'great teacher of humanity' entailed diplomatic frictions through the handing-out of Mao badges and booklets, which endangered some of the diplomatic friendships most carefully cultivated in an earlier phase: those with Algeria, Kenya, Zambia, Burma and Cambodia, for instance. In the first six months of 1967 China incurred quite pointless and counter-productive quarrels over incidents of this sort with at least twenty-five countries, many of them important to the more rational long-term manoeuvring of China as a Power. The degree of self-induced diplomatic isolation attributable to this excess of revolutionary zeal was well illustrated at the National Day celebration of October 1967, at which the only foreign leader of any status was the head of the Albanian delegation.

Such long-term portents for Chinese foreign and defence policy as could be seen through the haze of the cultural revolution were confused and ambiguous, but seldom reassuring. On the defence side, one result seemed to be a still more zealous striving towards an effective power of nuclear strike. Those military leaders who had favoured some caution about the use of resources for this purpose, and had inclined towards some reliance on the Soviet Union in advanced weapons-systems, such as Peng Teh-huai and Lo Jui-ching (both former chiefs of the General Staff of the People's Liberation Army) came under attack, along with Lui Shao-chi, for adhering to the 'revisionist line on science pursued by the handful of top party persons in authority taking the capitalist road'.[1] The desire to 'expose and repudiate' such 'capitulationist' views was expressed in the hurrying-on of the first Chinese hydrogen-bomb test of June 1967 and later ballistic-missile tests. On the other hand, the stress on self-reliance in the theory of 'people's war' remained one of the factors making direct Chinese intervention in the war in Vietnam improbable, at least short of a rapprochement between Hanoi and Washington or an unlikely degree of military downturn for the insurgents.

The two enclaves that had lived provisionally but in comparative peace on China's flank for the first sixteen years of the revolutionary government, Hong Kong and Macao, were both shaken by the storm on the mainland. The Portuguese authorities in Macao, after clashes between the police and Maoist demonstrators, were obliged to give undertakings which converted their status almost into that of *locum tenentes* for the Chinese government. In Hong Kong the British authorities were less yielding, and the situation towards the end of 1967 appeared to be settling into a more cautious process of attrition and bargaining. Economically speaking, the Chinese government had a good deal to lose in Hong Kong, and though it remained possible that the foreign exchange earnings from trade with the city might be sacrificed to some paroxysm of ideological feeling or domestic infighting, the omens were not clearly in that direction. Despite the Anglo–Chinese frictions in Peking, London and Hong Kong, Chinese exports to Hong Kong and imports from Britain both rose sharply during 1967. Thus, though it was impossible to disregard the evidence that the internal controls making for caution in Chinese foreign policy had become somewhat eroded in the course of the internal struggle, and might become further eroded, some countervailing evidence appeared to show that the conventional calculation of national advantage had not altogether been discarded. On the other hand, there was a discomforting revanchist quality in some Chinese attitudes during the cultural revolution, as exemplified in one slogan used at Hong Kong: 'Blood debts must

[1] *Liberation Army Daily*, 17 June 1967.

be paid in blood'. China has, in Chinese eyes, a good many such debts to collect. By this time Maoism seemed much more a Chinese than a Marxist phenomenon. Though he made use of an internationalist theory of revolution, Mao was not only 'the reddest red sun' for the revolutionaries to set their course by, but the inheritor of a specifically Chinese mandate to tutor the barbarian in wisdom and virtue.

Almost twenty years after the proclamation of the People's Republic, China appeared a profoundly unquiet Power, and a disquieting one. Its diplomatic isolation from the rest of the society of states was more complete than on the morrow of the revolution. Its strength in advanced weapons was still slight, compared with that of the other nuclear oligarchs, but was growing fast, as witness the American decision in 1967 to build an ABM system directed specifically against China. Alone among the dominant powers it had real reasons for wanting to challenge the entire power-structure of the world: reasons of national resentment, economic underprivilege and territorial irredentism as well as of ideology. The great diplomatic task of reconciling China's own concept of its place in the world and in the surge of history with the real structure of competing international claims and interests was hardly yet begun.

BIBLIOGRAPHY

BARNETT, A. DOAK. *Communist China and Asia.* New York: Harper & Row, 1963. (Paperback ed.: Vintage.)

CH'EN, JEROME. *Mao and the Chinese Revolution.* New York: Oxford University Press, 1965. (Paperback ed.: Oxford.)

FAIRBANK, JOHN K. *The United States and China.* Cambridge, Mass.: Harvard University Press, 1958. (Paperback ed.: Viking.)

LOEWE, MICHAEL. *Imperial China: The Historical Background to the Modern Age.* New York: Frederick A. Praeger, 1966.

SCHRAM, STUART R. (ed. and trans.). *Political Thought of Mao Tse-tung.* New York: Frederick A. Praeger, 1963. (Paperback ed.: Praeger.)

5·BRITISH
FOREIGN POLICY

F. S. Northedge

In the first chapter of this book we have described foreign policy as an interaction between forces originating outside the country's borders and those working within them. In Britain's case the former are peculiarly important, both because this country has been intimately involved in dealings with other nations since England became a naval Power under the Tudors and because British foreign policy has only rarely been affected by social strife at home. We must begin therefore with its world environment, or rather that environment as it has presented itself to British governments ruling a small, densely populated, highly industrialized island off the coast of Europe, uniquely dependent in the modern period on maritime trade and security and with an overseas Empire, in 1939, of 500 million people scattered through every continent, though reduced since 1945 to some thirty minor dependencies.

The most striking feature of this world environment since, say, the 1860s, when Britain was still at the height of her power, is the immense changes which have overtaken it, imposing mental readjustments which make understandable the disappointing record of British policy in the inter-war period and the decline in world status since. Britain, whom long participation in international affairs, early industrialization and world-wide international connections have made conservative to the bones, has faced changes in her external environment as revolutionary as any in history. These changes may be grouped under three heads: changes in the composition of the family of great Powers, changes in the size and distribution of the world diplomatic community, and changes in technology.

As to the first group, the unification of Germany in the 1860s, though it took more than a quarter of a century for its effects to be registered, changed the nature of Britain's task in Europe and opened the way to the eclipse of Europe by forces outside it. Before Germany became the greatest military Power on the Continent, British governments were able to throw their weight on this side or the other of the European balance, deciding, as late as 1877, whether there would be war in Europe or, if war was started by others, how long it would last and how general it would be. By 1914 that position was lost; the question for Britain then was not whether general war would ensue, but which of the two coalitions poised for war–the Central Powers or the Franco-Russian alliance–she would join. During the war Germany defeated or held at bay all her European rivals; only the certainty that the United States would fight on long after the Allies' exhaustion forced her to surrender. When America withdrew from the European balance almost as soon as Germany sued for peace Britain and France were left to do without Russian co-operation what they had failed to do during the war with it, namely contain Germany. Whatever British government had been in office in the 1930s the result would almost certainly have been the same; that Germany could not be contained without Soviet assistance, which implied Soviet paramountcy in Eastern Europe and hence the necessity for a United States presence in Western Europe. In turn, this meant a close alignment of British policy, and that of all West European states which wished to avoid Soviet control, with American policy after Germany's defeat in 1945.

This process was underlined by the parallel circumstance that Japan, who was able to dictate to the Western Powers with interests in the Far East, notably Britain, almost with impunity in the 1930s, could not be overthrown without American power and, at least, a formal Soviet undertaking, given at Yalta in February 1945 before the American atomic bomb was ready for use, to enter the struggle against Japan. With the final defeat of Germany and Japan in 1945 world politics were thus dominated by the rivalry between the United States and the Soviet Union, with Britain seeking to bind America to the defence of a weak and demoralized Western Europe and later to act herself, if not as a mediator in the Soviet–American tension, at least as its moderator. As Europe revived under Marshall Aid funds (1948–52), though divided along the lines of Western and Soviet occupation zones in Germany, Britain faced a new phenomenon: the tendencies towards integration among the states of Western Europe, first in the Coal and Steel Community created by an agreement signed in April 1951 and later, and more decisively, by the Rome Treaty signed in March 1957 for a European Economic Community. From this process British governments, Labour and Conservative alike, kept aloof, though they favoured international functional co-operation on the traditional model. Their reasons for doing so were partly ingrained mistrust of any European union of states, limitations imposed by Commonwealth ties, the anxiety not to consolidate the lines of division between Eastern and Western Europe and the wish to maintain an independent influence in Washington for the purpose *inter alia* of improving Western relations with the Communist world.

The United States acquiesced only reluctantly in British efforts for accommodation with the Soviet Union until, in the early 1960s, it began of its own accord to recognize its common interests with Russia in the avoidance of nuclear war. When the Kennedy administration (1961–3) showed signs of wanting a *détente* with Russia, it was not clear what role should be assigned to Britain in it; Mr. Kennedy appeared to need no lessons in diplomacy from London as his management of the Cuba crisis in October 1962 showed. At the same time, Britain, while welcoming evidence of disintegration in the Communist camp as Russia and China went their separate ways, saw a new factor developing: the rising power of Communist China, recognized by Britain herself in 1950 and by President de Gaulle in January 1964, embarking on the nuclear road in the 1960s and apparently seeking to revive the old Chinese hegemony in South East Asia, with serious implications for Britain's Commonwealth partners, Australia, Malaysia and New Zealand. The British government were able to prevail on the United States to agree to a conference in Geneva in July 1954 which dealt, along with the liquidation of the Korean War (1950–3), with the effects of the French defeat by the Communist Vietminh in North Vietnam. But the Geneva conference was a makeshift; the South Vietnamese regime refused to co-operate in holding all-Vietnamese elections in 1956, to which the Geneva conference had agreed, and as the North Vietnamese began to assist the Vietcong rebels in the south, the United States found itself, especially from February 1965, in an increasingly heavy military and economic involvement in South Vietnam as the point at which to hold Communism in Asia.

Britain was accordingly faced with a situation in which the East–West *détente*, for which British governments had worked so hard in the 1950s, was forced to mark time; in which she herself was supporting, with minor reservations, American policy in Vietnam, and hence compromising any efforts she wished to make towards mediating an increasingly grave threat to world peace; and in which she could in any event play only a minor role as far as the dominant tensions now appearing, those between the United States and China, were concerned. Meanwhile, President de Gaulle, having vetoed the British application to enter the EEC in January 1963, was extricating himself with impunity from the NATO alliance, the sheet-anchor of British policy in the post-war world, and aspiring to disentangle a new Europe, in which Britain had never shown genuine interest, from the old East–West conflict.

Such is the pattern of great-Power politics British governments have faced in the twentieth century. But the international scene as a whole has undergone change in terms of a dramatic increase in the number of states, many formed from the British Empire, and in consequence the enlargement of the area of international politics from its European confines. This process we call decolonization, dating its origins from the grant of independence to Burma, Ceylon, India and Pakistan by the British Labour government in 1947. But the Afro–Asian resurgence has been a problem for British Ministers since the First World War. Britain was engaged in a running fight with Egyptian nationalism from 1919 until the Suez crisis in 1956, interrupted by the Second World War in which Britain tried to satisfy Arab nationalism by restricting Jewish immigration into Palestine. Another similar conflict was that with Kemalist Turkey in 1920-2, culminating in the defeat of Entente designs to impose a Carthaginian peace on the Sultan. Yet another scene of conflict with extra-European nationalism was China, which after its nationalist revolution in 1911 lapsed into a civil war in the 1920s which took the form of a campaign against Western interests, the British being by far the most important, until Chinese energies were diverted into the war against Japan in the 1930s. In these areas Britain was fighting what in almost all cases turned out to be a losing struggle to retain her foothold in areas traditionally reserved to Western control.

After 1945 these conflicts with Afro–Asian nationalism con-tinued, exemplified by the Iranian nationalization of the Anglo–Iranian Oil Company in 1951 and the protracted struggle with Egypt over the British military base in the Suez Canal zone and the future of the Sudan. These tensions were, however, over-shadowed by the transformation of the British Empire itself into a multi-racial group of sovereign states. The decolonization process was less violent for Britain than for any other imperial Power, thanks to the existence of an anti-imperialist movement of long standing in the country, the well-established commitment to give independence to subject peoples as they became able to exercise it, British economic weakness at the end of the war and the wish to maintain a close accord with the United States with its well-known anti-colonial sentiments. But the creation of independent states out of the Empire weakened the Commonwealth; whereas the old Dominions, Australia, Canada, New Zealand, if not always South Africa, could be relied upon to regard sympathetically Britain's viewpoint in her most critical international controversies, the newer, non-aligned Commonwealth countries could not. These countries, in particular India and Pakistan, had their own quarrels, which Britain was unable to mollify, and other states, notably Russia at the Tashkent conference in January 1965, apparently were. The new states wished to ease the major international tensions; so did Britain. But Britain, in the eyes of many of these countries, was prevented by her support for American policies from taking the disinterested position the situation required. They sought foreign aid for their economic development while Britain was barely able to pay her own way in the world. There was a further occasion for misgiving which British Ministers tended to feel about the new states, namely their voice, quite out of proportion to their strength, at the United Nations, raucously denouncing Western colonialism while omitting to mention the Soviet brand, and threatening to make the world organization less of a concert of Powers and more of a futile talking-shop. Lord Home (now Sir Alec Douglas-Home) voiced the feeling when he spoke at the General Assembly as Foreign Secretary in 1961: 'If the emphasis is taken off the first duty of the United Nations, which is peace-making and security, and laid on the acceleration of independence and the eradication of colonialism, then it will sow the seeds of its own destruction'.

The third great change affecting Britain's international environment in this century is the technological revolution, so pervasive that only its more striking effects can be noted. The 1914–18 war demonstrated for the first time in any international conflict the application of modern machine industry to the primitive business of fighting, thus providing British foreign policy with its spectre of mass bloodshed which overhung it thereafter. The drive to avert at all costs the return to Armageddon was intensified by the coming of air warfare, placing in the front line the dense population of south-east England. At the same time, British naval power, the time-honoured defence against blockade and invasion, was brought into question by the submarine, the abolition of which by international agreement British governments unsuccessfully sought in the inter-war period. With the increase in the speed and costliness of vessels after the First World War and the United States determination to maintain primacy with Britain among the world's navies, Britain had no option but to concede parity in capital ships to that country at the Washington conference in 1921, which meant that in future no major British naval action could be launched without, at least, benevolent American neutrality. In the 1930s Britain was not only unable to bring naval power to bear on Japan, her alliance with whom she had allowed to lapse on American urging in 1921, but felt obliged, in order to divert resources into the air defence of Britain, to reach a naval agreement with Hitler in June 1935 which virtually condoned his rearmament in defiance of the Versailles Treaty.

These technological limitations to British power, however, pale into significance beside the rapid advances in missile and nuclear weapon technology, the beginnings of which appeared even before the Second World War ended. It has been recognized by all varieties of British opinion that there can be no adequate defence for the people of this country in the event of global nuclear war involving Britain. The 1957 Defence White Paper frankly said so and has never been repudiated in this respect since.[1] The £20 million spent annually in Britain on civil defence is an admission of the same fact. Although the conclusion drawn by unilateral nuclear disarmers is that Britain should withdraw from collective defence arrangements and declare herself, so to speak, an open country, majority opinion has supported successive post-war governments in holding that the deterrent force of NATO nuclear power, supplemented by Britain's own nuclear armoury, should be relied upon to discourage aggression. Here, however, is a paradox: namely, that while missile technology has brought the United States and the Soviet Union within each other's reach and hence made them less willing to incur destruction on their allies' behalf, it has also made more unconvincing Britain's efforts to provide her own delivery vehicles. The British solution, following the abandonment of the home-produced 'Blue Streak' missile in April 1960, was, by an agreement reached at Nassau in December 1962, to purchase American Polaris missiles for the equipment of four British-built submarines. Quite apart from the implications for this project of the new strides being made by the Soviet Union in submarine destruction, the question how, under these condi-

[1] Cmnd. 124, p. 2.

tions, the British nuclear deterrent could be described as independent was persistently asked by Opposition spokesmen at the general election in October 1964. Since forming his own government after his victory in that contest, however, Mr. Harold Wilson showed no sign of abandoning the British deterrent. In the Defence Review of 1966 another step was taken towards dependence on the United States when it was announced that the government proposed to maintain a military presence east of Suez, not by building another aircraft carrier as desired by the Minister for the Navy, Mr. Mayhew, who resigned on the issue, but by purchasing 50 F111 strike aircraft from the United States.[1] The technological revolution seemed inexorably to be increasing Britain's dependence on the American giant, while the American government's decision, announced in September 1967, to build a limited anti-ballistic missile defence left still farther behind such second-rank states as Britain.

The domestic setting

The internal environment of British policy is at once less complex and less significant than the external in the making of that policy. If a scale is imagined with states in which foreign policy is used by governments as a means of winning support at home at one extreme and those in which governments are free to pursue foreign policies with little interference from internal forces of opinion at the other, Britain's position is towards the latter end of the scale. Foreign policy, traditionally the private domain of the Crown, was the last royal prerogative to be ceded to Ministers responsible to Parliament, the surrender being complete only in the final years of Queen Victoria's reign. Since then the chief control of British foreign relations has rested with the executive, that is the Cabinet, in which Prime Minister and Foreign Secretary predominate. Public and Parliamentary interest in foreign affairs has much increased since 1918, but no British government has in these years failed to carry its policy through Parliament, the resignation of Sir Samuel Hoare as Foreign Secretary in 1935 through a public

[1] Cmnd. 2901.

outcry against the plan to partition Abyssinia being a rare exception. It is in the nature of the governing process, writes one authority,

> that Parliament can normally be consulted on foreign policy only after decisions have been made. Parliament does not share in the decision of whether or not to act; it approves or disapproves an action which has been started or completed . . . no Government with a Parliamentary majority has been forced to resign since 1885. . . . Even when the Commons is highly dissatisfied with the Government's foreign policy the Government is probably safe if its domestic policy is acceptable.[1]

With the reduction of Britain's relative world power after 1945 and the resulting shrinkage in the options facing the country, likemindedness between the two main parties on foreign policy has grown, exemplified by the attitudes of Labour and Conservative governments towards European union and East–West relations and by the assumption by the Labour government formed in October 1964 of the chief Conservative positions on the nuclear deterrent and the role of Britain as a world Power.[2] The resulting 'élitist' or paternalistic attitude of British politicians towards the wider public in matters of foreign policy is well brought out in the following excerpt from a former Minister of State's essay:

> It should, I believe, be possible for a government in this country to secure acceptance of its basic foreign objectives, by means of adequate exposition by the Prime Minister and Foreign Secretary in Parliament and to a less extent through the public relations machinery of the Foreign Office . . . they will, I think, find that public opinion deals very sensibly with broad policy issues. . . . It is no reflection upon the intelligence of the public

---

[1] Donald G. Bishop, *The Administration of British Foreign Relations*, Syracuse University Press, 1961, pp. 135–6.

[2] Bishop, *op. cit.*, Chapter 6; M. A. Fitzsimons, *The Foreign Policy of the British Labour Government, 1945–51*, Notre Dame, Indiana, 1953, pp. 24–26; F. S. Northedge, 'British Foreign Policy and the Party System', *The American Political Science Review*, Vol. LIV, No. 3, September 1960, pp. 635–58.

to say that in foreign matters they stand particularly in need of clear and honest leadership. In this respect, everyone in public life has a responsibility, but it is upon the leaders of the government that the main burden must inevitably fall.[1]

Besides the 'élitist' tradition and structure of government, the physical smallness of Britain, its detachment from Continental Europe, the existence of essentially national organs of communication such as press, radio and television, the racial homogeneity of the British and the centuries-old stability of institutions, have all served to reduce the incidence of violent schisms of opinion. Since the settlement of the Irish question in 1921 no alienated faction has existed in Britain which would rather make common cause with a foreign Power than endure its predicament. The significant feature of industrial unrest in Britain, as for instance during the General Strike in 1926 or the 'Hunger Marches' of the 1930s, is that it is almost invariably limited to internal issues, such as wages and employment, with barely any international overtones. Groups identifying themselves with international revolutionary movements, as the Communist Party or the British Union of Fascists, have never captured mass support. Neither during the Second World War, when the Axis Powers were appealing to traitors in all countries, nor during the Cold War, when the Soviet Union has invoked the international solidarity of the working class, has internal dissension seriously affected foreign policy.

This is not to say that public opinion in general or organized forces outside Parliament have never made their impact on British policy. The notable examples of the former's role are the influence of pacifist movements of opinion in the 1930s, which are generally regarded as having inhibited the National government from taking a firm stand against the Dictators, and the distinct electoral advantages to be derived in the post-1945 situation from pressing for 'summit' conferences as a means of reducing the risk of war with the Communist Powers; the influence of pressure groups, on

[1] Kenneth Younger, 'Public Opinion and Foreign Policy', *The British Journal of Sociology*, Vol. VI, No. 2, June 1955, pp. 169–75.

the other hand, can be seen in the role of the Right-wing 'Suez group' in Conservative Middle Eastern policies in the 1960s, of the Left wing of the Labour Party on East–West issues and on support for American policies in the Far East, of British mining interests in the Conservative government's dissent from United Nations action against the secessionist regime of Moishe Tshombe in Katanga during the Congo crisis in 1961–2, and of British textile interests in the matter of Japan's application to enter the GATT agreements.

But in many of these instances there are grounds for thinking the British Ministers would have followed broadly the courses which they did, even had no such pressures existed; hardly any British government, for example, could have enthusiastically opposed Germany in the 1930s after the tragic British losses in the First World War; equally, no British interest in the post-1945 world could have been served by intensifying still further the struggle with Soviet Communism. As for the force of sectional interests, it is notable that the 'Suez group' could not prevent the Churchill government from withdrawing from the Suez base in 1954 and the testimony of at least one student of the 1956 Suez crisis is that Eden's 'obsessive hatred of Nasser', coupled with a general British unfavourable image of Arab leaders, sufficiently accounts for the armed action against Egypt in that crisis.[1] More recently Mr. Harold Wilson's ability to maintain support for United States policy in Vietnam with both tiny and considerable Commons majorities, when that policy was intensely disliked by the Labour Left is an indication of the narrow limits within which organized sub-groups in Britain exercise an influence on foreign policy.

But by far the most important internal factor affecting this policy is the British economy. Since the Industrial Revolution turned England from an agrarian into an industrial and commercial nation, the country's standard of living has depended on its ability to sell goods and services to the rest of the world in return,

[1] Erskine B. Childers, *The Road to Suez*, MacGibbon and Kee, London, 1962, p. 230.

today, for a half of its food supplies and a sizeable fraction of the raw materials it consumes. Almost 40 per cent of the British working population is engaged in manufacturing industry, 10 per cent in engineering and the manufacture of electrical goods, with their heavy stake in foreign trade. Of a gross domestic product valued in 1965 at £30,392 million, £6,449 million worth was exported. Similarly, more than one-fifth of total personal spending went on imports from abroad.[1]

The problem of balancing the British financial account with the rest of the world has always been a serious one in the twentieth century, becoming acute after 1945. The United States and Germany had already begun to elbow Britain out of favoured markets before 1914; Japan became a serious competitor in the sale of textiles, especially in the Far East and other areas of low purchasing power, in the inter-war period; in the years since 1945 British exports have had a tough struggle in the face of competition from a variety of countries as modern techniques of manufacture and sales have spread throughout the world. World marketing conditions have moreover suffered many restrictions since 1914; after 1919 economic nationalism expressed in the high tariff policies of new states wishing to guarantee their economic sovereignty by building up their own sources of supply, was one factor, the economic depression of the early 1930s, which drove states to policies of *sauve qui peut*, another, the difficulties an old industrial country like Britain faced in adapting its techniques to new conditions, a third. These difficulties were intensified by the fact that a considerable proportion of British income from abroad, used for the payment of essential imports, came before the Second World War from dividends from accumulated holdings overseas; these were largely liquidated to pay for supplies during the 1939–45 war and to bridge the payments gap immediately after the war. The effect was that, after 1945 British exports had to rise some 65·7 per cent over imports in order to be in balance with the rest of the world. 'The scale of the loss and the structural adjustment required

[1] Central Statistical Office, *Monthly Digest of Statistics*, No. 247, July 1966, H.M.S.O., Table 14, p. 13; Table 1, p. 1; Table 3, p. 3.

was greater than that of any other country.' Yet the 65·7 per cent increase was attained by 1948 and was maintained, with ups and downs, until 1959.[1]

These economic factors have left their mark on British foreign policy in almost every issue facing British Ministers. After the First World War, following a brief Armistice-night vindictiveness towards Germany, the principal aim of Lloyd George, Bonar Law, Ramsay Macdonald and Stanley Baldwin was to 'return to normal', to have done with armaments and political feuding in Europe and resuscitate international trade and investment. In their dealings with the Dictators in the 1930s the National government sought above all else to lead Europe back to the peaceful international economy they regarded the rival coalitions of the pre-1914 period as having disrupted. 'The world would act wisely', said Anthony Eden (now the Earl of Avon) when Foreign Secretary in the 1930s, 'were it to turn from armaments competition to economic co-operation. . . . We definitely prefer butter to guns and we are prepared to do our best to secure that others have butter too in a world that has no need of guns.'[2] After the Second World War British balance of payments problems played a large part in the alignment of British policy with the United States, the source of supply of the chief scarce currency in the post-war world, the dollar; in the abandonment by Britain of an increasing number of overseas commitments, beginning with assistance to Greece and Turkey in February 1947, to the United States; in British pressure for restoration of full sovereignty to the Western zones of occupation in Germany; in the grant of independence to one British dependent territory overseas after another; and in sustained British pleas for a *détente* in the Cold War with the Communist states in order to reduce the costs of military defence. A direct line of thought links Lloyd George's efforts at the Genoa Conference in April 1922 to move the Bolsheviks out of enmity towards the West, and into trading with it, with Neville Chamberlain's belief

[1] Sir Roy Harrod, *The British Economy*, McGraw-Hill, New York and London, 1963, p. 30.

[2] Anthony Eden, *Foreign Affairs*, Faber and Faber, London, 1939, pp. 178, 187.

that, after her grievances under the Versailles Treaty had been redressed, Germany would take her place in a peaceful European economy, and with Lord Home's (now Sir Alec Douglas-Home's) belief as Foreign Secretary that when the 'thin Communist' was fattened by trade he would be amenable to deal with.

British style in foreign policy

Though much that needs to be said about the style, or inarticulate assumptions, of British policy is truistic and has been said before, it is too important to be overlooked.[1] We must begin with the fact that, as a sea-going people, with a vast overseas Empire to manage, the British, for a century at least, have venerated the *status quo*; their rule is *quieta non movere*. British policy, defending interests dispersed throughout the world, has opposed radical change while being prepared to make the best of it when it occurs provided it promises to endure. One thinks of the long British championship of Turkey at the Straits in the various phases of the Eastern Question, the desire to maintain the Austro–Hungarian Empire until the last possible moment in the First World War, the effort to restrict to the minimum territorial changes in Europe during the 1919 peace settlement. Since 1945 Britain has dissented from American proposals to liberate Eastern Europe, preferring to draw a veil over a *fait accompli*. 'We cannot change the Communism of Russia', Bevin said in 1948,

> and I am not going to try. We cannot pursue, and we have no intention of pursuing, a policy in Eastern Europe of trying to change by force many of the things done in those states with which we do not agree. Those things will be worked out in the process of time. But equally we are not prepared to sit idly by and see a similar process carried on over a weakened, distracted and disunited Europe.[2]

The associated British respect for international law and the sanctity of treaties reflects the trader's interest in the observance of

[1] For one account see F. S. Northedge, *The Troubled Giant*, G. Bell and Son, London, 1966, Chapter 23.

[2] The Labour Party; Report of the 4th Annual Conference, p. 195.

contracts and the imperialist's interest in the *status quo*. At the same time, there is the feeling that treaty engagements must not be too rigid if they are to command respect. One undertaking which British governments have always sought to avoid is that of defending the *status quo* in all particulars. This was the basis of British objections to President Wilson's conception of the League Covenant as a nexus of territorial guarantees, and to French appeals in the 1920s for pledges to crystallize post-war boundaries in Europe. 'Nations cannot be expected,' said Eden in 1936, 'to incur automatic obligations save for areas where their vital interests are concerned', and his words were used by Chamberlain in 1938 to avoid pledges to respect in detail the *status quo* in Eastern Europe.[1] Behind this, paradoxically, is the urge for stability, a particular order being more likely to last, the British think, if it allows for change.

British interest in stability and the *status quo* has prescribed indifference to the internal affairs of other states. As a rule, British Ministers do not concern themselves with the domestic arrangements of other countries; the question is rather whether foreign regimes are likely to last, whether their policies are, broadly speaking, in accord with British interests, and whether they will honour their cheques. When Neville Chamberlain said of Hitler in April 1939 'he is a liar' it was about the worst stricture he ever passed on the Nazi leader.[2] Hence the British aversion for interfering in foreign revolutions or civil wars, as the French in 1789, the Russian in 1917, the Nazi German in 1933, the Spanish in 1936, unless they actually threaten the balance of power, as the advocates of intervention in the Russian civil conflict in 1917 argued that it did; hence too the British practice of recognizing foreign states and governments as soon as they provide evidence of stability. These axioms reflect the trader's psychology when in a foreign

[1] *Documents on British Foreign Policy, 1919–1939*, ed. by E. L. Woodward and Rohan Butler, Third Series, Vol. 1, H.M. Stationery Office, London, 1949, Nos. 106, 114.

[2] Grigore Gafencu, *The Last Days of Europe*, Frederick Muller, London, 1947, p. 82.

country; he wants to know, not what the politics of the local ruler are, but whether he can keep the peace and create the physical security necessary for trade.

There is a final implication of Britain's historical character as a sea-going Power: its concern with the security of the world's maritime highways, vital residues of which remain even in the air and missile age. As the main nerve of French policy has traditionally been the Rhine, that of Japan the politics of mainland China, so British thinking was long dominated by the security of the great sea route to the Far East, through the Channel, the Atlantic and Mediterranean, the Suez Canal after its opening in 1869, the Persian Gulf, the Indian Ocean and Singapore Strait. As the United States was fortunate a century ago in having a friendly Power, Britain, dominant in the Atlantic and Pacific, so Britain has been fortunate in that her successor as the chief democratic nation, the United States, is also the world's leading naval Power. Furthermore, because of the great number of states bordering on the main sea routes, the British desire has been to harmonize the interests of as many states as possible with those of Britain, to have a friend in every port, and to do so, as Sir Eyre Crowe insisted in his famous memorandum of 1907, by identifying British policy as far as possible with the world's great causes.[1] The British hope is that too many nations will have their fates linked with Britain's to allow her to be ruined. The other side of the coin has been the persistent British aversion for partial alliances, for the organization of rival blocs of states, for permanent commitments, even in the Atlantic area, to a particular group of states. The Locarno Pact of 1925 by which Britain, for the first time, pledged herself to defend a particular frontier in Europe, was an almost perfect example of a British commitment. It bound Britain to defend each of the two chief European rivals against the other and hence ruled out partisan ties or military staff talks with either; it left Britain with full liberty to determine what action she should take in the event of a *casus foederis.*

[1] *British Documents on the origins of the War, 1898–1914,* ed. by G. P. Gooch and H. Temperley, H.M.S.O., London, 1928, Vol. III, pp. 402–20.

The second major feature of the British approach to foreign affairs, after its thalassic preoccupations, is its concern, one might say obsession, with the prevailing relations of power at the core of the international system. British public opinion, its Nonconformist wings in particular, may have revolted emotionally against the balance of power; but this has never seriously affected the British practice of it. The Labour Party could not have more vehemently rejected the balance of power than it did in the 1930s, yet its Foreign Secretary, Bevin, even if with dissent from his back benches, operated it successfully enough against the Soviet Union after 1945. Balance-of-power politics have two bases in British thought: the realization that any state dominating the European continent could afford to disarm on land and concentrate its resources on sea, and later air, power, thus jeopardizing British security; and the assumption that repose in Europe resulting from equilibrating the European Powers one against the other was essential if Britain was to have her hands free to defend overseas territories. These politics have expressed themselves in many characteristic British thoughts: the dislike of European union on the ground that it might take the form of a combination *against* this country; the hesitation about long-term alliances and the wish, if they must be contracted, to keep their structure as loose as possible;[1] and the aversion for splitting the world into blocs.

But by far the most characteristic British contribution to the practice of the balance of power is its tendency to seek what may be called the 'composition of the greatest Powers', the principle of systematically reducing frictions dividing the prevailing giants of the system and eliminating dissatisfactions between them. It is this attitude which explains why the British were remarkably generous towards Germany in the 1920s, looking upon that country as one of the leading states which had to be reconciled to the international order, and yet have been almost equally suspicious of Germany since 1945, since they now regard that country as a possible factor of discord between the greatest states of the present day, the

[1] For British policy in relation to NATO in this respect see Max Beloff, *New Dimensions in Foreign Policy*, Allen and Unwin, London, 1961, Chapter 3.

United States and the Soviet Union. As Mr. Macmillan said of his wish to take Britain into the EEC in 1961, 'we must be at the centre of power', because world peace, which since 1918 has been of the greatest interest to Britain, depends not so much on the goodwill of the lesser states as on that of the true giants of the system.

British politicians in office, though not always in Opposition, tend in fact to think 'in power terms', in ratios of strength between states, more often than in moral or ideological terms. The prejudice of British politicians is to minimize the ideological pretensions of foreign regimes, to consider instead their actual capacity to do harm or good and their disposition, derived from concrete interests, to do either. In every British Foreign Secretary lives the faith that foreign states incited to world domination by political doctrines, once dismissed by Aneurin Bevan as 'ritualistic exercises', will sooner or later realize the practical advantages of peaceful co-operation. Hence the traditional British response to revolutions and ideologically inspired upheavals abroad: alarm perhaps, but refusal to act unless general security is threatened, and even so, tardily. 'We shall be found in our place', wrote Castlereagh on the subject of intervention in foreign revolutions in May 1820, 'when actual danger menaces the System of Europe, but this country cannot, and will not, act upon abstract and speculative Principles of Precaution'.[1] Lloyd George, defending his wish to bring to an end Allied intervention in Russia in 1919 after the danger that Germany might profit from the revolution had passed, might have used the same words.[2] It is not, of course, true to say that in concentrating upon power considerations rather than on ideological differences British Ministers have always judged them correctly. But where they have failed to do so this has often been due to neglect of the ideological component in power. It is generally recognized today that in the 1930s the National government

[1] Harold Temperley and Lillian M. Penson (eds.), *Foundations of British Foreign Policy*, Cambridge University Press, 1938, p. 63.

[2] Parliamentary Debates (Commons) Vth Series, Vol. 114, Cols. 2939–46 (16 April 1919).

might have taken the measure of Nazi Germany sooner had they not tended to write off its ideology as an atavistic distraction from serious business.

British political style, resembling a series of geological strata laid down one on top of the other through time, harbours many strange inconsistencies and paradoxes. One of these is the conflict between the balance-of-power principle and the newer notion that in the final resort the interests of all states are reconcilable, and that no essential tension exists between the interests of other states and those of Britain. Britain's security depended in the modern period on her weight being thrown against the strongest Power of the day in Europe. But with the First World War came the realization that British strength, even with France acting as the stone of attrition, was no match for Germany without the assistance of Russia or America, or both; and since for different reasons the help of neither country was readily available in the 1930s, British policy sought to reconcile the Powers and was reluctant to admit until almost too late that a coalition had somehow to be organized against Germany. It is a remarkable fact that the Conservative Party, the party *par excellence* of the balance-of-power in the nineteenth century, came, after 1918, to prefer the principle of reconciliation, so much so that Duff Cooper saw fit to resign from the government in October 1938 because his Conservative colleagues had, as he alleged, abandoned balance-of-power principles. Since 1945 Britain, as a loyal member of the Atlantic alliance, has played a prominent part in the European balance, but the realization that she can play only a minor role in controlling it has disposed British Ministers to seek to render the division of forces between East and West more flexible.

From this overlaying of the traditional British practice of the balance of power with newer drives to reconcile the interests of all nations with each other and with Britain has sprung one of the most persistent features of British diplomacy; its remarkable fluctuations in attitude towards other Powers, from conciliation and compromise to hostility and war to the death, from naïve credulity in the good faith of other states to unrelenting struggle, and back again. Walter Lippmann's rebuke that democracies are 'too belligerent in war, too pacific in peace' suits Britain above all other people. In the course of the Paris Peace Conference in 1919 British policy switched from intense anti-Germanism, the policy of 'squeezing Germany until the pips squeaked', to siding with Germany against France and the East European successor states. When the Conference opened in January the British case was based chiefly on the claim for reparations, the trial of the Kaiser and the surrender of German colonies; yet as early as 25 March Lloyd George was calling for a treaty drawn up 'as if we were impartial arbiters, forgetful of the passions of the war'.[1] Throughout the 1930s British Ministers believed that Hitler was doing no more than removing the objectionable features of the Versailles Treaty, which the British government had themselves condemned in 1919. By 1940 they had dedicated themselves to the destruction of Nazism in a way that astounded even Hitler, who concluded from their former behaviour that they would come to terms after France collapsed. Towards the end of the war, Winston Churchill was being charged by the American delegation at Yalta in February 1945, not without reason, of wanting to 'gang up' against Russia; his Fulton speech in March 1946, warning of Stalin's intentions in Europe, had a generally cool reception in the United States for the same reason. Yet, two months after Stalin's death in March 1953, Churchill pressed for a 'private conference' with the new Soviet leaders 'not overhung by a ponderous and rigid agenda', and was accordingly condemned by many Americans and West Germans for being 'soft on Communism'. Again, in November 1957 Harold Macmillan as Prime Minister was saying in Parliament that 'the threat of Russia and Soviet Communism had never been so great or the need for countries to organize themselves against it so urgent';[2] a year later he was embarking upon a continuous series of demands for 'summit' conferences which culminated in the Paris East–West meeting in May 1960

[1] Peace Conference (Paris), 1919, Cmd. 1614 (1922), p. 5.
[2] Parliamentary Debates (Commons), Vth Series, Vol. 577, Col. 40 (5 November 1957).

which ended before it began. Small wonder it is that other countries often complain that they do not know where they stand with Britain.

The second major inconsistency in British style is the tension between the policy of the 'composition of the greatest Powers' and the championship of small nations. Generally speaking, British governments have not scrupled to sacrifice weak countries to compensate other great Powers. This was the British attitude towards Poland in 1919, Czechoslovakia in 1938 and Eastern Europe as a whole since the war; Britain was always the most willing of NATO states to draw a veil over Stalin's European gains between 1945 and 1948 and negotiate with Russia on that basis. Superimposed upon this tendency to use small states as pawns in great-Power politics have been, firstly, the British belief that the maintenance of Britain's world position depends upon its being identified with good causes, to which we have already referred, and the defence of small nations has been a 'good cause' since 1789; and, secondly, the romantic popular nationalism which took the British middle classes by storm in the mid-nineteenth century, voiced by Gladstone, Bright, Cobden and most Liberal leaders of the day, and expressed in the welcome given to such patriots from the Continent as Louis Kossuth and, later, T. G. Masaryk. The interaction between these forces, the composition of the greatest Powers and the defence of national self-determination, was crucially illustrated by the Munich conference of September 1938. Munich was an act of compensation on the eighteenth-century model; it was acceptable to British opinion partly because of the feeling that the nationalism of a small East European state, Czechoslovakia, ran the risk of alienating a great Power, Germany, whose co-operation was essential to peace. At the same time, in the act of compensating Germany Britain was giving expression to the national principle which had caused many liberal-minded people to side with the smaller states in 1919.

The pattern of British interests

Foreign policy style reflects values historically developed in a country and articulated by its leaders of opinion. It is also related to interests in that the persistent effort to defend interests promotes a particular style; style is a satisfactory or congenial manner of handling the country's interests. We must therefore now consider some of the dominant interests which British governments, with more or less approval from public opinion, have defined as vital.

At the head of the list we must, of course, place, as with all other states, territorial integrity and political independence, or in other words the security of the home base from foreign invasion and rule. This is the first of vital interests in that the British have been and are willing to fight for it, with allies or alone. National security is, however, rapidly becoming, if it has not become, the only interest on behalf of which Britain would readily fight with the full extent of her national resources, and it must be quite clear that this interest is really at stake. In 1914 Britain went to war, not so much owing to any immediate threat of invasion, but in order to maintain a voice in a European conflict which was already breaking out. In 1939, however, she went to war, not to preserve a balance of power, but to defend herself against what seemed inevitable invasion should Germany succeed in bringing all Europe under her control. Since 1945 the *casus belli* for Britain has been definitely limited to actual armed threats to British independence or that of her NATO allies, with which Britain's own independence is now indissolubly linked.

As for overseas possessions on behalf of which Britain is willing, if not to go to war, at least to use force, these have been drastically reduced from the massive Empire as it stood in 1939. Today, although Britain still has dependent territories for whose security she is responsible in every continent, these have shrunk to a mere handful: in the Mediterranean, Gibraltar and the two British sovereign bases in Cyprus, though the latter are used in conjunction with NATO naval commands in the Mediterranean; in Africa, Rhodesia, so long as Britain refuses to accept that country's unilateral declaration of independence of November 1965 and hence still has some technical responsibility for Rhodesia's security; in Central America, British Honduras and the British Caribbean island group, including the Bahamas and Bermuda, though these now fall within the United States defence sphere; in the South Atlantic, the Falkland Islands and South Georgia; in the Far East, Hong Kong and a number of scattered island dependencies in the Pacific. Bilateral defence agreements involving the possible use of force include those with Malta and Libya, the scale of both of which are to be reduced, according to the 1966 Defence Review; with the Republic of South Africa under the agreement of June 1955 by which Britain gave up the Simonstown naval base and accepted with South Africa joint responsibility for defence of the sea routes round Southern Africa;[1] and with Malaysia until the end of 1971. Britain also leases naval bases in Libya and Singapore, now headquarters of the Far East Command, though the post-devaluation economy measures announced by the Prime Minister on 16 January 1968 included the withdrawal of British forces from Singapore by the end of 1971. In addition, British forces are to be withdrawn by the same date from the states of the Persian Gulf with which Britain also had joint defence arrangements.

Besides these commitments to defend British territory and overseas dependencies and bases are the undertakings through collective defence arrangements which have grown up since the war within the framework of Article 51 of the UN Charter. It is a curious commentary on Britain's economic weakness in the 1960s that she has treaty engagements to act against common dangers to security with 24 other countries; 14 under the North Atlantic pact of 1949, three (Iran, Pakistan, Turkey) under the CENTO (formerly Baghdad) pact of 1955, and seven (Australia, France, New Zealand, Pakistan, the Philippines, Thailand, the United States, together with the three former states of Indo-China, in so far as they all form part of the designated treaty area) under the SEATO agreement of 1954. In addition, Britain, like France and the United States, has more than once undertaken to maintain its rights, including the right of free access, in Berlin, as for instance in the declaration of 14 December 1958.[2] These pledges, unlike the British guarantee to Poland in 1939, by no means take the choice

[1] Cmd. 9520 (July 1955).   [2] Germany No. 1 (1959), Cmnd. 634, p. 21.

of war or peace out of Britain's hands; the CENTO and SEATO commitments are little more than promises to consult and even the NATO treaty leaves it open to member-states to determine what form their assistance against armed attack shall take. But some provision to fulfil these commitments must be made.

The principal question affecting the security interests of Britain, however, is their relation to the second vital British interest, peace. Peace is not a vital interest for Britain if by that is meant that under no condition would it be sacrificed. According to the 1958 Defence White Paper, which would still seem to be valid in this respect, Britain would fight with all her power, including the use of strategic nuclear weapons, against a major attack, not only upon these islands, but also upon allies, even if this were launched with conventional weapons only.[1] There is no substantial section of absolute pacifist opinion in Britain. Yet Britain has a stake in peace at least as heavy as that of any other country, both on account of her hideous vulnerability in wartime and because of the losses in life, wealth and world status which she has already sustained in two world wars. British policy must be, as Lord Avon once described it, one of 'peace at almost any price'. Here, then, is a further paradox: that, while nuclear weapons are, on the admission of successive governments since the war, unable to defend the country if the crisis comes, defence policy is based on the assumption that any war involving Britain *must* be nuclear since, like other West European countries, she cannot contemplate warfare in Europe at lower than the nuclear threshold, as seems implied in strategies of flexible response. At the same time, no British government has favoured the spread of nuclear weapons to other countries, or enthused over the acquisition by France of an independent nuclear weapons system, or regarded with anything but suspicion proposals, such as the scheme for a multilateral nuclear force (MLF), for giving West Germany a say in NATO nuclear strength.

Along with the British interest in peace is its corollary: the interest in pacification and disarmament. Pacification, meaning

[1] Cmnd. 363, p. 2.

the systematic effort to remove the grievances of rebellious Powers by negotiation, has been expressed in British policy in three ways since the war. First, British Ministers have sought to use the United Nations, as they tried to use the League of Nations, not so much for the organization of punitive measures against recalcitrant states, but for conciliation and quietly negotiated compromises; Britain's application to the Security Council for mandatory economic sanctions against Rhodesia in December 1966 reflected African pressures within the Commonwealth rather than any definite British belief in their efficacy. Britain never agreed with American efforts, though she may have acquiesced in them, to use the UN as a machine for waging political warfare against the Soviet Union in the late 1940s, or to organize voting majorities in the General Assembly against the Communist states, though she stood with the United Nations in the action in Korea in June 1950; she has persistently called for Communist China's admission into the organization. Secondly, British governments during the most intense periods of the Cold War were more active than those of any other NATO state in calling for talks at heads-of-government level with Soviet leaders and in doing so anticipated the East–West *détente* which developed after the Cuba crisis in October 1962. Although more recently Britain has strongly dissented from President de Gaulle's decision to withdraw French forces from NATO commands, the talks he held with Soviet leaders during his 12-day visit to the Soviet Union in June 1966 were fully consistent with the long-standing British wish to come to terms with Communist leaders, pressed in NATO circles in the late 1950s when de Gaulle was unable to give his support. Thirdly, British pacificatory policies have been expressed in a search for specific tension-easing agreements with the Soviet Union, concerning military disengagement and denuclearized zones in Europe, non-aggression pacts and other such arms control arrangements. The 'Eden Plan' for a zone of limited military forces and installations in Central Europe, presented to the Geneva 'summit' conference in 1955, and Macmillan's proposal for the limitation of forces and weapons in an agreed area of Europe which he took to the Soviet Union in

February 1959 are typical examples.[1] Finally, Britain played an important part in the launching of the three-Power nuclear test ban negotiations in August 1958, and although it is not yet known exactly what part Britain played in the talks, there is no doubt that the British delegation proved fertile in expedients to keep them going until partial success was attained in August 1963.

As for disarmament, strong forces have combined to make it a persistent preoccupation. In the period between the wars Britain's fear of naval competition, first from Japan and the United States, later from Nazi Germany, made her a leading participant in the Washington naval talks in 1921 and in the negotiation of the London naval treaties of 1930 and 1936. At the World Disarmament Conference which met in 1932 and had petered out by 1934 the fear of an arms race in Europe resulting from Germany's refusal to accept its forcibly disarmed status under the 1919 peace settlement made Britain an active mediator there too. Since 1945 the outpacing of this country in armaments by the two super-Powers and fear of the spread of nuclear weapons, and hence of the loss of Britain's position as member of a small nuclear club, have all given the United Kingdom a special role in disarmament talks. In these she has proved only marginally more willing, if willing at all, to accept the lower verification requirements demanded by the Soviet Union, and her present unreadiness to abandon her nuclear force is no encouragement to other countries to renounce nuclear weapons. Nevertheless, whenever the call is made for yet another round of disarmament talks, British Ministers, as the appointment by this country of the world's first Minister for Disarmament shows, are generally prepared to echo it.

Thirdly, after security and peace as vital British interests, comes the perennial British demand for representation in the highest councils of nations. The British world role, on which all governments since the war have either expressly or by implication insisted, is in the final resort the demand for a seat at tables where

[1] Misc. No. 21 (1955), Geneva Conference, Cmd. 9633, Annex I, pp. 99–101; Soviet Union No. 1 (1959), Cmd. 689, pp. 2–3.

questions affecting the entire international community are settled. The claim is made on various grounds: Britain's contribution to the maintenance of international order in two wars; the contribution she continues to make to the maintenance of peace in areas outside that in which the British Isles are situated; long experience of world affairs, especially in dealing with non-European peoples; the fact that Britain remains a leading commercial Power and a banker for the Sterling Area, a nuclear state and one with world-wide connections even in her present straitened conditions. Britain had little difficulty in maintaining her position at the apex of the international pyramid in the inter-war period; it was for her to say at any time during the late 1930s whether there would be war with the Dictators and on what issues. During the Second World War she kept her seat at conferences of the leading Allied Powers and was recognized as a world leader when given permanent membership of the UN Security Council when the Charter was framed in 1945. Britain did lose effective say in the occupation of Japan in 1945-51 though formally represented on the Far Eastern Commission in Washington and (in a Commonwealth delegation) on the Allied Control Council in Tokyo. It is, however, testimony to Britain's ability to hold her place at the highest level even in the Far East that she secured the co-chairmanship with Russia of the Geneva Conference on Korea and Indo-China in 1954 and also steered the conference to its conclusion despite the strongest aversion from its proceedings of Secretary of State Dulles.

After the accession of President Kennedy to the White House in January 1961, however, some fear was expressed in Britain that he might seek to come to terms directly with the Soviet Union without giving Britain access to the talks; this fear was to some extent confirmed when the President met Mr. Khrushchev alone in Vienna in June 1961. There seems little doubt, too, that in any future conference between the Western Powers, chiefly represented by the United States, and the Soviet Union or China or both together, Britain would necessarily play little more than an ancillary role. But equally there is no doubt that the government would assert a right to be there, and hardly less doubt that it would be conceded.

Another example of the British concern with maintaining a foothold in world-wide centres of international decision-making is the effort to keep in step with the three main international associations in the West since the war: the Atlantic Community, Europe and the Commonwealth. The desire of British government has been to avoid any internal tightening of these groups which might confront Britain with a choice between one and other of the three. A certain strain has appeared between the Commonwealth and the Atlantic connection in that a number of the newer Commonwealth countries, especially since the intensification of the Vietnam conflict in February 1965, have regarded Britain as having sacrificed its traditional role as a mediator by aligning herself too closely with the United States. The chief strains have appeared, however, between the rival attractions of Europe, on one side, and of the Commonwealth and the Atlantic Community, on the other. As integration in Western Europe went forward after the formation of the Coal and Steel Community in 1951, British Ministers faced the dilemma whether they wished to have Britain considered as essentially a European Power, which meant sooner or later severing the Commonwealth connection, or whether they should maintain merely an associative relationship with the new Europe, thus giving point to those Europeans who claimed that Britain always wanted the best of both worlds and therefore should be accorded no special favours.

Even if Britain decided that on entering the EEC she could make arrangements to meet the problems of countries like Ceylon, Ghana, Hong Kong, India, Mauritius, Nigeria, New Zealand, Sierra Leone, which were peculiarly dependent on favourable trade relations with Britain, the fact remains that British membership of the European communities, if this is agreed by France, must serve to weaken Britain's special relationship with the United States. It is hard to see how a British Prime Minister could go to Washington to argue a specifically British point of view while year by year Britain was being absorbed more deeply into a West European union. The British dilemma over Europe, however, precisely illustrates the persistent desire to maintain representation at the highest international level and the problems it creates. Before the Macmillan government's decision to apply for membership of the EEC in 1961 one of the strongest arguments against doing so was that it would destroy British hopes of exercising an independent influence on world affairs at the highest level, or more exactly of steering United States policy into courses in the interests of peace and stability. By 1961, with President Kennedy's accession to office, this had become a less convincing argument. It was replaced by the claim that the Europe of the Six, now developing more rapidly than most British observers had deemed possible, would become a new focus of world power in which Britain must have a hand if she were not to be by-passed by the main lines of diplomatic communication. Thus the reasons for and against joining Europe turned to a large extent on how far this move would affect the time-honoured British place in centres where issues affecting the whole international community are decided.

It is unnecessary to dwell in detail on the fourth and final group of interests vital to Britain, the economic. As we have emphasized, a country as dependent on international trade and as vulnerable to changes in world economic and financial conditions as Britain cannot but be intensely concerned with the international economy. Hardly any important act of a British Foreign Secretary is not in some way affected. What the British expect from the world economy is a high level of demand for the kind of industrial products and services, such as shipping, banking and insurance, in which Britain specializes; the reduction as far as possible of barriers to international trade and the avoidance of inward-looking economic blocs with little in the way of intercourse between them; the reduction of international tensions which oblige the Powers to place restrictions on their trade with unfriendly states; the maintenance of a high level of purchasing power and employment among Britain's trading partners; and the reduction of the world's military budgets in order to leave more spending power available for peaceful trade.

Conflict clearly exists between economic interests of this kind and the requirements of security. To maintain good relations with allies, especially the United States, for defence purposes for instance, British governments have had to agree to more controls on trade with Cuba, the Soviet bloc of states and Communist China than strictly economic conditions would have prescribed. It is also interesting to see how strong moral or moralistic ideas in Britain and especially in the Labour Party have on occasion led to the sacrifice of economic gain to principle, a notable case being the government's agreement in December 1967 to continue the embargo on the sale of arms to South Africa which the United Nations had decreed, even though the deal was estimated at £200 million. This was done despite evident disagreement in the Cabinet and largely to placate the rank-and-file of the Labour Party.

In the next decade

Before the major overhaul of British policy which accompanied the Labour government's announcement on 16 January 1968 of economy measures to make devaluation of the pound work, the central issue of that policy in the immediate future appeared to be whether the country should continue to try to maintain its position as a world Power, though clearly in the second or even third rank; or whether it should merge itself in Europe and limit itself to strictly regional interests, while not excluding the possibility that a united western Europe, with Britain and possibly other Efta countries as members, might still play a part in world affairs comparable to that of the two giants.

Before the election of the Wilson government in October 1964 Labour spokesmen had persistently criticized Conservative pretensions to keep Britain 'seated at the top table' in international affairs. Almost immediately on becoming Prime Minister, however, Mr. Wilson began to talk much the same language. At the Lord Mayor's dinner at Guildhall on 16 November, for instance, he used the phrase: 'we are a world Power, and a world influence, or we are nothing'.[1] How far this reflected the inevitable tendency in foreign affairs for an Opposition to borrow the Government's policies when in Government themselves, or the need to maintain foreign confidence in the pound, or the realization that if Britain were to reduce her external commitments too quickly the result might look more like a rout than an orderly retreat, is impossible to say. Nevertheless, the strain on the pound during the following three years led to a withdrawal from Aden in 1967 and proposed withdrawals from the Persian Gulf and the Far East in 1971 in a manner which did seem like a rout.

Mr. Wilson was not lacking in reasoned arguments on behalf of the world role and the 'East of Suez' policy on other occasions. Speaking at a meeting of the Parliamentary Labour Party on 16 June 1966, he argued that Britain still had commitments outside Europe which made her more than a European Power, commitments to Commonwealth countries like Malaysia and to states situated in areas of key economic importance, like the sheikdoms of the Persian Gulf; that Britain was a world banker and could never disinterest herself in world-wide economic and trading conditions with all their political overtones; that Britain was a populous and still wealthy country which lived by its world-wide business; and that, as a nuclear Power, Britain remained a considerable military force and moreover had the kind of reputation abroad which enabled her to intervene to quell unrest where intervention by other Powers would be resented.

There was also the argument that Britain, perhaps more than any other country, was well placed to help consolidate the East–West *détente* owing to her traditional influence in Washington and the respect still paid to her in Moscow; that, in consequence of her long-standing relationship with the United States, it was for Britain to keep the bridge intact between that country and Europe, especially when they threatened to drift apart as a result of the growth of neutralism in Europe and America's preoccupation with Asia; that it would be dangerous to stand aside and leave the United States to fight it out 'eyeball to eyeball' with Communist

[1] *The Times*, 17 November 1964.

China, when Britain had already done so much to improve relations between the West and the Soviet Union; and that, as a country with the strongest interest in peace, Britain had a special duty to help build up the United Nations and equip it as an effective peace-keeping institution.[1]

The arguments urged against the world role by its critics – these being mainly in the Labour and Liberal parties, though the then Conservative 'shadow' Defence Minister, Mr. Enoch Powell, with some qualifications stood with them – were partly that it did not make sense in Britain's weakened economic situation and that the attempt to maintain military forces East of Suez from an inadequate financial base was to increase further the chronic pressures on the pound and make the country even more a pensioner of the United States; and partly that pursuit of a world role which must ultimately be abandoned on account of its cost prevented Britain from seizing opportunities for leadership in a western Europe that was moving gradually towards a unity Britain would find increasingly hard to penetrate. The risk was, the critics thought, that Britain would fall between two stools: unable to make a success of an independent world role and excluded from a Europe which, as the old East–West confrontation died away, stood out as an entity comparable, in economic strength at least, to the two giants. Alongside this major debate, however, the Labour Left, while opposing the East of Suez policy, was also unenthusiastic about joining the European communities.

To some extent this debate had always been unreal. On the one hand, the Wilson government in its Defence Review of February 1966 made clear its determination to cut its overseas defence commitments to the bone. This decision became even more unequivocal after the economic crisis in the summer of 1966, which resulted in the introduction of a severe 'squeeze' in July, and more so still after the devaluation crisis which resulted in the reduction of the pound's value by 14·3 per cent in November 1967 and the Government's cuts in overseas defence spending in January 1968. The British withdrawal from Aden in November

[1] *The Times,* 17 June 1966.

1967; the reduction in British forces in Malaysia after the ending of the confrontation with Indonesia in August 1966, followed by the decision to withdraw all forces from Malaysia and Singapore by the end of 1971; the cancellation of the contract for 50 FIII aircraft from the United States in January 1968 on the assumption that they would no longer be needed in view of the proposed winding up of the East of Suez policy; the principle laid down for the first time in the 1966 Defence Review that Britain could no longer contemplate a war outside Europe without allies; the decision to reduce forces in Germany unless there was substantial assistance with the foreign exchange problem: all showed that circumstances, rather than reasoned argument, were forcing Britain to reduce her commitments in proportion with her resources. The impression was inescapable that the government were being driven by events rather than doing anything to control them.

On the other side of the coin, the critics of the world role, in so far as they advocated a retirement into the new European system, were handicapped by the fact that France still held the key to Britain's entry into Europe, and so far from Britain's reduction of her overseas commitments being regarded in Paris as making her more truly European, the economic troubles which underlay that action were paraded by President de Gaulle as showing that Britain was not really strong enough for membership. When the French Foreign Minister, M. Couve de Murville, at a meeting of the Council of Ministers of the six Common Market states in Luxembourg on 23 October 1967, made known the President's still unfavourable attitude to Britain's membership he pointed to the state of the British economy and the role of sterling as the reasons. This was brutally confirmed by de Gaulle himself at his press conference on 27 November when he refused even to open negotiations on Britain's entry into the EEC.

At the same time, other pressures were forcing on Britain a radical reconsideration of foreign policy and making the idea of a world role less convincing. First, there was the ever-growing disparity in military strength between the super-Powers, on the one hand, and second-rank countries like Britain and France, on the other. The decisions of the United States and the Soviet Union (the former being made without consulting Britain) to install limited anti-ballistic missile systems, a field in which Britain and France as independent states could never hope to compete, showed how wide this gap was becoming. Moreover, the veto placed by the US Congress in 1967 on Britain building ships for the American navy as a method of financing the British purchase of American FIII strike aircraft, intended in the 1966 Defence Review to be the chief instrument of British air power in the 1970s, underlined the increasing unreality of British efforts to maintain an independent military capability remote from Europe.

Secondly, the general outstripping of Britain by the United States in military and economic terms and the heavy American involvement in Vietnam in the mid-1960s, a conflict which Britain could neither mediate nor assist the United States in winning, tended to empty the concept of the 'special relationship' of its last remaining contents. In October 1967 Lord Chalfont, the British Minister in charge of British negotiations for entry into the European Economic Community, was saying that Britain made no further claims on the United States by virtue of the 'special relationship', and that Britain had henceforward to think, not so much of the United States and herself, as of the United States and Europe, of which Britain hoped to be a part.[1] As these final Anglo–American links weakened, Ministers became more sensitive to the economic penetration by US capital of the more advanced sectors of British industry. If Britain did not succeed in joining the EEC, this penetration–or 'economic helotry', as Mr. Wilson described it in a speech at the Council of Europe in Strasbourg in January 1967–would grow.[2] But if, as some proposed, Britain sought a form of economic union with the United States and Canada as an alternative to the EEC, it would probably grow even more.

Along with the Anglo–American 'special relationship', Commonwealth unity was being eroded, too. The old idea that the

[1] *The Times*, 10 October 1967.   [2] *The Times*, 24 January 1967.

Commonwealth could ever form a single trading preference area, another alternative to Britain's entry into Europe, seemed less and less convincing. The Commonwealth still accounted for some 30 per cent of Britain's overseas trade, but it was a diminishing fraction, it covered older lines of manufacture rather than newer and it was becoming less important in the total economies of most Commonwealth countries than their trade with countries outside the Commonwealth. The declining defence commitments of Britain also reduced the meaning of the Commonwealth even for some of its oldest and most loyal members, such as Australia and New Zealand, which were being absorbed into America's defence strategy in South East Asia. Moreover, the Commonwealth as a political entity received a sharp blow from the Rhodesia crisis which entered its acute phase with the illegal declaration of independence by the Smith regime in November 1965. A Zambian diplomat's description of Britain as a 'toothless bulldog' tended to sum up African nationalist reactions to British reluctance to use force against the Smith regime, while British public opinion did not warm to a Commonwealth which asked Britain virtually to risk ruin in order to establish a moral principle in Rhodesia.

Hence, the four major alternatives to British membership of the west European communities – a north Atlantic economic union to include Britain, the United States and Canada; a strengthened Efta; an economically integrated Commonwealth; or a continuance of Britain's present international position – have not increased in attractiveness since the first British application to join the Common Market in 1961. This very fact was, of course, a strong card in France's hand in negotiating over the British application to join the EEC, and since, if Britain were allowed to join, France would risk losing the hegemony in the European communities she has hitherto enjoyed, she could be relied upon to play that card for all it is worth. British pressure for entry was therefore likely to be continuous, and so, for the same reason, was French resistance to that pressure.[1] But in the last resort it may well

[1] Written in January 1968.

be two other factors which will decide the future of British foreign policy.

The first is the economic. The question whether Britain can surmount her 'stop-go' pattern of economic crisis and reach an upland of growth will govern every aspect of foreign policy in the next ten years. To some extent this is a matter of British psychology as well as of resources and skills; the attitude of reclining in no doubt hard-earned affluence and leisure is inappropriate for any considerable state in the strenuous modern world. But there is also, secondly, the question whether British Ministers will continue to have ideas about world affairs and argue policies which command respect in the world's capitals. British prestige in 1945 was due, not only to British courage in 1940, but to the fact that Britain, though belatedly, had been right about Hitler and the prospects of surviving against him. As war ended in 1945, Britain was right about Stalin and his ambitions in Europe when Roosevelt took the unrealistic view; was right about the necessity to co-exist with Communism when Dulles wanted to destroy it; was right, as American leaders later agreed, about the need to accept the non-alignment policies of the new Afro–Asian states. Other countries, the United States not least, could reflect that if they rejected British advice on foreign policy they might have cause to regret it later. But Britain has made grievous errors in foreign policy since then: in Egypt in 1956, and in miscalculating the viability of European union since the war until it was too late. More recently, British Ministers have tended to use foreign policy initiatives with a view to improving their public relations at home. Until they return to attempting to see the international situation as it is, not as they think the voter would like to see it, they cannot command the respect abroad which is essential to the successful performance of any kind of role.

BIBLIOGRAPHY

ALLEN, HARRY C. *The Anglo-American Predicament*. New York: St Martin's Press, 1960.

BISHOP, DONALD G. *The Administration of British Foreign Relations*. Syracuse, N.Y.: Syracuse University Press, 1961.

CAMPS, MIRIAM. *Britain and the European Community, 1955–1963*. Princeton, N.J.: Princeton University Press, 1964.

GOODWIN, GEOFFREY L. *Britain and the United Nations*. New York: Manhattan (Royal Institute of International Affairs), 1958.

HÜSLER, ANGELO. *Contribution à l'étude de l'élaboration de la politique étrangère britannique: 1945–1956*. Geneva: Droz, 1961.

MILLER, JOHN D. B. *The Commonwealth in the World*. 3d ed. Cambridge, Mass.: Harvard University Press, 1965.

NORTHEDGE, F. S. *British Foreign Policy: The Process of Readjustment, 1945–1961*. New York: Frederick A. Praeger, 1962.

————. *The Troubled Giant: Britain Among the Great Powers, 1916–1939*. New York: Frederick A. Praeger, 1967.

SETON-WATSON, ROBERT W. *Britain in Europe, 1789–1914*. New York: Cambridge University Press, 1937.

STRANG, WILLIAM. *Britain in World Affairs: The Fluctuation in Power and Influence from Henry VIII to Elizabeth II*. New York: Frederick A. Praeger, 1961. (Paperback ed.: Praeger.)

————. *The Foreign Office*. New York: Oxford University Press, 1955.

TAYLOR, A. J. P. *English History, 1914–1945*. New York: Oxford University Press, 1965.

WOODHOUSE, C. M. *British Foreign Policy Since the Second World War*. New York: Frederick A. Praeger, 1962.

WOODWARD, ERNEST L. *British Foreign Policy During the Second World War*. London: H.M. Stationery Office, 1961.

6·FRENCH FOREIGN POLICY

Dorothy Pickles

In 1948, General de Gaulle accused the Fourth Republic of having no foreign policy, by which he meant that governments were too weak and too divided to have either any long-term coherent plan, or the authority to carry one out. Governments of the Fifth Republic have had both a goal and the internal authority to move towards it, in so far as external circumstances allowed. But it is General de Gaulle's plan, and he alone decides on the pace and the direction of the advance. If, however, foreign policy is defined more broadly to include, either alongside or in the absence of specific planned ambitions, a conscious image of what is or ought to be the country's place in the world, or some general guiding principles or attitudes determining or influencing decisions on specific issues, then France can be said to have had under both regimes foreign policies whose patterns have constituted a continuous tradition discernible throughout much of her history. It has helped to form present-day attitudes and still helps to mould French thought along certain lines, to encourage Governments and public opinion to remain in behavioural ruts, or to evolve new policies by modifying older patterns rather than by breaking entirely new ground.

Aims
French thought in the field of foreign affairs has been dominated by two basic traditions, variously described as those of movement and stability, introversion and extroversion, conquest and moderation. At certain periods they have co-existed and overlapped, at others one of these has predominated to the virtual exclusion of the other. The more positive and dynamic tradition holds that, by virtue of her history and geography, and perhaps also of her natural temperament, France is destined to play a leading role in

187

Europe, and has the right to claim certain 'natural frontiers'–the Rhine, the Alps and the Pyrenees. For more than three centuries there have been recurrent echoes of such claims–for instance, by Richelieu, Rousseau, Danton, Carnot, Clemenceau and General de Gaulle; and the claims have sometimes been advanced to justify policies of aggrandizement and aggressive wars, particularly during the reigns of Louis XIV and Louis XV.

The more static tradition, which predominated from 1815 up to the fifties of the present century, is that of a basically satisfied power. It is a theory of 'natural equilibrium', which emphasizes preoccupations with security, the will to peace and the maintenance of the *status quo*. France's policies at the Paris peace conference in 1919 were a clear expression of both these theories, with the regretful conclusion that the second was imposed by the facts of the time. As Clemenceau put it in the Chamber of Deputies on 15 September 1919,

> We all know instinctively that expansion to the Rhine was the tradition of our ancestors. . . . That is where we ought to have been. . . . It is not the fault of the revolutionary armies that we could not stay there, nor is it our fault that if, today, when I seek to reach the Rhine, I find German lands between it and me and am obliged to take this fact into account.

Taking the fact of Germany into account, in the sense of trying to ensure the security of her eastern frontier, has been France's main preoccupation for the past century, at times to the virtual exclusion of everything else. The conditions posed by France as constituting effective security may often have approximated to the claim to 'natural frontiers', but there is, nevertheless, a significant difference of tone between seventeenth- and twentieth-century arguments. At Versailles, and a quarter of a century later, following the Second World War, this preoccupation with security led to claims to occupy the Rhineland and to remove the Saar from the sphere of German sovereignty. But France did not seek the political annexation of either, and in 1946 she was proposing, not French, but international, control of the Ruhr. There have been aggressive actions and attitudes which, though explicable in terms of the search for security, have appeared to the outside world as possible manifestations of a French desire for hegemony in Europe – the occupation of the Ruhr, for instance, in 1923, and the present Gaullist intention that France shall be (*de facto* if not *de jure*) the sole nuclear power in continental Europe. But throughout most of the life of the Third and Fourth Republics, French foreign policy was undoubtedly aiming first and foremost at security from German aggression. Except during periods of acute fear of Germany, or during periods of international tension arousing traditional aggressive statements or a sense of national humiliation (the Fashoda, Agadir and Suez incidents), the general public was neither aggressive nor, indeed, primarily interested in foreign affairs. It became, and has remained, a commonplace that in France elections are never won on foreign-policy issues.

From the end of the eighteenth century onwards, foreign-policy attitudes have been increasingly coloured by a third tradition, which is not, strictly speaking, an aim, but an innate conviction. Its importance is extremely difficult to evaluate, but it is certainly a feeling that runs deep, and that has had at times a considerable impact on French policies. It is the belief that France is not only a natural political leader in Europe, but also a natural cultural leader, that French ideas and civilization should be exported to less favoured nations, at first in Europe, and, with the coming of the colonial era, to overseas possessions. Like the two dominating traditions, this belief has been used to justify conquest. The revolutionary leaders, for instance, believed that they had discovered the secret of good government, and their claims to 'natural frontiers' were strengthened by claims to be fighting to bring liberty to other countries that, like France, had the right to be free. 'All the plans for French hegemony that I know of,' wrote Carlo Laroche, 'are plans for perpetual peace; the revolutionary conquest itself is a crusade.'[1] Napoleon justified expansionism by a mixture of nationalism and zeal for popular approval. In his *Mémorial de Sainte Hélène*, he predicted that

[1] *La Diplomatie française*, Presses universitaires de France, 1946, p. 121.

the first sovereign who, in the midst of the first great struggle embraces in good faith the cause of the people will find himself leader of all Europe, able to do as he wills.

The patriotism of nineteenth-century democrats also included the belief in France's right and duty to emancipate oppressed nations, and so justified expansionism. Louis Blanc, for instance, held that it was her duty 'to spread out, to overflow'.[1] And in the twentieth century, the Communist leader, Thorez, quoted with approval the statement by Jaurès that Napoleon, 'by throwing Europe into violent confusion had given her new life'.[2]

The theory of France's civilizing mission still served in many French minds to justify the retention of quasi-colonial rule in North Africa, long after world opinion had come to regard the end of Empire as inevitable. And it still plays an important role in the relationships that have been built up between France and her former overseas possessions and protectorates. Britain has tended to try to export Parliamentary government to her former colonies and to train local administrators. France has exported teachers in their thousands, and has imported overseas political leaders who, as members of French political assemblies, have been trained in French ways of thought and then have returned to lead their countries when they became independent.

The period after the Second World War brought radical changes in France's position in the world which have modified to some extent these traditional modes of thought. Although technically on the side of the victors, France emerged from the war economically, psychologically and politically only on the fringe of great-Power status. She was not represented at Yalta or at Potsdam. She had to fight for the right to share in the occupation of Germany. She was faced with a tremendous task of economic reconstruction and modernization, jealous of Great Britain's 'special relationship' with the United States, and of her advance in

[1] *Histoire de dix ans*, V, p. 504.

[2] *La Mission de la France dans le Monde*, Editions sociales internationales, 1938, p. 65.

the nuclear field, yet unable to catch up the ground lost by four years of occupation. The first reaction to this situation, among the predominantly Left-wing governmental parties during the early post-war period, was to fall back on the tradition of leadership in the field of ideas, and, in default of power, to seek to play the role of a mediator–as, for example, in European disputes such as that over Trieste–or to avoid taking sides irrevocably with either of the two 'hegemonies'. Even after the Cold War had become an inescapable fact and the Marshall plan had ranged France indisputably on the American side, there remained strong neutralist tendencies in Left-wing circles. By the early fifties, however, the majority of moderate and non-Communist Left-wing opinion had found a new road (or rather an old road, adapted to new times and new methods) to French security, to French leadership in Europe, at first perhaps only in the field of ideas, but already in the minds of some a road leading to the recovery of French power and prestige in Europe. This was the road to an 'integrated' Western Europe, governed by supranational institutions.

By the time the Fourth Republic entered its second decade, quarrels over the organization of Europe, the political and military deadlock reached in the Algerian war, and the inability of the traditional parties to provide stable government or coherent policies had convinced many Frenchmen, including a number on the Left as well as on the Right, that the regime was doomed. Some looked to General de Gaulle, as representing the last hope of extricating France from the Algerian war without bringing civil war to France. Others looked to him to provide a new regime and new policies. The traditional parties intended to get rid of him once he had served their purposes. He intended to get rid of their influence and to mould French opinion to serve his purposes. By the end of 1962, it was clear that General de Gaulle was the definitive victor in this struggle for power, and the Fifth Republic, whose policies up to then had been limited by the demands of the Algerian problem, was free to undertake foreign policies decided and dictated by him.

General de Gaulle's own speeches and writings show quite

clearly that his foreign policy is based on a certain number of assumptions, beliefs or goals, all of which are basically in line with traditional French attitudes. First, whatever reverses France may suffer, she remains in his view potentially a great Power, and her destiny is and will always be to realize this potentiality. In the present world situation, however, she can do so only on certain conditions. She must be economically and politically strong and stable. She must also be the leader of a united Europe, and this requires the pursuit of common European defence and foreign policies, but the rejection of integrated institutions. In the Gaullist view, only national States have the authority to carry out policies and to inspire the loyalty of armies.[1] Supranational institutions are regarded by General de Gaulle as 'myths, fictions and empty show',[2] or as 'the chimera' of 'an intolerable and impracticable fusion'.[3] Only after a long period of intergovernmental co-operation along traditional lines will it be possible to envisage any kind of federal European Government. Sully's Grand Design for Europe and that of General de Gaulle are nearer to each other in spirit than are the modern Gaullist and supranationalist conceptions of Europe.

Another assumption is that the frontiers of this united Europe will not remain those of the six members of the EEC, however useful these are as a starting point. Sooner or later, co-operation must be extended to countries behind the Iron Curtain, not excluding Russia, in the hope that, one day, the frontiers of the new Europe will approximate to the historical frontiers of the continent. At this future, unspecified date, when countries of the Eastern bloc are assumed to have abandoned 'the dominating ambitions of an out-of-date ideology',[4] it will be possible to establish 'from the Atlantic to the Urals, a *détente*, perhaps an *entente*'.[5] Looking forward, he says,

[1] Press conferences of 5 September 1960 and 15 May 1962, and speech to the *Haute Ecole des Etudes Militaires* on 3 November 1959.

[2] Press conference of 4 February 1965.

[3] Press conference of 4 February 1965.

[4] Declaration at Bonn, 4 September 1962. [5] Speech at Poitiers, 15 June 1963.

I see Europe as she is, stretching from Gibraltar to the Urals, from Spitzbergen to Sicily, and not limited to a Franco–German grouping, that would be viable only under a German hegemony, and with the frontiers of Charlemagne.[1]

It is only within this wider Europe that it will be, in his view, eventually possible to eliminate the main obstacle to European strength and influence, namely, the division of Germany.

Another belief is that this wider Europe must have a truly world role, including the sharing of peace-keeping activities with other great Powers, influence throughout a wide area, including Africa and the Middle East, and responsibility for providing aid and culture to under-developed nations.

Aims so imprecisely formulated and so variously interpreted cannot provide more than a guiding light, and in Gaullist France the President alone is able to relate them to the day-to-day and medium-term activities that go to make up foreign policy in the accepted sense of the term. At what stage Britain–now outside the European, and in what the General considers as the 'Anglo-Saxon', camp–is envisaged as joining his Europe, the exact form that co-operation will eventually take in the 'wider Europe', the time schedule for the achievement of a European defence and foreign policy, in either the narrower or the wider European framework–all these and many other questions are never clearly answered. It is not even certain that the General himself believes that the goal is attainable. The extent to which, in his mind, these aims are far-distant objectives, or a basis for decisions on immediate policies, or merely ambiguous or grandiloquent phrases forming part of the deliberate ambiguity and the grandiose image that go to make up his 'public face'–these are points left in the main for press and public to interpret. Thus Gaullism involves a perpetual focusing of attention on the personality, leadership and declarations of the President. And this is an essential element in his methods.

Machinery and methods

Like the principles of French foreign policy, the machinery of

[1] Press conference of 7 April 1954.

its decision-making has been subject, at least during the present century, to influences and traditions that also have their distinctive patterns. General de Gaulle and governments of the Fifth Republic have not formally abandoned traditional ways, though they have modified some of the patterns. Republican Presidents, though constitutionally irresponsible, exercise formal powers in the field of foreign policy, but they have also had varying degrees of political influence, and sometimes more influence than would be acceptable in a British constitutional monarch. The formal powers can be dismissed in a sentence, since, under all three recent Republican constitutions, they have required a Ministerial counter-signature. The difference between the practice of the Third and Fourth Republics on the one hand and that of the Fifth on the other is that, whereas Presidents of the former regimes were the mouthpieces of governmental decisions, under the Gaullist regime the position has been reversed. The Ministerial counter-signature constitutionalizes the President's decisions, but it is the Ministers who have constituted themselves his obedient mouthpieces.

This change is a break with Republican tradition, though a less spectacular one than is often assumed. Where the control of foreign policy is concerned, there have been two contradictory Republican traditions. The first, that of executive control, was inherited from the personal diplomacy of kings and emperors. It helps to explain the tendency, under the Third and Fourth Republics, for Deputies to regard foreign policy as being in the main a Presidential or a Prime-Ministerial responsibility, except during periods of tension when foreign policy became a dominant political issue. The tendency of some Prime Ministers of the Third Republic to take the portfolio of Foreign Affairs themselves strengthened their position *vis-à-vis* the President. Between 1920 and 1939, of fifty-eight effective Prime Ministers, sixteen were also their own Foreign Ministers. Even a strong President, however, could not stand up to a strong Prime Minister, and in the only two known cases of a head-on clash, the President resigned.[1] During the later years of the Third Republic the President's influence in general

[1] President MacMahon in 1879 and President Millerand in 1924.

declined, to an extent that justified the description of the Presidential function as being that of 'a mute and powerless onlooker'.[1]

The two Presidents of the Fourth Republic were stronger personalities, whose influence was considerable, but this was due mainly to the political weakness of the regime. The Fourth Republic's attitude to the control of foreign policy was dominated by the second tradition, inherited from the Revolution, that of parliamentary domination of the executive. Great importance was attached to the role of the Foreign Affairs Standing Commission of the National Assembly. This body, set up at the beginning of the century, has always enjoyed great prestige among the Standing Commissions. It has usually included a high percentage of former Prime Ministers or Foreign Ministers; it has certain rights to receive information, including the right to summon high officials, and to *ask* Ministers to appear before it. Ministers usually find it impolitic to refuse these requests, and, even under the Fifth Republic, important policy statements have often been made to the Commission before being made to the National Assembly.

In practice, it is not possible to make any hard-and-fast distinction between these two traditions, because political realities rather than political theories have tended to determine where effective power really lies. Under the Fourth Republic, political factors were responsible for two main weaknesses in the process of decision-making. First, governments were paralysed by party divisions and harassed by too many urgent problems, and so alternated between a situation in which they had too little power and one in which they had too much. No coherent policies were possible, because governments were too short-lived, and because it was possible for compromises to be reached only when there was an imperative need for urgent decisions to be taken. The normal situation was that of hesitation, deadlock and delay, as, for instance, over the projected European Defence Community, which was eventually turned down by the French National Assembly almost four years after the introduction of the original government

[1] Roger Pinto, *Eléments de droit constitutionnel*, Morel & Corduant, Lille, 1952, p. 328.

proposal. But government action was, nevertheless, sometimes possible precisely because the legislature was so often impotent. Ministers could sometimes succeed in presenting the Assembly with a virtual *fait accompli*, and so by-pass the parliamentary control that could have been exerted over governments if party divisions had been less great. For instance, M. Schuman delayed seeking parliamentary ratification of the treaty setting up the Coal and Steel Community until it was politically impossible for the legislature to turn it down. Individual Ministers sometimes managed to survive successive Ministerial reshuffles and changes of government. In the forties and fifties, M. Bidault and M. Schuman, who belonged to the same party, were both Foreign Ministers in several governments and managed to establish a degree of continuity that other Ministers could not achieve, partly because they remained in office longer, partly because, except for bitterly contested issues such as the EDC, political interest was mainly centred on internal quarrels.

The second weakness in the field of decision-making arose from the disproportionate amount of time that Ministers were compelled to devote to party quarrels. This had serious repercussions on the efficiency of departmental administration. Sometimes too much had to be left to high officials on the spot, who were then in a position to present the Minister with a *fait accompli*. Examples are the deposition of the Sultan of Morocco in 1953, the arrest of the five Algerian nationalist leaders in 1956 and the bombing of Sakhiet-Sidi-Yussef in 1958. In all these cases, actions carried out by officials were subsequently covered by the government. At other times, there was merely inaction. There are some Ministers, wrote the former Ambassador in London, M. Massigli, in 1958,[1]

who no longer work with their departmental heads, but only

[1] *Quelques maladies de l'Etat*, Plon, 1958, p. 51.

For an analysis of the working of the Ministerial *cabinet*, *v.* chapter III and pp. 55–60 of Alfred Grosser's study, quoted on the following page. For a brief description of the institution, *v.* the author's *France: the Fourth Republic*, Methuen, 1958, pp. 99–101.

with their own personal *cabinets*, if, indeed, they do not rely entirely on their own inspiration.

This was the kind of situation that resulted in the sending of General Navarre to Indo-China without any real instructions, and to the refusal of M. Grandval to accept the post of Commissioner-General in Indo-China, because he could not discover what his functions were to be.[1]

Though the processes of decision-making during the Fifth Republic have been spectacularly different, they have been no less dependent on political factors. Whatever the importance that General de Gaulle attaches to what he calls 'the personal equation' –and no doubt it has been of great importance–as long as the constitutional and political machinery for defeating governments and electing Presidents remains intact, even he is unable to act without the consent of the National Assembly, and the subsequent ratification of the electorate. The chief weakness of decision-making under the Fifth Republic has been that it has reflected no lasting evolution either of opinion or of machinery, but merely the use of existing machinery by the President for his own ends, a use that is possible only as long as the majority of French citizens and French Deputies remain content to let General de Gaulle do their thinking for them. Whatever has been gained in coherence, consistency or drive is, therefore, his personal achievement, and, with his disappearance from office, or with a change in political attitudes, there could simply be a reversion to the preceding situation.

It is true that the 1958 Constitution does give the President three personal powers in the field of foreign policy that were not possessed by his predecessors. No counter-signature is required to exercise emergency powers (article 16), to accede to or refuse a governmental or parliamentary request for a referendum (article 11), and to submit to the Constitutional Council any international agreement containing provisions that appear to him to be contrary to the Constitution (article 54). But the first was intended to

[1] Examples quoted in Alfred Grosser's *La IVe République et sa politique extérieure*, Armand Colin, 1961, p. 53.

be used, and can constitutionally be exercised, only in carefully defined circumstances, and the second applies, as far as foreign affairs are concerned, only to the ratification of a treaty that would affect the working of internal institutions. Neither the second nor the third confers any real powers on the President; they merely allow him to submit the question at issue to another body–in the one case either Parliament or the electorate, in the other the Constitutional Council. Since the President, once he has assumed emergency powers, remains the effective judge of their extent and duration, article 16 is, on the other hand, a potential source of considerable power. But there is no guarantee that this power will not disappear in some post-Gaullist revision of the Constitution. General de Gaulle had used them only once up to 1968.[1]

The President's methods, then, have consisted essentially of the use of existing machinery or of personal influence, with the consent of Parliament and of public opinion. He has transformed the chairmanship of the Cabinet, traditionally a formal right, into real personal leadership. He has been able to by-pass the Cabinet by using inter-ministerial committees under his chairmanship in order to present it with ready-made policies. He has been able to maintain his grip on public opinion by using Presidential tours, speeches, press conferences and so on to focus attention on his personal leadership, and so has made the Gaullist movement dependent on him for its electoral success. Since he has been his own most successful public-relations officer, what he says forms part of a permanent electoral campaign. The extent of his impact on foreign policy must be judged mainly in the light of what he has actually done to modify European and Atlantic policies and to find a new world role for France.

Content: (1) European and Atlantic policies

Throughout the fifties, all Frenchmen would still have subscribed to General de Gaulle's statement in 1944 that 'the fate of Germany is the central problem of the universe'. France's post-war foreign

[1] For a brief period in 1961, and with general approval owing to the special conditions created by the Algerian war.

policy was founded on, and limited by, the perpetual fear of Germany, and even in the sixties the eyes of politicians as well as of French diplomatists still remained, in Harold Nicolson's phrase, 'eternally fixed on the blue line of the Vosges'.[1] But during the intervening years there had been a considerable evolution in French opinion regarding the means by which the problem of Germany could be solved. During the early post-war years, French governments tried to deal with the problem along traditional lines by occupation of the Rhineland and the economic separation of the Saar from Germany, by instituting international control of the Ruhr arsenal, and by preventing Germany from restoring a central government. By 1949 it was already clear that three of these French safeguards would not be achieved, and that the fourth (the economic separation of the Saar) would shortly disappear.

For the overwhelming majority of Frenchmen, then, French post-war 'Europeanism' was primarily a political device for solving the German problem, though there was, of course, a great deal of genuine support for the idea of a politically united Europe for other reasons as well. Three things helped to divert the original French-sponsored movement in favour of rapid political federation into less ambitious channels. The first was the failure of the European nations themselves to agree to entrust more than symbolic functions to the Council of Europe, which, therefore, ceased to represent, even in the minds of 'Europeans', an embryo European Parliament. The second was the refusal of the six governments to accept the draft European constitution, agreed upon by the *ad hoc* committee set up by the Common Assembly of the European Coal and Steel Community and the Consultative Assembly of the Council of Europe. And the third was the failure between 1950 and 1954 to provide for a re-armed Germany within a European framework. After the defeat by France of the much amended proposals for a European Defence Community, therefore, French opinion turned by general agreement to the road of economic integration. The initial experiment of the Coal and Steel

[1] *Diplomacy*, Home University Library, Oxford, 1963, p. 150.

Community was followed by that of the European Economic Community, which, under the 1957 Treaty of Rome, was to achieve a Common Market by 1970. By the time the organs of the EEC began to function at the beginning of 1959, General de Gaulle was already President of the Fifth Republic, and French policies within the EEC have therefore been Gaullist policies.

Up to the mid-fifties, French opinion had been bitterly divided over both the concept and the area of the 'Europe' that was regarded by all but the extreme Right, the Communist party and a minority of Socialists as offering the only basis for a final settlement of the German problem. To some elements on the Left, the concept of a 'Europe' excluding Great Britain could not provide an adequate framework within which to contain the growing economic power of Germany. For some, the whole idea of German re-armament, whether within a European or a NATO framework, was unacceptable. For others, it was acceptable only if Great Britain was a member of, or closely associated with, the Europe of the Six. By the time the Rome Treaty had been in application for a year or two, however, virtually all French opinion had become reconciled to the EEC as the basic unit of a future united Europe. Even Communist political objections weakened in face of the universal expectation of economic benefits for France within the Common Market.

General de Gaulle considered the Common Market a useful aid in consolidating French economic and political stability, and still more a basis for the extension of France's role of leadership in Europe to the political and defence fields. Once the Algerian war was ended, and the French army was back in France and in process of modernization, his hands were free for a more active French policy in these fields. He concentrated on three essential tasks: the prevention of all integration, economic, political or military, that would reduce France's control over her own foreign policy; the detachment of France from existing obligations in the Atlantic alliance, which in his view made the United States the effective controller of European defence; and the extension of the concept of Europe beyond the frontiers of the Six, in order eventually to break down the *de facto* division of the world into two mono-lithic spheres of influence.

These policies were rendered more generally acceptable than they would otherwise have been, thanks to a number of factors; to the climate of French opinion that had developed during the fifties; to the effects on that opinion of the apparent recession of the Soviet threat from 1963 onwards; and to the President's skill (complemented by the efforts of Gaullist propagandists) in using both these factors in ways enabling him consistently to out-manoeuvre the opposition parties. Again and again, he was able to present to the mass of the electorate the image of a Gaullist move-ment united under his leadership, as against disunited opposition parties, unable to put forward any agreed or attractive counter-proposals.

The reliance of the Fourth Republic on the Atlantic alliance had been dictated by post-war conditions. French opinion had always been critical of the organization of NATO, and particularly of what was regarded as France's second-class role within it. Com-munists and neutralists were hostile from the start to the whole conception of the alliance. All other parties resented bitterly the criticisms by NATO allies of France's North African policies, and especially of her Algerian policies. In 1958, there were angry speeches in the National Assembly, including threats that France might even withdraw from the alliance. But at this date, France was not yet in sight of becoming a nuclear Power, and most of the French army had been involved for over ten years in colonial-type wars. France's position in NATO was thus virtually that of a sleeping partner, and she was unable to undertake the needed modernization of the army while the Algerian war continued.

By 1963, the Algerian war was over and French forces were in process of being sent back to France. The modernization of the army could, therefore, begin. The French so-called deterrent was now about to become operational, and a Gaullist nuclear strategy was now in existence, which provided popular though not plaus-ible arguments in support of French claims to a position of nuclear equality within NATO, not least with Britain, whose 'special relationship' with the United States in the nuclear field had always rankled with French opinion, on the Left as well as on the Right. Some Gaullist spokesmen were also using the near-existence of an operational French nuclear force to justify a position of European nuclear independence of the United States. They argued that France should be an equal partner in the alliance with some share of control over the use of nuclear force. Yet, at one and the same time, they refused to accept any nuclear role for Germany, on the ground that France's deterrent would provide an embryo European deterrent. They also refused French support for either a multi-lateral or a multi-national NATO nuclear force, on two main grounds: that it was militarily useless, or worse, and also that the proposal had been put forward by the United States for political reasons, precisely in order to avoid any *real* sharing of nuclear responsibility. Another important change was the Gaullist assumption, from 1963 onwards, that the nuclear stalemate justified the belief that no major Russian threat of nuclear war existed in the near future. The President, indeed, stated that the defence of Europe had now become a secondary consideration for the United States.[1] From 1964 onwards, he argued that the danger of nuclear war had now shifted to the Far East, a theatre in which France, disapproving as she did of the Vietnam war, had no intention of getting involved.[2] Gaullist strategists were by then busily engaged in demonstrating that a relative degree of immunity from limited nuclear aggression would be conferred on Europe by the French deterrent alone.[3] In the unlikely event of a major attack, France's strategic position was still regarded as ensuring United States intervention in defence of Europe, whatever the relations between France and her allies. In other words, the stage was set for the claim to 'national independence', put forward by General de Gaulle in

[1] In particular, in his press conference of 14 January 1963.

[2] Press conference of 21 February 1966.

[3] V. article by General Gallois in *International Affairs*, October 1963, 'The *Raison d'être* of French Defence Policy'; also *Le grand dessein national*, by Louis Vallon, pp. 179–90, and speech by M. Pompidou in the National Assembly on 2 December 1964.

his broadcast of April 1965 in far more categoric terms than he had used up to then.

In the meantime, a number of steps had been taken by General de Gaulle to withdraw active French support from integrated NATO commands. Rocket-launching sites and stocks of nuclear arms were not accepted on French soil because France had no say in their use. Units of the Mediterranean and Atlantic fleets were removed from NATO command. Troops returning from Algeria did not rejoin NATO forces in Germany but remained under national control in France. By 1963, the only effective French contribution to NATO integrated forces was in the field of air defence. France refused to take part in the NATO multilateral mixed-manned force proposed by President Kennedy, and also refused a private offer of American aid in French nuclear construction. And France reminded Germany in 1964 that if she were to join the proposed multilateral NATO force, as she had expressed her willingness to do, this would be regarded by France as tantamount to a rejection of what the President called 'European Europe', because it would demonstrate her prior loyalty to Atlantic and American-dominated policies.

In spite of considerable opposition in both press and parties to Presidential methods, and of growing disquiet in 'European' circles regarding France's isolation within the alliance, the President nevertheless succeeded in winning support for his policies, not only from the mass of the electorate, but also in some sections of the opposition. For instance, the Gaullist policy, from 1964 onwards, of seeking a wider Europe by encouraging a *détente* and co-operation between France and the Soviet Union and the countries of Eastern Europe, together with his Far Eastern policy (his recognition of China and his opposition to the Vietnam war) were popular with the Left in France, and particularly with the Communist party. Moreover, his increasingly anti-American tone also appealed to a number of elements on the Left, not restricted to Communist and intellectual 'fellow-travelling' circles. As leader of the main opposition grouping in 1964 and 1965, M. Defferre was no less anxious to ensure French independence of American domination, though he saw the danger more in economic than in military terms. And M. Lecanuet, as leader of the Centre opposition, demanded that the supranational Europe that he wanted to see should be an equal partner of the United States within the Atlantic alliance.

Though the President avoided for the most part the grossly exaggerated claims for the French deterrent put forward by some of his supporters, he did not contradict them. His own plans for concerting European defence and foreign policies, while unpopular with the opposition because they emphasized the need for inter-governmental and not supranational institutions, also emphasized France's right to equal partnership, along with two other themes dear to 'Europeans'. These were the rejection of any nuclear role for Germany and the deferment of any consideration of German reunification to some far-distant future.

It is this context that helps to explain why France's decision in March 1966 to withdraw entirely from NATO (though remaining a member of the Atlantic alliance) failed to arouse active opposition in France, even from the Left-wing opposition Federation, led by M. Mitterrand. There were some routine and somewhat half-hearted protestations of loyalty to the Atlantic alliance, but the majority of French opinion seemed quite resigned to the fact that, once taken, this decision was likely to prove irreversible. Much of the Gaullist argument in favour of 'national independence' appealed to the less politically educated sections of opinion, while the orthodox parties had no alternative to offer other than the hope of some future European deterrent, supranationally controlled. Opposition parties, however, proved unattractive for a number of reasons. First, the opposition still presented to the electorate the old image of quarrelling parties manoeuvring for electoral advantage, and so were not seen as constituting a serious alternative Government. Second, the proposals themselves were, in their own way, as unrealistic as Gaullist policies. Ten years of expenditure and research had been put into making the French deterrent what it was. No conceivable government could be expected to scrap it, particularly as most Frenchmen in all parties shared the Gaullist view that the Cold War no longer constituted any real danger to France. And no united Europe existed to which nuclear control could be entrusted. Third, Gaullist criticisms of the existing structure of NATO were, by and large, accepted, and all sections of opinion supported demands for its reorganization. There was also some sympathy for this view among France's NATO allies. The difference between them was that General de Gaulle clearly no longer believed that the United States was likely to consider any reorganization along the lines that he was proposing.

In the short run, then, the President's NATO policies seemed to do him no harm on the home front. Indeed, in the 1967 general election, they almost certainly improved his position. After the first reactions to the President's announcement, France's NATO partners showed no inclination to weaken any further the remaining links between France and themselves. But they were conscious of the enormous problems that the decision would entail. There were, in particular, the difficulties of co-ordinating French policies with those of the remaining members of NATO, by means of complex bi-lateral negotiations, the dislocation and expense caused by movements of troops, commands and headquarters from France to other allied countries, and the impossibility of effective strategic planning to meet possible emergencies. If they had found France a difficult member of NATO to live with, they realized that it was going to be even more difficult for NATO to live without her. Nor was it clear what, in fact, French membership of the alliance without membership of NATO would henceforth involve, other than the retention by France of a veto.

France's partners in the EEC had to face additional problems in their efforts to live with her. Between 1960 and 1965, the President's plans for Europe caused several important clashes with the other five. First, his proposals for the co-ordination of European defence and foreign policies through what were called the Fouchet Plans for institutionalized co-operation between the six governments were eventually rejected by the Five in April 1962. The main reason was that they suspected that the General intended to use these institutions to strengthen inter-governmental at the expense of supranational institutions, and also as a means of undermining existing European institutions and weakening NATO. All that came out of this initiative was a 'first instalment' of co-operation along the proposed lines through the Franco–German treaty, signed in January 1963. This provided for periodic meetings at Head-of-State, Ministerial and official levels, but did nothing during the following years to harmonize French and German foreign policies. On the contrary, differences between the two countries were intensified both by the President's attitude to NATO and even more by his apparent opposition to any moves towards German reunification in the foreseeable future, and by his intention to maintain discrimination against Germany in the nuclear field.

Another clash was over the President's attempts in 1965 to prevent the implementation of the provisions of the Treaty of Rome making possible decisions by qualified majority on a number of matters as from January 1966. For seven months, France boycotted the EEC institutions. And the agreement finally reached at the end of January 1966 was, in reality, no more than an agreement to differ, accompanied by the pious hope that where, in the view of any member, a matter coming within the scope of these provisions was of 'vital national interest', then discussions would continue for a reasonable period in the hope of reaching an agreed solution. No provisions were made to meet the situation that would arise if no agreed solution or compromise could be reached. French opinion, therefore, interpreted the agreement as a victory for the French point of view, although concessions by France on one or two minor points served the Five as face-saving formulae in support of the thesis that both sides had made concessions.

Another clash arose from the attempt by France to reduce the importance of the *de facto* role that the Commission had come to play in the EEC. Having first successfully challenged the initiatives taken by the Commission in 1965, both to speed up the transfer of the administration of the agricultural fund to the Community and to extend the powers of the European Parliament in order to include some degree of supervision of the administration of this fund, France laid down, during the period of her boycott of the EEC, ten additional conditions that, in her view, ought to govern future relations between the Commission and the Council of Ministers. The general objectives of most of these were accepted by the Five. Some really did not do more than state as an explicit requirement what was already normal current practice. Some underlined more explicitly the French desire to restrict the Commission to the role of an obedient executive – for example, requirements that henceforth the credentials of Heads of Missions of non-member states should be presented to the Presidents of the Council and of the Commission together, that powers delegated to the Commission by the Council in certain defined fields should not include the Commission's right to exercise discretionary powers, and that the Commission should not canvass public support for its proposals before they had been considered by the Council of Ministers.

The cost of these French victories was a decline of confidence within the EEC in the organization's ability, while General de Gaulle remained in power in France, to make any significant advance towards the supranational Europe that remained the objective of the other Five. France's relations with her partners were strained, and Franco–German tensions in particular were greatly increased. Germany was paying the largest single contribution under the EEC agricultural agreement, while France was to derive by far the largest share of the expected benefits. Moreover, French fears that Germany might become a nuclear Power in Europe or in NATO remained wholly unallayed. It appeared, therefore, more and more probable that, in face of France's Atlantic policies, Germany would sooner or later be forced to choose between her loyalties to the European cause and to the Atlantic alliance as it was understood by France's partners.

The meeting in January 1967 between General de Gaulle and the new German Chancellor opened up a promise of greater Franco–German cordiality, but the abortive attempts by Great Britain during that year to open negotiations on membership of the EEC did nothing to improve France's general relations with her EEC partners. All of them expressed their desire that there should be (at least) negotiations with the British Government and not, as in 1963, what amounted to a French veto. Once again, however, the French were able to impose their point of view.

As far as French opinion was concerned, however, the President's European policies, though criticized by 'Europeans' in all parties, increased rather than diminished his popularity—except for the brief period preceding the Presidential elections of 1965, when no settlement of the EEC quarrel seemed in sight. French farmers' expectations of benefits from the EEC agricultural common market certainly far outweighed, at least for the time being, their cost in terms of the bad feeling created in the EEC, and of possible obstacles to the smooth working of EEC institutions in the future. Other Gaullist attitudes popular throughout France were the General's hostility to any German claims to a nuclear role, and his clear statement[1] that German reunification was primarily a European problem, and one that could be solved only in a relatively distant future, when Europe had created a wider framework within which German reunification could no longer threaten French security or that of other European countries.

Nor was the stagnation of Franco–German relations seen as something wholly regrettable. A Europe dominated by France and Germany had always been regarded by extreme Left-wing opinion as a Europe that would eventually be dominated by Germany alone. French attempts from 1964 onwards to encourage Franco–Soviet rapprochement and to build up contacts with countries of Eastern Europe, whether or not they were in the President's mind a possible alternative to his policy of Franco–German reconciliation or complementary to it, were, therefore, welcomed on the Left, and certainly brought some dividends in the form of votes in the Presidential election. Some fears were expressed from time to time regarding the possible dangers both of setting Germany an example in nationalism and of creating a situation in NATO that

[1] Press conference of 4 February 1965.

risked strengthening Germany's position in it. But French opinion seemed to be very little disturbed at the prospect of weakening allied defence by encouraging a massive withdrawal of US forces from Europe, so convinced were most Frenchmen of the irreversibility of the apparent East–West *détente*, and of the forthcoming disappearance of the Cold War.

Content: (2) A world role

The President's claims to a world role for France were, indeed, popular for psychological as well as for political reasons. They helped to assuage the feelings of resentment and frustration created by France's economic and political weakness and her difficulties in the field of foreign policy throughout most of the life of the Fourth Republic. She had been publicly criticized in NATO and the UN; she had felt humiliated by President Nasser as well as by the United States; she had been described as 'the sick man of Europe', with an out-of-date economy, an unstable currency and with budgets and foreign trade in perpetual deficit. Under the Fifth Republic, it was France's turn to criticize the UN as ineffective and NATO as outdated, to read lessons to the British and the Americans on how to reform their currencies and restore their trade balances. Between 1959 and 1968, General de Gaulle's policies outside the European and Atlantic fields included proposals for international currency reform, censure of the UN, and a whole string of international agreements, ranging from those with the Soviet bloc to those with Latin America.

During the fifties, France's policy in the United Nations had shrunk to periodic attempts to prevent French North African policies from being debated, or alternatively to prevent the voting of resolutions hostile to France. Gaullist UN policy took a more aggressive line from the start. General de Gaulle was at first accusatory, not to say abusive, referring to the UN as the 'so-called United Nations' or the 'disunited Nations'.[1] From 1960 to 1965, he became unco-operative and didactic, on both juridical and political grounds. France insisted that the Charter did not authorize

[1] Press conference of 5 September 1961.

military or peace-keeping action by decision of the General Assembly; action must be decided on by the Security Council alone. In other words, the 1950 'Uniting for Peace' resolution was invalid. Intervention in the internal affairs of states was outside the competence of the UN, and intervention concerned with the relations between states ought to be limited to cases where there was a direct threat to world peace. It should not include military action, because the UN was not equipped to use force effectively.[1] In other words, disputes between the mother country and dependencies should be dealt with by the state juridically responsible, and quarrels between sovereign states should be dealt with by negotiations between the parties concerned. France, therefore, refused to accept UN decisions relating to the Congo, Cyprus, the Dominican Republic, Rhodesia and South-West Africa or to pay any dues resulting from these decisions. She refused to recognize the right of the Secretary-General of the UN even to take conciliatory initiatives in the case of the dispute in 1961 between France and Tunisia, on the ground that he was exceeding his powers, since any right to act belonged to the Security Council alone. From 1964 onwards, General de Gaulle supported the admission of Communist China to membership of the UN, and also to a proposed concert of the five nuclear Powers on whose agreement, in his view, the maintenance of peace really depended, and ought to depend.

Gaullist hostility to UN (or 'summit') conferences on disarmament followed logically from this position. Although, up to 1961, France was represented at UN disarmament conferences, from the point at which the Gaullist nuclear force came near to becoming operational, General de Gaulle regarded policies of nonproliferation as being essentially designed to discriminate against lesser nuclear powers. Disarmament conferences were regarded by him as both ineffective and harmful; ineffective, because disarmament could be achieved only through the agreement of the nuclear Powers themselves; harmful, because in the absence of any

[1] Speech by M. Couve de Murville to the General Assembly on 29 September 1965.

intention on the part of the USSR to disarm, large disarmament conferences (and even 'summit' conferences) became no more than propaganda platforms used by the USSR to appeal to the un-committed nations. France thus refused to attend the proposed eighteen-power disarmament conference that began its sittings in 1962, understandably referred to by General de Gaulle in his press conference of 23 July 1964 as 'the useless and interminable Geneva conference'. She refused to sign the 1963 test-ban treaty, described as an empty gesture by nuclear Powers anxious to prevent France from using essential tests.[1] In 1968, she did not sign the non-proliferation treaty.

In 1965 and 1966, after a French Ministerial absence of three years, the Foreign Minister, M. Couve de Murville, attended the sessions of the UN General Assembly, indicating that France now intended to take an active part again in what she regarded as the legitimate activities of the UN. He insisted once again, however, on the limitations of such activities, adding that even legally per-missible actions should be taken by the Security Council 'with discernment' since they were not always politically expedient.

Belief in the need for great-Power control and in the ineffective-ness of large international organizations also characterized Gaullist attitudes to international monetary problems. But, as so often happened, the French President's intervention in the matter in-volved, along with some not unfounded technical criticisms of the working of the existing system, a number of political objections, based on considerations of French prestige and status, together with positive suggestions for reform that aroused concern among his allies and even among some of his supporters at home. He objected to the greater freedom of action in monetary matters that the United States and (in theory) Britain enjoyed, thanks to their position as the possessors of generally acceptable reserve currencies. The French Government, therefore, refused for some time to agree to any reforms—whether through increased payment facilities under the control of the International Monetary Fund, or through the creation of additional credit under the control of the Group of

[1] Press conferences of 15 May 1962 and 29 July 1963.

Ten–until the United States and Britain had eliminated their balance-of-payments deficits. The French government sought to make additional payments facilities dependent on control by the Group of Ten, that is, by an organization including only the major industrial Powers, instead of by the International Monetary Fund, whose members include representatives of under-developed countries. France was also, implicitly if not explicitly, making her agreement to additional credit facilities conditional on modifications of the voting system in the Group of Ten as a result of which the EEC would obtain an effective veto power. It remained to be seen whether the economic consequences of the 1968 May 'revolution' would make her more accommodating in the future.

Naturally, Gaullist insistence, both in the United Nations and in international monetary organizations, on the right of the richer and more powerful nations to predominate won little sympathy among the uncommitted nations. Nor were these sympathetic to France's claims to nuclear power. But Gaullist policies outside these fields were much more attractive to them and so helped to increase France's standing in their eyes, even in the United Nations, in spite of the unpopularity of her attempts to restrict its functions. Indeed, one French journalist commented that, by 1965, France had become 'the leading neutralist Power'. 'In the present climate,' he added, 'French nuclear explosions make far less impact than bomb explosions in Vietnam.'[1] Gaullist anti-Americanism, France's reputation as a 'decolonizer', her policy of 'aid and trade', both to her former dependencies and to other under-developed countries among the uncommitted nations–all these were regarded favourably in the 'Third World'. More important still in their eyes was the

---

[1] *Le Monde*, 28 and 29 August 1966; article by Camille Fondère.

The first clear statement of France's Vietnam policy was made by the Prime Minister, M. Pompidou, in February 1964, in which he said: '. . . we think that the future of the Western world, and its interest too, lies in a neutralism that will protect the country [i.e. Vietnam] from ideological conflicts . . .'. The most spectacular statement was made by General de Gaulle in his Phnom Penh speech in September 1966, the gist of which was repeated in his press conference of 28 October of that year. He then urged the withdrawal of United States troops from Vietnam as a prior condition of any effective peace negotiations.

French policy, involving, from 1964 onwards, Franco–Soviet rapprochement, recognition of Communist China and support for her admission to the United Nations, and French advocacy of the unity and neutrality of Vietnam.

General de Gaulle undoubtedly regarded increased French prestige in the uncommitted world as a contribution to France's recovery of world status and frequently spoke of aid to under-developed countries as an essential function of a great Power. Though France did, in fact, devote a higher proportion of her national resources to supplying overseas aid (most of it to her former dependencies in Africa and Madagascar), and though for most ex-French African States this aid was essential to their survival as independent nations, this fact did not prevent periods of acute tension in the relations of some of them with France. In 1961, there was a short period of actual fighting between French and Tunisian troops over the future of Bizerta, and aid was at times reduced or suspended in all three North African territories, owing to their unilateral decisions to nationalize the property of French residents without prior agreement on the amounts or methods of compensation.

Nevertheless, French relations with French-speaking African states certainly did reveal the continuing predominance of France's economic, political and cultural influence in these areas. It is more doubtful, however, whether the trade-and-aid policy, either in these areas or in the wider field, particularly in the Middle East and in Latin America, could help France to obtain what General de Gaulle was seeking, that is, world recognition of France's historical and political right to consider Europe, Africa and the Middle East as her legitimate sphere of influence.[1] France's resources were so limited that it was ludicrous to regard her as a possible rival to the

[1] Declaration of 17 August 1950 (quoted in *De Gaulle et l'Europe*, by Roger Massip, Flammarion, 1963, p. 151); also press conference of 28 March 1949, and speech to the *Institut des Hautes Etudes de Défense Nationale* on 20 January 1967, in which he spoke of the need to achieve a 'coherent' Europe, including all European countries, and so bring about a 'tri-polar' world – the United States, Europe and Asia.

United States. This was plainly evident during the French President's month-long tour of Latin America in 1964, with its succession of agreements for technical and cultural co-operation and for economic aid. The most that could reasonably be hoped for was a modest degree of publicity for France, together with some assistance to French foreign trade, and a small drop in the bottomless ocean of South America's economic needs.

Where the President's Far Eastern policies and his campaign for Franco–Soviet *détente* and rapprochement were concerned, it was never easy to estimate what his predominant aims were. How far was this attempt to thaw out the cold war really seen by him as the achievement of the preliminary condition for progress towards his goal of 'Europe from the Atlantic to the Urals'? How far was it inspired merely by anti-Americanism, and how far also by the need for him to increase support for Gaullism at home? The policy of East–West *détente* brought a series of technical and cultural agreements, whose content was modest, and certainly not commensurate with the publicity they received. The President's statements on Vietnam were both vague and negative, and thus comprehensibly irritating to American opinion. He rejected the role of mediator and admitted that the conditions for a possible negotiated settlement did not exist. He did not indicate how they could be created (even his proposal for the withdrawal of United States troops from Vietnam was not intended to apply to the immediate future), nor how his hoped-for guarantee of peace by the great Powers could be made any more effective than the 1954 Geneva agreement had proved. Nor did he explain how, if circumstances ever called for the implementation of the guarantee, it would be possible to prevent an even greater risk of escalation into major war than that which he claimed already existed in 1966 and 1967.

Uncertainties of Gaullist foreign policy
General de Gaulle's statements of policy on Vietnam constitute only one of many examples of the difficulties of interpreting either his real purposes or the degree of success of his foreign policy.

Some of the difficulty stems from his ambivalent constitutional and political role. On the one hand, according to the Constitution, the President of the Republic is politically irresponsible, irremovable during his seven-year period of office, and above the political battle. On the other hand, he is regarded by Gaullists and opposition parties alike as the real head of the Government as well as the Head of State. He himself has claimed both roles. Elected by universal suffrage, he has considered himself as spokesman for the whole nation and its main unifying factor. Yet he has openly claimed government policies as his own (and these claims have been supported by Prime-Ministerial statements) and has been the most influential defender of the Gaullist majority, as well as the most devastating critic of its opponents. Which role is uppermost in his mind at any given moment is known only to him.

The essence of Gaullism, therefore, cannot be isolated. It is at one and the same time a personal vision of the President, the political programme of a party pledged to unquestioning support of as much or as little of the vision as he cares to disclose, and also the target of opposition parties no less in the dark, and agreed only in rejecting it.

Another factor making any objective assessment of the success or failure of Gaullist foreign policy impossible is the uncertainty surrounding the future of the regime. If it disappears with General de Gaulle's death or retirement, then much of his foreign policy may prove no less ephemeral. But how much? It will not be possible, until his unique form of personal rule has ended, to know how much of what he was able to do was his personal achievement, how much was made possible by the combination of exceptional circumstances and an exceptional man, and how much really does (as he often claims) represent French opinion and will be continued by his successors.

At least, the striking differences of tone and method – the General's 'style', as the French put it – ought not to be allowed to mask the very real degree of continuity between the foreign policies of the Fourth and Fifth Republics. Decisions to modernize the French economy and the army and to make France a nuclear power were taken before General de Gaulle returned to power. The Treaty of Rome, too, was already in application when he became President. France's ambivalence regarding British membership of European institutions did not date from the discussions relating to her membership of the EEC. French attitudes to Britain were largely formed in the early fifties, at the time of the setting up of the Coal and Steel Community and of the abortive proposal for the European Defence Community, and differences of opinion became even more marked during the abortive negotiations for a European Free Trade Area.

Circumstances, too, played their part. General de Gaulle's foreign policy was hampered for the first four years of office (exactly as that of governments of the Fourth Republic had been) by the overriding need to end the Algerian war. From 1962 onwards he enjoyed a degree of freedom of action that no Prime Minister of the Fourth Republic had ever had. The elections of 1962 gave the Gaullist party a virtual majority in the National Assembly, and with the support of the *Républicains indépendants* a narrow Gaullist majority still existed after the 1967 elections. The 1968 elections gave the Gaullist party an overall majority. The world situation was evolving in the way that was to make possible his policy of *détente* between East and West, as well as his intransigence within the Atlantic alliance. Up to 1968, France's financial and economic situation reinforced her political stability. The 1968 student and worker strike movement could introduce new political as well as economic problems.

Opponents of Gaullism like to present Gaullist foreign policy as essentially traditionalist and nationalist. In the sense that it rejects the idea of supranationalism as a possible basis for French foreign policy this is true. But nothing justifies the view that, in the interim period before such supranational institutions become a fact, any conceivable non-Gaullist governments would fight less hard for the satisfaction of French national interests. No doubt, the 'style' would differ. But there is no evidence that the bulk of the French nation does not welcome the results of his policies in the EEC or that subsequent governments will reverse his policy towards NATO. On the contrary, it has been suggested that one reason for his decision to leave NATO in 1966, instead of in 1969, was to ensure that this policy would be irreversible after his death or retirement. The popularity of Gaullist *détente* policy is due, in great part, to the traditional desire to ensure France's security against Germany by a rapprochement with Central and East European countries. Even the most ardent 'Europeans' and Atlanticists have not been so committed to the West that they would not welcome additional safeguards in the shape of something of the traditional Franco–Russian friendship.

In at least two ways, Gaullist foreign policy can claim to have brought a real change. No doubt, decolonization was inevitable, but it is extremely doubtful whether any leader but General de Gaulle could have completed it as rapidly and with so little political opposition. *L'Afrique francophone* may never become the *Communauté francophone* dreamed of by Presidents Senghor and Bourguiba. But at least eight years after the achievement of independence by all African states except Algeria, and six years after independence came in Algeria, the Fifth Republic's standing in these former dependencies was still high. Second, General de Gaulle succeeded during those years in giving France at least the illusion of being once again a great Power. In so far as they existed, the foreign policies of the Fourth Republic had been, as Alfred Grosser has convincingly demonstrated, essentially expressions of a sense of national weakness.[1] However unrealistic General de Gaulle's policy of 'national independence' may be, it would never have been possible, nor won so much support, if there had not existed a more confident psychological atmosphere. That, General de Gaulle has been largely (though not exclusively) responsible for creating.

How long lasting these achievements will be is another matter. If General de Gaulle's foreign policy has to be judged on the basis of Europe's position in relation to the Atlantic or the Urals, then it

---

[1] *La IVe République et sa politique extérieure*, pp. 397–406.

must be said that no discernible progress has been made. Franco–German co-operation, intended in 1962 to be the first instalment of the Gaullist Europe, was in 1968 still tentative and unreliable, though the Franco–German climate had become visibly more co-operative since the change of leadership in Germany. Gaullist plans for closer European co-operation in foreign affairs had come to nothing. European co-operation in aid to under-developed countries had got no further than adding Nigeria and Tanzania to the list of African associate-members of the EEC. Even on the Gaullist assumption that the East–West thaw was irreversible, there was no reason to believe that the modest proportions of existing co-operation could be greatly increased. Apart from the (possibly only temporary) coincidence of French and Soviet views on a number of current problems, such as Vietnam, France's departure from NATO and her desire to keep Germany a divided and non-nuclear power, the two countries remained as divergent as they ever had been on major issues such as the status of East Germany, the existence of the French nuclear force and proposals for a European deterrent. Nor was there any evidence that the Soviet Union either attached sufficient importance to France to want to cultivate closer relations or had any real confidence in the permanence of French anti-Americanism. General de Gaulle's Far-Eastern policies, though popular at home as well as in Cambodia, Laos and the uncommitted world generally, did not seem likely to achieve any positive results. And his recognition of China had brought no discernible dividends at all.

Paradoxically enough, what had contributed most to increasing General de Gaulle's stature and France's standing abroad was not his foreign, but his internal policies, while it was at home that his foreign policies had been most successful, for they had greatly contributed to his own prestige and authority. For many Frenchmen, the most important contribution that Gaullism could make would be in the internal field, by helping to remove from French internal politics the recurrent obsession with constitutional change that has done so much since the war to weaken France's influence in the world.

In 1968, it was still by no means certain that the Fifth Republic would outlive General de Gaulle. The surprising thing was the increase in the number of Frenchmen who, in 1968, still looked to de Gaulle, rather than to Gaullists or anti-Gaullists, to solve France's problems.

BIBLIOGRAPHY

Background

ASSOCIATION FRANÇAISE DE SCIENCE POLITIQUE. *La Politique étrangère et ses fondements.* Paris: Armand Colin, 1954.

DUROSELLE, JEAN-BAPTISTE. "Changes in French Foreign Policy Since 1945." Pp. 305–58 in STANLEY HOFFMAN et al., *In Search of France.* Cambridge, Mass.: Harvard University Press, 1963.

GROSSER, ALFRED. *La IVe République et sa politique extérieure.* Paris: Armand Colin, 1961.

PICKLES, DOROTHY. *French Politics: The First Years of the Fourth Republic.* London: Royal Institute of International Affairs, 1953.

THOMSON, DAVID. *Democracy in France Since 1870.* 4th ed. New York: Oxford University Press, 1964.

UNIVERSITÉ D'AIX-MARSEILLE, CENTRE DE SCIENCES POLITIQUES DE L'INSTITUT D'ETUDES JURIDIQUES DE NICE. *Les Affaires étrangères.* Paris: Presses Universitaires de France, 1959. (Part I: "Les fondements du pouvoir politique dans la conduite des affaires étrangères.")

WOLFERS, ARNOLD. *Britain and France Between Two Wars: Conflicting Strategies of Peace Since Versailles.* New York: Harcourt, Brace & World, 1940. (Paperback ed.: Norton.)

FRENCH FOREIGN POLICY

Foreign Policy of the Fifth Republic

BEAUFRE, ANDRÉ. *Nato and Europe.* New York: Alfred A. Knopf, 1967.

DE GAULLE, CHARLES, *War Memoirs of Charles de Gaulle.* 3 vols. Vol. I: *Call to Honor 1940–42* (1958); Vol. II: *Unity 1942–44* (1959); Vol. III: *Salvation 1944–46* (1960). New York: Simon & Schuster.

GROSSER, ALFRED. *French Foreign Policy Under De Gaulle.* Boston: Little, Brown, 1967. (Paperback ed.: Little, Brown.)

KULSKI, W. W. *De Gaulle and the World.* Syracuse, N.Y.: Syracuse University Press, 1966.

L'Année politique. Annexes, 1959–68. (Press conferences of the President of the Republic.)

PICKLES, DOROTHY. *The Uneasy Entente: French Foreign Policy and Franco-British Misunderstandings.* New York: Oxford University Press, 1966.

WILLIS, F. ROY. *France, Germany and the New Europe, 1945–63.* Stanford, Calif.: Stanford University Press, 1965.

7·WEST GERMAN FOREIGN POLICY

Philip Windsor

West Germany is unique among the countries considered in this book in that it is in no sense a great Power. Other countries have seen their power shrink or falter in the post-war world; with most the title of power rests on a traditional or indeterminate ascriptive courtesy; there is no country whose actual resources, current influence or conjectural power can be measured, in the same terms, against those of any other. But West Germany, whose economic resources are formidable, whose military machine is a major power factor in the policies of the Atlantic alliance, and in the development of East–West relations, and whose potential strength has long complicated relations within the European Economic Community, is entirely without the interests, responsibilities and prestige of a major Power. It is, Willy Brandt said during the Federal elections of 1964, an economic giant but a political dwarf.

Yet it is one of the most important countries in the world. The United States, the Soviet Union, Britain and France, and many countries in both Eastern and Western Europe, must all take account of West Germany's interests and reactions in framing their own foreign policies; they all pay it the dubious compliment of regarding it as the once and future king of Europe–unless they are careful. And this attitude reflects the first reason for Germany's importance, its potential power. The existence of a united Germany has been a dominant problem in European politics for the greater part of a century. Indeed, the 'German problem' has been no more than a series of attempts by the other major Powers to adapt to the creation of a country potentially stronger than any of them, and capable in two wars of holding out for years against the combined strength of most of the other major Powers in the world. The emergence of the two super-Powers in the years after the Second World War has finally destroyed Germany's pre-eminence; but the economic and military strength of a reunified Germany would, in the eyes of both these Powers, and particularly Russia, mean a major shift in the structure of international relations. Each side in the Cold War has been determined to prevent the other from gaining the alliance of a reunified Germany; and the Cold War, if it can be defined at all, can best be defined as a struggle to control the future of Germany. The other conflicts which were contained in the Cold War – the ideological clash, the struggle for the allegiance of the 'Third World' – have been resolved or at least suspended; but not the conflict over Germany. On the contrary, every attempt at a *détente*, every step towards a relaxation in Europe, has only emphasized how persistent this conflict is. It looks, in the autumn of 1967, as if it might eventually be resolved through the policies of the two German states themselves, but it can not be done without a fundamental revision of attitudes among the other Powers concerned. Hitherto, the major Powers, in Europe and beyond, have been able to unite only against Germany, but if they have not been fighting her, they have never been able to agree on what to do with her. During the period of the Cold War, they have consistently rejected all proposals for reunification, lest they be to the advantage of one side or the other, but have not yet agreed, though the Soviet Union has now been demanding that they should for ten years or more, on the permanent division of the country. The result has been that the Soviet government has been willing to talk *détente* only on a basis which was unacceptable to the Western Powers, who have insisted that any real *détente* in Europe was conditional on German reunification; and thus every attempt to liquidate, or even palliate, the Cold War, has only emphasized its underlying conflict.

This pattern indicates the second major reason for Germany's importance. It would look at first sight as if the Federal Republic had been practically impotent throughout the history of the Cold War – as if the potential strength of a reunified country had conspired with the interests and concerns of other Powers to keep it in a position of permanent weakness. But while it is true that Germany has not had the power to decide its own future, it has been perfectly capable of preventing anyone else from doing so instead. It has seldom been able to take any positive action to advance its own interests, but it has frequently blocked possible agreements among the other Powers which it thought might damage these interests. In other words, Germany holds the key to the future of the Cold War, or to the *détente* which might follow it. Every understanding between the two sides intimately concerns Germany, whether in the field of arms control (in which its own territory would be of fundamental importance) or of concerted economic policies such as those which Khrushchev or some voices in the American government have at different times proposed (and where the Federal Republic would have a paramount part to play) or of a much looser form of political and economic relations between the two halves of Europe (in which the relations between East and West Germany would be crucial). In other words, the future of the relations between the major Powers of the world depends to a very high degree on the policies and attitudes of Germany, which is not a world Power but whose interests are of world-wide importance. It is this position which makes of Germany a country in a class by itself, and which makes its foreign policy peculiarly important. In general, though, these remarks apply only to West Germany. The East German state has been, and in many ways still is, too firmly under Russian control to be said to have a foreign policy of its own. It has certainly taken initiatives in Eastern European affairs and in intra-German relations which can not always have been pleasing to the Soviet government, but these initiatives have never been able to withstand Russian opposition. Even today, when the East German government is beginning to enlarge its own freedom of action, it can only do so within the limits allowed by the Soviet Union, which continues to control much of its economic and foreign policy.

West Germany, in contrast, has partly by its own efforts and partly through the active encouragement of the United States, developed an independent position within the Western system and a policy towards the Soviet Union and Eastern Europe which has been quite distinctive from that of its allies. For many years, this policy has been more distinctly negative than that of any other European Power. It is also quite capable of becoming more fluid and pragmatic. But, generally speaking, the West German government has used its power to insist that no measure of *détente* was acceptable that might even be held to imply the recognition of East Germany; that *détente* was more or less identical with German reunification; and that since any interim measures of agreement could only help to strengthen the East German regime by granting it a certain legality, it was better to make no concessions at all unless the Soviet Union were already prepared to concede the reunification of the country. In other words, all or nothing—and one might sometimes be forgiven for thinking that if it had not been for the infuriating legalistic pedantry of the German government and its ludicrous posture of devotion to a cause which it did everything to hinder, it might have been possible long ago to liquidate the Cold War and restore some meaning to the word Europe.

Clearly, this is to oversimplify; but it is true to say that for many years one of the most important countries in the world, a country which occupied a central position in the relations of the other major Powers, devoted its energies and influence to having practically no foreign policy at all. This apparent paradox can only be understood if the context of German foreign policy is examined from the inside as well as the outside. For, even granted Germany's peculiar importance and peculiar position, it was not necessarily bound to exercise the restrictive and negative influence that it did. Indeed, the government's chosen foreign policy was challenged almost continuously inside the country from the moment it began. And while it is a truism to say that, in most countries, foreign policy represents some kind of internal consensus, in Germany foreign policy was precisely the area where opinions and convictions inside the country have been most sharply divided. And this in turn reflects the almost conscious precariousness of the West

German state: of its social stability, of its political institutions, of its economic prosperity. It is surely only in Germany that a general election could have been won on the slogan: No Experiments; and a tricky and venturesome foreign policy was precisely the kind of experiment that much of the electorate feared most, as something that would endanger all the rest. But equally, a large minority, and one by no means confined to the official Opposition, feared exactly the opposite: that if Germany deprived itself of an independent foreign policy, if it were content to be a good ally and wait for its protecting Power, the United States, to solve the German problem in its own good time, if it were content in short, as one observer put it, to become a depressing mixture of America and Belgium, then the social stability and democratic institutions would in the long run be much more seriously endangered by frustrated nationalism and a sudden readiness to experiment on every hand. So the long, and, with one brief period of suspension, almost continuous debate on Germany's foreign policy that has gone on within the country has really been a debate about Germany's future. As one popular Left-wing writer in Germany has expressed it: 'Seventy million people can't just sit in two waiting rooms for ever'. And the fact that it was a Left-wing writer who said this underlines the paradox of the debate: it has been the Social Democrats who in traditional terms have been by far the more 'nationalist' of the two great parties. For they have, for the greater part of the Federal Republic's existence, insisted that Germany must not mortgage its future on the support of the Atlantic alliance and its integration generally into the Western world. The Christian Democrats, on the other hand, have been primarily concerned with assuring the security of Germany by working as closely as possible with the leading Western Powers in the Atlantic alliance and the European Community.

Now both these parties, the opposition and the government, were equally concerned for the *internal* stability of German society. One has only to read the private comments, the *obiter dicta*, even some of the public speeches of Adenauer, or Schumacher, the first leader of the Social Democrats after the war, or Ernst Reuter,

West Berlin's most famous mayor, to realize their concern for the future of the country they were re-creating, their mistrust of a national identity which seemed to be founded almost exclusively on economic prosperity, and their determination that the sick romanticism of the Nazis should never again gain a hearing in Germany. But the remedies they prescribed were different. For Adenauer, and thousands like him, the secret of the future lay in a rapprochement with the 'hereditary enemy', France, and with a determined effort to integrate Germany's resources with those of her neighbours, so that Germany would neither be tempted nor be able to 'go it alone' again. Equally, Germany's military potentialities were to be integrated either into a European system, or into NATO. But for Schumacher, this was a false, if not a disastrous, solution. The fate of the Weimar Republic had shown what could happen if a democratic system of government were combined with the loss of national independence, or with a restrictive set of international commitments.

So Schumacher embarked on a course of preventive nationalism. In an attempt to forestall the emergence of a new brand of Right-wing nationalism, he made himself the champion of a national alternative to the integrationist policies of Adenauer. His own record as an unswerving opponent of the Nazis, who left the concentration camps at the end of the war a sick and crippled man, gave him a moral qualification for this role, and even those who disagreed with him most profoundly might have been thankful that in assuming it he robbed both the traditional nationalists and the post-war Communist party of the exclusive appeal which they might otherwise have enjoyed. But this is not to suggest that he was merely playing a part. There might have been times when it looked as if the basic principle of Schumacher's policy was an equal and undifferentiated hostility to all the occupying Powers, and a still greater hostility to the 'Chancellor of the Allies' as he delighted in calling Adenauer. But he was genuinely concerned both for the future of East Germany and for the future temper of West German democracy; and he saw far more clearly than Adenauer that one could not simply integrate West Germany into a Western bloc and then hope that East Germany would somehow be 'drawn towards' it. Integration with the West meant, in his view, an end to any hopes of reunification for the foreseeable future. And in these circumstances, how stable would German democracy prove to be?

Looking back, there is no doubt that he was right in most of his prognostications. German democracy has proved remarkably stable, but for years it was fed on the illusion of a future negotiation from strength, which would one day confine the Russians to their own frontier and bring East Germany back into the fold. This illusion collapsed on the night that the Berlin wall was built, and the country has since then been deeply divided on many questions of foreign policy; it has become disillusioned with its allies, and a new and not insignificant grouping of Right-wing nationalists has emerged, which could prove to be a real political force. How far Schumacher was right in assuming that in the circumstances of the Cold War, and in view of Western as well as Russian policy towards Germany, there was any real choice, is a different matter. It would have been exceedingly difficult for any German government to start playing all the occupying Powers off against each other and work out its own policy for reunification in association with none of them; and it may be that Adenauer was simply bowing to the inevitable and making the best of it. But the point here is that a choice *was* made, and it was made within an internal context.

Both Adenauer and Schumacher approached the question of Germany's foreign policy as part of the question of the internal future of the German state. Indeed, the two were practically indistinguishable, and in taking a decision about the one they were also exercising a form of guardianship over the other. Equally, their approach to the problem of East Germany reflected their judgment about the nature of West German society. It is this inextricable interaction between the internal and the external aspects of policy-making which distinguishes Germany so sharply from most other countries, where it is possible for parties to differ sharply on internal requirements and priorities, but to unite in promoting a bi-partisan (or multi-partisan) foreign policy. This has been true in the post-war years in France, Britain and the United States. It has seldom been true in Germany. Even when both the major parties were committed to Western European integration and to the Atlantic alliance (which took a long time to happen) their view of the *implications* which this position held for East Germany and for their relations with other Eastern European states were still wide apart. There has never been a true consensus on foreign policy in Germany. This is because the context is unique.

The structure of policy-making

In the years between 1945 and 1950, West Germany made a fundamental choice. Broadly speaking, this was a choice between security in the context of partition, and the prospect of reunification in a context of great insecurity. As I have suggested, Germany, or the German leaders, did not have much of a choice. It would be more accurate to say that the Western Powers made certain decisions about Germany, and that the men inside the country who then emerged as leaders were those who were willing to co-operate in implementing these decisions. The decisions themselves were natural, humane and sensible. Perhaps they were inevitable. What they amounted to was a recognition by the Wester n Powers –Britain and the United States more or less in concert, and subsequently joined by France–that Germany was essential to the economic recovery of Europe, and that if they waited for agreement with the Soviet Union, Germany's recovery and that of Western Europe as a whole could be delayed indefinitely. They themselves had a fundamental choice to make: between attempting to preserve the wartime alliance with Russia in the post-war world–but at the expense of Europe–or getting on with the reconstruction of Western Europe–but at the expense of the alliance with Russia, and at the risk of splitting Europe in two. By the time the Marshall Plan was proposed, and the Eastern European countries were forbidden by Stalin to accept American aid, the choice became one between including Germany in the Western European economic structure, or treating it as a country apart for the sake of an increasingly nebulous chance of co-operation with the Soviet Union. What was by now certain was that the whole of Germany could not be included: it would only be the three Western zones. In 1948, when the Western powers introduced currency reform in Western Germany,[1] they had virtually decided on the creation of a West German state. The fact that as a direct consequence of currency reform they then engaged in an exhausting struggle with the Soviet Union – the Berlin blockade – only gave added point to their decision; and by a significant historical coincidence the draft of the West German constitution was duly completed on the day the blockade was lifted.

Now this pattern of events was highly consequential for the future framework of German foreign policy. Most of the new German leaders had emerged before the new German state was created. They came into prominence by working with the Allied authorities in their zones – and by fighting the Allies in the interests of the population behind them. They came to control the essential machinery of political power before they were elected to national office. And by co-operating with the Allies in a series of (urgently necessary) economic decisions, which were also willy-nilly foreign policy decisions, they had made the basic choice in German foreign policy before there was even a Federal Republic to make these decisions for. In other words, German foreign policy after the war did not begin as an organic process of choosing between priorities in the German community; it began at a high level of collaboration with external Powers.

This fact had two long-term consequences. It meant first of all that the basic framework of German foreign policy had already been established by the time the new state was created: it meant that West Germany had entered upon a process of partnership and integration with the Western world, and the main emphasis of foreign policy in the ensuing years would be on the development of this partnership *as a means* to securing greater freedom and a

[1] There is evidence to suggest that Britain and the United States had decided to go ahead with currency reform in their zones shortly after the Marshall Plan was announced in June 1947, and that in the intervening months they were waiting for France.

higher degree of sovereignty for the Federal Republic, but *also* as an end in itself. In Adenauer's view the two objectives were practically identical, and from that time on every relaxation of control, every concession to German sovereignty, went hand in hand with a fuller German commitment to the process of Western integration–until at last the whole process culminated in German rearmament exclusively within the framework of NATO and entirely according to NATO plans.

The second consequence was that for years German foreign policy was extremely centralized in its direction and control. The men, and above all the one man, who had won both the confidence of the German people and of the occupying Powers were entrusted by both with the patient task of extending German liberties. To the Germans Adenauer was able to demonstrate that greater freedom went together with more integration–hence his almost Bismarckian stature in Germany and the extraordinary reputation he achieved by doing what was not after all a particularly subtle or complex diplomatic job. To the Western allies and the Western Europeans he was able to demonstrate that Germany now had a responsible and stable government, one which was ready to participate in the constructive reshaping of Europe, and which could be relied on as a staunch ally–hence the extraordinary position he was accorded abroad, and particularly in the United States, as the spokesman of the new Germany and Europe's leading statesman. Adenauer began early to enjoy an enormous prestige, both at home and abroad, and with the prestige went power. For years he was the virtual dictator of German foreign policy, and he was almost a dictator in the classic sense of the word: one who was granted supreme powers in order to restore the civic security of his country.

These two interacting consequences–Germany's commitment to European integration and Adenauer's very close control over German foreign policy–did not mean that he was acting with the whole nation behind him. Rather, it meant that he had been virtually granted powers to play a lone hand by the mass of the electorate, but that he did so in opposition to what in other countries and in normal circumstances would have been very powerful pressure groups. There was first of all the SPD. More will be said about its role in German politics, but it is essential to appreciate that the SPD was, and is, a very powerful party, exercising control over most of the important cities and many of the state governments in Germany, constituting a large proportion of the Bundestag, and exercising there in addition to the standard functions of an opposition a considerable influence on policy-making through its representation on various governmental committees. There were, secondly, large sections of the CDU itself, that loose coalition of interests and opinions, many of whose members have been well to the left of some sections of the SPD in their attitudes to Eastern Europe. In matters of foreign policy, Adenauer ignored the one and rode roughshod over the other. But these were by no means his only adversaries. On the wide range of foreign policy he had also to contend with the other party in German politics, the Free Democrats, who came increasingly to represent the influence and interests of the powerful industrialists of the Ruhr, anxious to extend their trade and investment to East Germany and Eastern Europe. In the early years of the growth of the West German economy, when an enormous and unsatisfied home market provided the captains of industry with plenty of scope for their activities, these pressures were muted; but they were already beginning to be felt by the mid-1950s, and at the same time the Free Democrats underwent a series of changes culminating in a *coup* which left them more firmly committed than before to a new though ill-defined Eastern European policy. Here, too, Adenauer fended off his potential supporters for the sake of what was coming to appear to many German politicians a narrow, inflexible and unprofitable policy. In other words, his view of Germany left little room for a normal consideration of 'national interests'.

That much for the broad range of German policy. On more specific questions, he also ignored sectional interests. On the matter of German rearmament in particular, a step which Adenauer himself proposed in 1950, it might be thought that he had the influential remnants of the Wehrmacht behind him. Far from it. In fact, the leaders of the old army, men like Guderian, were much closer to Schumacher and the more intransigent sections of the SPD in their attitude than they were to Adenauer. By 1950–five years after the war, but only one year after Germany had been reconstituted as a state–Schumacher's position had changed from his earlier hostility to all the occupying Powers to a vaguer identification of West Germany's interests with those of the Western world. Not that this meant either integration in Western Europe or German rearmament, but it did mean that the Western Powers, and especially of course the United States, would be obliged to defend the Federal Republic from any threat of a military attack. And more than this, it meant that Germany must be *defended*, not occupied and liberated later. Schumacher declared in fact that Germany's defence lay on the Vistula, not on the Rhine. With this, the Wehrmacht officers agreed. They had little interest in a West German deterrent-or-defence force, which would have left the country open to Soviet occupation while it acted as the first line of defence for Western Europe. In these circumstances, few of them showed any real desire for German rearmament, and in 1950 Guderian insisted that German reunification was more important than any contribution which the Federal Republic might make to Western defence. In fact, the professional military approach was much closer to that of the Social Democrats than to that of the government. Both emphasized the primacy of the aim of reunification; both argued that the only effective defence for Germany would have to take the form of a counter-attack.

In contrast, the government insisted that West German rearmament must be purely defensive, and that its main function should be to make a Soviet attack on Western Europe more difficult and more costly–that it should in other words deter the Soviet forces from trying a *coup de main*. Along with this went a willingness to see German forces incorporated in a supranational framework like that of the European Defence Community, or, subsequently, NATO. In the question of German rearmament, above all others, Adenauer demonstrated that he was anxious to re-cast the whole framework of Germany's 'interests', to place these interests in a Western international context, and to ensure that any extension of German sovereignty or German power did not mean any increase in German self-sufficiency. And in following this line of policy, he was willing to ignore or alienate the natural champions of these interests, and force them to accept 'his' process of integration. It was no small political achievement to form the Bundeswehr out of the nucleus of former Wehrmacht officers—whose political reliability had already been tested by several years of fundamental opposition to Adenauer's political views.

Obviously, this achievement was not without its price. Long years were spent in domestic political battles, about the pace of the re-armament programme, about the nature of West Germany's defence, and later, about the delays in the programme which these very battles themselves involved. But it was an instance of the way in which Adenauer's conception of Germany's true interests induced him to take up arms against his own potential supporters. He seems to have relished these struggles anyway. How was it, though, that he was able to win most of them hands down? I have indicated the basic framework within which he operated, and his ability to take advantage of historical circumstances to impose his will. But how was policy made?

The most striking fact here is that the Foreign Ministry had very little to say. When Germany's first independent Foreign Minister, Heinrich von Brentano, first took office, he was expected to have a considerable say in foreign affairs. At that time, in 1955, he was indeed thought to be chief candidate in the succession to the Chancellor himself. In fact, though, it was his tenure of the Foreign Ministry which destroyed his stature inside the CDU by making it plain that he was little more than Adenauer's chief clerk. Far more influential was the former Under-Secretary in the Ministry, Walter Hallstein. He had been the Chancellor's personal assistant before 1955, and continued to enjoy direct contact with him over Brentano's head after that time. In 1957 Bonn severed diplomatic relations with Yugoslavia because that country had decided to recognize East Germany. The decision was Hallstein's and the step was taken while Brentano was still considering what to do. But

Hallstein was almost the only man from inside the Foreign Ministry who had the ear of Adenauer. Otherwise, he had a tight ring of personal advisers drawn from very different walks of German life: a Cardinal, a banker, a couple of civil servants. The only other professional diplomatist who belonged to this 'magic circle' was Herbert Blankenhorn, who has filled the two key posts of Ambassador to NATO and Ambassador in Paris and is now Ambassador in London. The most notorious of these advisers was that well-known ex-Nazi, Hans Globke, who enjoyed a position of special confidence and provided all the enemies of the Federal Republic with a rich store of ammunition.

But it was not only a question of advisers. The Foreign Ministry seemed to be of less account in furnishing the information and judgments upon which decisions were based than either the German secret service (the Gehlen organization) or the Ministry of Defence. The process also worked in reverse: there were times when Adenauer refused to show the Foreign Minister the texts of letters he had received from Khrushchev or Eisenhower because they were addressed to him personally. The Foreign Ministry in fact remained, almost throughout Adenauer's time in office, a purely administrative machine. Diplomatists with ideas above their station found that they had been appointed to obscure South American Republics; others, if they were really important men like the Federal Ambassador in Moscow, were simply recalled and retired.

But this demotion of the Foreign Ministry could not have been accomplished without the acquiescence of the Bundestag. It is hard to say why the German parliament played such a minor and ineffective role for so long. Even the Bundestag Foreign Affairs Committee was, in comparison with some others, of little importance: so much so that its first two chairmen, both of whom were figures of great note in German politics and one of whom, Kiesinger, is now Chancellor, were reduced to continual requests for more information about what the government was doing. And this in spite of the fact that the Committee in theory has the right to take part in the formulation of foreign policy and has frequent discussions with members of the Cabinet and senior officials in the Ministry. This is not to say that it was never consulted: of course it was. But so, on occasion, were the leaders of the Opposition, and on much the same basis. They were all given the chance to air their views–in the hope perhaps of a word of congratulation if their views happened to coincide with those of the old man. In fact, the relative ineffectiveness of the Committee itself represented a measure of acquiescence on the part of the Bundestag. Why?

The answer seems to come back again to the fact that the different groups and parties in the Bundestag were presenting radically different views of Germany and therefore of German foreign policy; and the foreign policy debates in particular have generally been fierce and frequently abusive. In these, the contending groups were competing for the ear of the electorate and it is worth noting that in Germany the most important debates have always been broadcast and are now sometimes televised. In such debates the parliament is less concerned with particular issues or with the day-to-day conduct of foreign policy than with the general principles on which members believe it should be based. The result has been a series of well-rehearsed general arguments (which could hardly fail to bore the listening electorate) and a paucity of concrete proposals or criticisms. Moreover, the fact itself that these debates have been debates of principle tended to ensure that all criticism was directed at Adenauer, and that he therefore dominated the arena. In these circumstances it was easy for him to ensure not only that he took personal charge of the government's case but also that he practically imposed the rules of debate. Only once, in 1957, did this land him in any personal discomfiture; normally he seemed to enjoy pitting himself against the combined ranks of his critics, and needless to say his policy remained quite unaffected. What it all amounted to was that the Opposition were concerned to keep the idea of an alternative alive; not to present a series of practical or detailed alternatives. It was not remarkable, if this was the case, that the most cogent tactical criticisms came during the Adenauer era not from the SPD but from within the ranks of the CDU. And again these were mostly voiced not in Bundestag debates, but in the private forums of the *Fraktion* (parliamentary party) meetings.

These were the general conditions at the national level which enabled Adenauer to dictate German foreign policy for so long and to carry his views, however negative they might be, against those of his more flexible critics even from within his own party. This was exemplified in 1957 when the Chancellor abruptly rejected the Rapacki Plan for a form of nuclear disengagement in Europe. He was fiercely criticized for doing so by a fairly influential group within the CDU under the leadership of Dr Eugen Gerstenmaier, who has been both Chairman of the Foreign Affairs Committee and President of the Bundestag.[1] But the Plan had already been rejected.

There was also another factor which played a significant part. This was the extraordinary power of the Ministry of Defence and of its Minister, Strauss.

It is worth dwelling for a moment on the role of the Ministry of Defence not only because it helped to make of Strauss a key figure in German politics, but also because the interaction between defence and foreign policy in Germany has been even more direct than in most other countries. The chief, and for long the only real, field of German foreign policy has been Western Europe and the Atlantic alliance. The Federal Republic had suspended its foreign policy in Eastern Europe; it was not allowed to be a member of the United Nations; for a long time its policies in the Third World seemed to be no more than a series of bribes to indigent nations not to recognize the DDR. West Germany had staked everything on NATO and the Western world. In these circumstances a decision on defence policy could be a significant act of foreign policy. Britain, for example, can justify its defence contortions east and west of Suez by pointing in each case to the foreign policy requirements imposed by the other. Germany had no such choice. A particular defence commitment implied a particular commitment in foreign affairs. Thus the decision to arm the Bundeswehr

---

[1] An office which, unlike that of Speaker in Britain, confers real political influence.

with what were euphemistically called 'the most modern weapons', which was taken in 1958, implied a still closer working partnership between the Federal Republic and the United States than had existed before, and this was to have very considerable consequences during the whole period of tension between the American and French governments.

Now, many decisions of this nature were taken on the basis of military criteria, and sometimes by the Ministry of Defence rather than the Foreign Ministry. This was the case, too, with the Multilateral Force, where Strauss was the first European Defence Minister to announce his support for the plan. Others were still considering it at the time; it was, after all, a decision which could only be based on an assessment of foreign policy requirements. Militarily it made little sense. But Strauss professed to be convinced by the military arguments, and proceeded to impose these on the Foreign Ministry. The fact that the Foreign Ministry was in any case likely to lend its support to the plan does not make any difference to the fact that the Defence Ministry was pre-empting it. On another occasion, though, Strauss had proposed a five-point plan of his own, which accepted the principle of disengagement, and contravened all the military provisions for the defence of Germany which NATO strategy demanded. This was a blatant case of his exceeding his powers and embarrassing the Foreign Ministry. This time he incurred the wrath of Adenauer–but even so waited until he was in the United States a few weeks later before repudiating what he had said. But this was a rare instance of action *against* the mainstream of Adenauer's policy. In general Strauss was the Chancellor's most powerful ally, and helped to ensure that decisions in foreign policy could continue to be taken outside the range of pressures and political compromise which were normal in most democratic countries.

The power of the Minister of Defence, taken in conjunction with the other factors I have outlined, suggests why it was possible for the control and direction of foreign policy to remain unaffected by the many-sided criticism which it encountered in Germany for so many years. The structure of German policy-making was in this, above all other fields, singularly authoritarian. German foreign policy remained in consequence singularly restricted.

But this does not mean that the pressures for extension or change were repressed. On the contrary, West Germany seems to have been more capable than most other countries of rapid adaptation to the needs of the moment; and this applies not only to the official policy of the government but also to the declared policy of the political parties. Both at governmental and at party level policy declarations and principles could seem to remain extraordinarily rigid for years on end, and then suddenly switch to an almost complete reversal without any apparent difficulty.

The Hallstein Doctrine, for example, which made it a basic principle of German foreign policy that the Federal Republic could not remain on friendly terms with any country which recognized the DDR, seemed for years after its first enunciation in 1955 to be immutable. In 1964 the Erhard government announced that it was seeking to establish friendlier relations with the states of Eastern Europe all of which were actually allies of the DDR. In 1967 the Federal Republic opened diplomatic relations with Rumania – ten years after they had been broken off with Yugoslavia which had had the temerity merely to recognize the DDR. But the Hallstein Doctrine has not been dropped. There is little doubt that if any state in the under-developed world recognized East Germany it would immediately find its relations with the Federal Republic were severed, and that its economic aid was suspended.

Again, the SPD has been through two or three fundamental modifications of policy. From adopting a predominantly 'nationalist' stance in the years immediately after the war, and opposing the 'Europe of the clerics and cartels' which it declared was being created by the Christian Democratic parties in France, Italy and Germany, it swung to a markedly pro-Western orientation during the mid-fifties. At the same time, it had not abandoned its hopes of German reunification, nor its opposition to the form that was finally adopted of German re-armament. In 1959 it could still produce a *Deutschland plan* based on the assumptions of a reunified and neutral Germany. By 1960 it had dropped all this in favour of more or less straightforward loyalty to the Atlantic alliance—and this was the period during which the almost continuous debates on the nature of German foreign policy were briefly suspended. But within two or three years the SPD was reconsidering the importance for Germany of the alliance, and its implications for an Eastern European policy. At the time of writing it has joined its chief enemy in a 'Grand Coalition' and supplied the Foreign Minister, though apparently without any real commitment to more than a mildly experimental foreign policy.

All this has indicated that although Adenauer was able to establish a rigid, and perhaps rather simplistic, foreign policy and to defend it for years on end against all comers, this was really a personal achievement which he owed to the peculiar conditions of post-war Germany; and this achievement in itself helped to strengthen the underlying pressures which he had repressed for so long. German foreign policy could be a good deal more volatile than it has appeared. To appreciate this, one needs to understand something of the structure of German politics.

The workings of German politics

Each of the three major parties—the Christian Democratic Union, the Social Democrats and the much smaller Free Democrats—is more of a coalition than a united political party. All of them have been subject to struggles for power and internal take-overs, in which the warring factions represent not only a set of temperamental affinities or vaguely ideological alignments, or even disputes over particular issues, but a genuine group of interests. These interests in turn are the expression of particular forms of financial backing, of press ownership and/or support, and of regional party organization. The way to the top in German politics does not lie in getting a seat in the Bundestag, in performing years of faithful service as an obedient poodle, and in eventually being given a chance to display one's talents in an obscure ministry: it lies in getting control of a regional seat of power and using it as a springboard to the upper flights of the party. If one can secure control of such a region one's future is assured. The Chancellor's displeasure can suspend but not destroy the political life of a well-entrenched boss; and the most effective way of spending one's time in the wilderness is to go and run an important city, keep one's name in the news, and wait for the next power struggle.

The most notorious instance of a success which was based on more or less absolute regional power is, of course, that of Herr Strauss. With his control of Bavarian newspapers, of the powerful Bavarian wing of the CDU, the Christian Social Union, and his bunch of obedient followers in the *Fraktion*, he was well able to afford 'retirement' after the Spiegel affair. It simply enabled him to develop a powerful attack on the Erhard government from outside the area of governmental responsibility, and to play at being king-maker when the crisis came. But this is only an extreme form of a normal mode of political conduct. Adenauer's case, as Mayor of Cologne, was perhaps untypical because of the extraordinary circumstances in which he came to power. But most eminent politicians have their regional seat: Willy Brandt in Berlin; Kies-inger in Baden-Wurttemburg; von Hassel, the Minister of Defence who succeeded Strauss and stayed on in the Erhard government, in Schleswig-Holstein; Helmut Schmidt, one of the leaders of the SPD, for long its spokesman on defence matters and one of the principal architects of the Grand Coalition, in Hamburg; and Erich Mende, the leader of the Free Democrats, in Düsseldorf. Many of these careers represent a two-way process: from city or state to the Bundestag, and back again if opposition palls, or office does not materialize. But the return to one's city never implies a retirement from national politics.

Obviously, this is not the only way to achieve distinction. Some men, like Krone in the CDU, Ollenhauer who succeeded Schu-macher as leader of the SPD, or Wehner, the ex-Communist who is now the SPD's chief theoretician, and champion of a rapproche-ment with East Germany, have worked their way up through the central party machine. But men like these, though they are capable of exercising great influence, seldom wield real power.

In any event the structure of politics here means that many of the really decisive power groupings in any conflict over a particular decision, or struggle for control of the party, are found outside the parliamentary framework. Pressure groups among members of the Bundestag are not unknown, but they are normally *ad hoc*, quick to coalesce and dissolve over very particular issues; and if they are more permanent this usually means that they represent a regional seat of power which happens to coincide with a particular political outlook. (Again the most notable example has been the 'Gaullism' of the CSU deputies from Bavaria.) The consequence of this political structure is that while debate inside the Bundestag may often be muted, and at other times diffuse and general, there is plenty of scope for discussion and argument in the other forums which party and state politics provide. Party discipline may be important at the Federal level, but it is not, as is the case in more centralized countries, an impediment to real discussion.

The second consequence has already been suggested: men who cannot abide a particular set of policies or who are worsted in a particular conflict do not go out into the wilderness. They might retire to their own territory, but from here they still take part in the political game and in the framing of subsequent decisions. Thus a commitment to a particular line of policy does not necessarily imply that all those with any say in the party will automatically be found on platforms to defend it. On the contrary, it is possible for a group of critics to form a nucleus of potential ministers and officials who will be there to carry through the new decisions when they have been made. This has been particularly noticeable in the SPD: Brandt, for example, is the natural successor to Ernst Reuter, the first Mayor of West Berlin. He did not follow him directly in this office but he was marked out as Reuter's heir from a very early stage in his political career. Towards the end of his life Reuter had been embroiled in fierce arguments about foreign policy with the leadership of his own party. (He was much more unambiguously pro-Western than Schumacher, and indeed his views on foreign affairs came fairly close to those of Adenauer.) These disputes had little effect on the leadership of the SPD at the time; but later, when it became clear that the premises of the party's foreign policy were really untenable, Brandt was able to

emerge from West Berlin as the man who could convert his comrades to a more up-to-date view, and eventually capture the
leadership for himself.

These two consequences combined, then, to create a reservoir of
potential change in German foreign policy. And because the
Foreign Ministry had been condemned for many years (even after
its official formation—which was not until ten years after the war)
to relative impotence, there was none of the entrenched commitment to a particular form of policy, or inertia in the face of change,
that is to be found in better-established Foreign Offices. It could be
accused no doubt of a lack of imaginative sympathy with new
ideas, but not of ingenuity in resisting them.

Oddly enough the real inertial force was the German public
itself. In its unwillingness to frame any view of contemporary
Germany and its place in the world, in its dogged devotion to
Adenauer—at least until the last year of his office—as the Grand Old
Man to whom everything could safely be entrusted, and in its lack
of human understanding or concern for the population of the
DDR (unpleasantly exemplified by the sale of tourist mementoes
at the Berlin Wall), a great part of the German public remained
sublimely unconcerned with the most important issues in Germany's foreign policy, content to pay lip-service to the idea of
reunification, and then retreat into its contemplation of the *Wirt-
schaftswunder*. This was certainly one reason for the SPD's continued failure at the polls (though if present trends continue in
Germany's demographic voting patterns the country should have
a permanent socialist government after about 1975) and it certainly
provided Adenauer with a reliable base of public support; but in
the end this inertia did not mean any well-articulated public resistance to the idea of change—only to certain symbolic changes like
the recognition of the Oder–Neisse Line. Rather, it meant a certain
alienation of the decision-making processes within the parties from
the public to whom they might have been expected to appeal. It
meant that they were able to present, and the public was prepared
to accept, a set of *faits accomplis*. This generalization applies more to
the CDU than to the SPD, which has a more activist tradition—but

that is another way of saying that the CDU was primarily a voters' party and the SPD, a members' party. (Except in Berlin where the position was reversed.) And as far as the voters went the debates within the parties were almost as remote as the arcane processes of decision in a department of state. This was not for want of trying within the party leadership: they did their best to present the issues to the public; but it was an indication of the public attitude.

Part of the trouble was, of course, that public energies were syphoned off rather than stimulated by the idea of reunification. It is all very well to commemorate the East German rising by proclaiming that 17 June shall be observed as 'Day of German Unity', and to draw comfort from the fact that this day is also observed in many of the American states where there is a large German population. But speeches and rallies on 17 June, where they do not actively stimulate an undesirable form of German nationalism, tend to leave the impression that one's duty has been done for a while, and that there is nothing more to do. They do not promote any active examination of German foreign policy, or suggest any questions as to whether it really is contributing to German unity. Similarly the activities of such moderate, well-organized and officially supported pressure groups as the *Kuratorium Unteilbares Deutschland*—which is basically composed not of individual but of group members, trade unions, student organizations and so on— exist to keep the idea of reunification alive and to feed the illusion that something is being done about it. Here again, the *notion* of reunification seems to be separated in public attitudes from the conduct of foreign policy.

The net result of this separation between parties and voters, coming on top of the structure of party politics itself, was that the parties discussed and adopted policies in a sort of political void. The existence of pressure groups, in the peculiar circumstances of post-war Germany, tended to confirm rather than to call into question the remote and quasi-authoritarian nature of German political decisions. Paradoxically, this process was strengthened by the gradual absorption of Germany's traditional independent local press into a near-monopolist newspaper chain and a few mass-circulation magazines. This certainly helped to weaken the regional support of some of the politicians, but it did little to stimulate serious discussion of political issues. All in all, the parties were left free to change, or adapt, their policies–though without much hope of exercising any immediate influence on the electorate. They could only hope, by the gradual accretion of change, to induce a long-term adaptation of attitude. So German political life under Adenauer was marked by a number of almost violent changes in party programmes, and by a curiously static temper in the electorate at large. But this also explains why the changes which followed Adenauer's retirement were comparatively rapid and caused comparatively little friction. The pressures had been building up for years.

What were the main lines of the party development? The CDU, it will be clear, had coupled its programme of Western integration with economic recovery, re-armament and domestic stabilization. No real crises occurred within the party until after the Berlin Wall was built. Only then, when the CDU lost three-quarters of a million votes in the subsequent elections, and found that it could not govern without the support of the FDP, did it become clear that the old Adenauer formulae in domestic and foreign policy were beginning to lose their magic. Hitherto the CDU had never issued a single comprehensive statement on its foreign policy. Germany was still accumulating strength, along with the whole Western world, for that great negotiation in the sky which would finally induce the Russians to go home. The Berlin Wall ruined this legend. Thereafter, there were still no formal policy statements; the emphasis still lay on continued Western integration–though the Federal Republic was now beginning to feel the stress of being torn between France and the United States: integration was no longer a simple idea; but within the party a fierce discussion had begun of Germany's Eastern policies. These discussions coincided with a movement for Adenauer's retirement and promoted a continuing political crisis from which the CDU is still suffering. Since then two governments have been manoeuvring

244

for compromise among conflicting groups, whose relative emphasis lies on France or on the United States, on a new policy towards
Eastern Germany or on the continued priority of Western integration, but none of whom seem to have developed any idea of how
to combine a policy towards Germany's Western neighbours with
a new approach towards her Eastern brethren.

The SPD had taken a more sophisticated view of the dynamics
of the Cold War than had the CDU. It considered that the main
impediment to reunification lay in the tensions of the Cold War
itself, which the policy of the CDU seemed to be striving to maintain. In their view the formula of building up strength in order to
negotiate should be reversed: concessions would have to be made
by each side in any case, and no harm would be done if West
Germany, or its Western allies, began the process. A progressive
reduction of Cold War tensions could eventually lead to a withdrawal of troops from Central Europe, and thus to reunification.
The *Deutschlandplan* of 1959 was the culmination of this argument,
and presented the sequence advocated by the SPD. A four-Power
conference would create a standing commission of representatives
from both German states on a basis of parity (first Western concession); the commission would then prepare an all-German peace
treaty along with proposals for a European security system; meanwhile controlled disarmament could begin in a zone which would
initially comprise the two Germanies, Poland, Czechoslovakia and
Hungary. The armed forces of these states would be restricted in
size and levels of armament, and nuclear weapons would be
banned (an echo of the Rapacki Plan). This would be followed by
the withdrawal of foreign troops from the area. There would be
unrestricted inspection to ensure that all these provisions were
observed. (A good combination of concession, in that the Soviet
Union itself would not be open to inspection, and insistence on
what the Western powers regarded as non-negotiable in such a
context–that is the right to inspect). These were the first crucial
stages. Thereafter a sort of European collective security system was
envisaged which would enable the states covered by the plan to
withdraw from the NATO and Warsaw Treaties. After this the

245

all-German commission could begin to co-ordinate the economies of the two countries and later create a Parliamentary Council—again on the basis of parity of representation. This could draw up a constitution for a reunified country, after which there would be free and secret elections.

I have sketched this plan in some detail because it was, in the context of the time, a sophisticated and sensible document—it had the courage to reverse the normal order of Western demands which *began* with free elections and did not even guarantee that a United Germany would not become a member of NATO—indeed, Dulles insisted that it would have to—and safeguarded the essential interest of the two Germanies while being prepared to make concessions of timing and priorities in the interests of the Soviet Union. It was also highly representative of the predominant tendencies in SPD thinking throughout the 1950s. But within a year it had more or less been forgotten. Obviously it had one glaring weakness: there was nothing in it to suggest that it *would* lead to reunification. The whole procedure might be followed, disarmament might begin, the two German states might form their commission, but having got that far and having secured the military neutralization of Germany, why should the Soviet Union take the gratuitous risk of unifying the country? In one sense this is to put the question the wrong way round, because it is clear from the provisions of the plan that long before this Soviet troops would have been withdrawn from East Germany, and with them the main vehicle of Soviet influence there; either the Soviet Union would agree at the beginning to the plan, in which case it would leave East Germany to decide whether it wanted reunification, or it would not, in which case its troops would stay. But in another sense the question is the right one to ask, for the very concessions envisaged by the SPD and particularly that of parity in representation, implied that the Soviet Union had an overriding interest in the evolution of the plan and that it would have means of exerting political and economic pressure on the DDR long after its troops had been withdrawn. The plan, then, did not really offer reunification.

Moreover it came out at a time when the Berlin crisis was well under way. It was unfortunate for the SPD that the final formulation of its hopes for reunification should appear just at the time when Khrushchev was brutally insisting on an immediate and definitive recogniti on of the fact that Germany was divided. But it was also rather fo rtunate for the Berlin wing of the party, coming as it did after a series of efforts by Brandt to 'modernize' its approach to both domestic and foreign affairs. There is no doubt that Khrushchev helped Brandt to capture the leadership of the SPD and to swing the party more or less behind Adenauer's foreign policy. (It is worth noting, though, that the *Deutschlandplan* has never been formally repudiated.) But the end result of the events of 1959–61 has been to divide the SPD on its own priorities and to promote a crisis within the party over its foreign policy, just as the same events did inside the CDU. Since then different wings of each party have resembled each other more closely than they have some of their opponents on the same benches.

This is not quite true though of the FDP. It began as a looser conglomeration of liberal and national tendencies than even the CDU. But since 1959 (when the party also produced a *Deutschlandplan* some of whose features were similar to those advocated by the SPD, but whose priorities were quite different) the party has been much more homogeneous and dynamic than either of the others. This is because it was captured in the most spectacular of all the party revolutions that have happened in Germany since the war by its present leader, Erich Mende, and his Düsseldorf group of 'Young Turks'. Some of these have suggested that political relations should be established forthwith between Bonn and Pankow; in general they have repeatedly stressed that Germany's most immediate task, taking precedence over the Atlantic alliance and over the European Community, should be to sort out its own future. His revolution accomplished, Mende tarnished his electoral image in 1961 by joining the CDU in a coalition government, after swearing throughout the campaign that he would do no such thing.

But the real difficulty with the FDP has been that many of its ideas for closer working relations between the two German states, which were revolutionary when they were proposed seven or eight years ago, have now become commonplace in both the other parties. As the revolution in attitudes towards Germany's foreign policy has continued since Adenauer's retirement, the FDP has gradually become less and less distinct from the other parties. Equally, its very definition as a party with a particular and separate approach, as a homogeneous political entity, has positively robbed it of electoral support in a country where parties have such a broad-based and generalized appeal. To be a member of the FDP is to be a little peculiar, and it means that one's political attitudes are far more readily identifiable by the outsider than if one were a member of the CDU or even the SPD. One sign of the disaffection Mende's control has ultimately produced is the emergence in Germany of a self-consciously and self-righteously nationalist party which has gathered in a good deal of the support that might once have gone to the Free Democrats. In fact it now looks as if the FDP is never likely to become a mass party, but to survive as a kind of perpetual Anti-Corn Law League, a political ginger group, devoted to one or two issues at a time. These issues will, of course, concern the relations between the two Germanies.

This is a general summary of the way the parties have evolved in Germany over the last few years, and of the kind of pressures which have emerged in the post-Adenauer period. It indicates that in the end German political parties have not, so far as foreign policy is concerned, developed into consistent political groupings with a consistent political attitude. Each of the two major parties has undergone revolutions of leadership and orientation, each of them is divided along roughly parallel lines. This is partly a result of the extraordinary rigidity of the Adenauer years, partly of the structure of German politics. In each case the party is confronting some decisive choices, and in each case it is anxious to delay making these choices for as long as possible. Their general approach is symbolized in the fact that both are working together in 1967 in a cautiously experimental coalition government. What are their areas of choice?

The areas of choice

Since the crisis in the Erhard government and its ultimate down-fall, most people in Germany would agree that the task of the Federal Republic is to develop a strategy which connects a settle-ment of the German question with the extension of a *détente* in Europe and with provisions for European security. The Erhard government, although it ostensibly fell on a set of proposals for dealing with an economic crisis (not much of a crisis by British standards), was really brought down by a crisis over foreign policy. The unfortunate Erhard had tried to combine the Atlantic orienta-tion of the post-war years, the close relationship with France of Adenauer's last period, and the demands for better relations between the two Germanies which had been growing since the Berlin crisis, with an opening to Eastern Europe. This kind of eclecticism was perhaps inevitable in the circumstances of the moment; but like all forms of eclecticism it was bound to be a failure in the end. Erhard was brought down by an unholy alliance between Strauss and Adenauer, and his Foreign Minister fell with him. This alliance, which was the political spearhead of the move-ment known as 'German Gaullism' and whose stronghold was the Bavarian CSU, did not however have any coherent alternative to offer. The trouble with the German Gaullists has been that, unlike de Gaulle himself, they tended to combine a resentment of Ameri-can leadership with a persistent belief that the Cold War had some-how been diminished and ought to be increased. But they could not have it both ways: vigorous prosecution of the Cold War depended ultimately on the United States; European self-assertion and a close alliance with France depended in the end on a *détente*. This is a lesson which Kiesinger, Erhard's successor, has been quick to learn. He has made the alliance with France the basis of a new relationship between Germany and Eastern Europe. It might not be quite true, but Kiesinger manages to act convincingly as if it were true, that the interests of Germany and France are pretty well identical: both want to prosecute a smaller European *détente* within the larger framework of the *détente* between the two great Powers, and neither is anxious that the two great Powers should get on so

WEST GERMAN FOREIGN POLICY

well that they arrange the future of Europe without consulting the Europeans themselves. In these respects, then, Kiesinger is both a Gaullist and a champion of *détente*. This leaves the original group of German Gaullists little room for criticism; and Kiesinger's tactical success has been indicated by the fact that his Foreign Minister is Willy Brandt, while Strauss has been shunted off into the Ministry of Finance.

But this success has blurred what is really a new division which cuts across party lines. This division has been summarized by a German authority[1] as that between 'integrationists' and 'reunionists'. The integrationists are those who continue to give priority to the manner in which Germany's relations with her Western neighbours are to be defined. There is plenty of room for division within this group, notably on the relative importance of France and the United States in the current political situation; but essentially it agrees on the precedence of the Western European and Atlantic world over the question of German reunification. The integrationists include the Adenauer circle, Strauss and his followers and the SPD in South Germany. It is in fact primarily a phenomenon of Southern and Western Germany, and has roots in the catholicism of those areas. The reunionists, on the other hand, give priority to the establishment of one German state, or at least to the creation of a healthy relationship between two German states in which the DDR would be open to West German influence. They are prepared to sacrifice or ignore some aspects at least of Western European integration for the sake of this aim. Representatives of this group include the FDP as a whole, Wehner's followers inside the SPD, Gerstenmaier's adherents inside the CDU, and parts of the North German CDU in general. Kiesinger and Brandt have succeeded hitherto in doing something to satisfy each of these groups; but there is little doubt that if they were forced to make a choice both would belong to the first.

It will be seen that of the parties only the FDP has really made a choice. The others are both divided. Everybody agrees that some kind of strategy should be developed to combine the Eastern and

[1] Dr. Georg Bluhm of the University of Kiel.

Western objectives of German policy as far as possible. But a combination of this nature would be little short of a miracle; and Kiesinger's tactical success looks at the time of writing as if it has been little more than a holding operation.

The kind of difficulty which this holding operation has produced has been best exemplified in Willy Brandt's old fief of Berlin, where dissatisfaction with the policies of Brandt himself has produced a running crisis, both in the relations between Berlin and Bonn (and here Brandt is frequently stigmatized as the local boy who has succumbed to the political temptations of the capital) and in the wider question of how far Berlin is qualified or able to carry out its chosen role as mediator for the Federal Republic in its dealings with Pankow. This crisis has produced serious internal disturbances in Berlin. It has also led to something of an upheaval in the political councils of East Berlin.

The present situation is not exactly a suspension of foreign policy on Adenauer's lines, but it could hardly be described as energetic. The basic difficulty is that no real choice *can* be made until the Federal Republic is prepared to define its future relations with the DDR. At present it is waiting on the development of *détente*, both on a great-Power and on a European level. It seems still to believe that the road to Pankow runs through Washington, Moscow, Prague and Bucharest, and that Paris too is following this route and helping to explore it for Germany. The proposition that the road from Bonn to Pankow runs across the German frontier has not yet been admitted. And this means that the Federal Republic is still content to depend for the formulation of its foreign policy on a set of variable factors which it can do little to influence or control. Many changes have happened since Adenauer retired, but in some important respects German foreign policy is still in a state of suspended animation.

BIBLIOGRAPHY

BRENTANO, HEINRICH VON. *Germany and Europe: Reflections on German Foreign Policy*. Translated by EDWARD FITZGERALD. New York: Frederick A. Praeger, 1964.

FREUND, GERALD. *Germany Between Two Worlds*. New York: Harcourt, Brace & World, 1961.

GROSSER, ALFRED. *The Federal Republic of Germany: A Concise History*. Rev. ed. New York: Frederick A. Praeger, 1968. (Paperback ed.: Praeger.)

HISCOCKS, RICHARD. *Democracy in Western Germany*. New York: Oxford University Press, 1957.

——. *Germany Revived*. London: Gollancz, 1966.

JAKOBSEN, H.-A., and STENZL, OTTO. *Deutschland und die Welt*. Munich: Deutscher Taschenbuch Verlag, 1964.

MOCH, JULES. *Histoire du réarmement allemand*. Paris: Robert Laffont, 1965.

PLESSNER, HELMUT. *Die verspätete Nation*. Stuttgart: Kohlhammer, 1962.

RICHARDSON, JAMES L. *Germany and the Atlantic Alliance*. Cambridge, Mass.: Harvard University Press, 1966.

SPEIER, HANS. *German Rearmament and Atomic War: The Views of German Military and Political Leaders*. New York: Harper & Row, 1957.

STRAUSS, FRANZ-JOSEF. *The Grand Design: A European Solution to German Reunification*. New York: Frederick A. Praeger, 1967.

WINDSOR, PHILIP. *City on Leave: A History of Berlin, 1945–62*. New York: Frederick A. Praeger, 1964.

8·THE FOREIGN POLICY OF INDIA

Peter Lyon

India is new, big, populous, poor, non-aligned, parliamentary and important. Each of these qualities vitally affects her foreign policy. Not least is this because there is an intimate but very complex interplay between India's changing internal order and the changing international order.

India is a new state, and a new, strange and sizeable shape on the political map of the world. This independent political entity in international affairs, India's 'newness', India as presently shaped, dates only from independence in August 1947. Indian official publications still often contain such passages as: 'Nature has made India a distinct geographical entity', and yet in political terms this unmistakable geographical entity, this distinctive geographical individuality, can only be seen as such if India and Pakistan are regarded as a single whole, which they are not, or by ignoring Pakistan altogether, which is what many Indian politicians would often like to do, but find it difficult in fact to do. India is a new state, albeit the seat of ancient civilizations, but in what sense is she a nation-state? And how does her nation-statehood affect her foreign policy? Pakistan, as we shall need to explain further, provides at once the chief limitation on and the antithetical expression of India's nationalism. India's foreign policy begins and ends with Pakistan; but it cannot, of course, be entirely explained by reference to Pakistan. Even so, Pakistan is an important factor in the domestic and foreign policies of India, challenging India in the region of South Asia, in Asia generally and in the world at large, provoking from India at times a kind of descant generally quite distinct from the general opera of India's foreign policy. What then is this general opera?

Its main libretto was, until 1964, provided in Jawaharlal Nehru's

253

voluminous speeches: as a prospective foreign policy in the days before independence, in fact from the late 1920s onwards, and then continuously from 1947 until Nehru's death in May 1964. In the recently published memoirs of a distinguished Indian diplomat we are given substantial quotations and excerpts from a private note written to him, in January 1947, when as one of the two first newly appointed ambassadors of India (the other was the ambassador to the United States) Nehru gave some practical advice and set out some general guide-lines of India's foreign policy.

The note[1] dealt with a variety of matters such as the use of a flag and a national crest (neither of which India then possessed), the dress to be worn on ceremonial occasions, the propriety of attending Commonwealth meetings and the scale and manner of entertainment. The new ambassador and his staff were asked to remember that they should function 'as Indians and not as imitation Englishmen'. 'Our ambassadors', wrote Nehru, 'will represent a great country and it is right that they should make others feel that they do so. But they also represent a poor country where millions live on the verge of starvation. They cannot forget this nor indeed should they do anything which seems in violent conflict with it.'

Nehru's note also contained a broad enunciation of India's foreign policy which K. P. S. Menon says he cannot refrain from quoting at length because 'it contains the seed of that policy of non-alignment or non-involvement or positive neutrality, which was to become a robust tree and under which many a state in Asia and Africa was to shelter from the storms and stresses of a divided world, and at the same time to try to alleviate them'. It is curious that such a perceptive and experienced Indian diplomat, writing in 1964, should still regard Indian non-alignment as having acted as a kind of diplomatic anti-upas tree, under whose shelter many were protected from the otherwise withering effects of great-Power policies; but it is more significant here to notice what Nehru was writing in private to one of his chief envoys in 1947.

[1] See K. P. S. Menon, *Many Worlds. An Autobiography*, Oxford University Press, 1965, pp. 229–30. I am grateful to the author and to his publishers for kindly permitting me to reproduce these passages.

'Our general policy,' Nehru explained, 'is to avoid entangle-
ment in power politics and not to join any group of Powers as
against any other group. The two leading groups today are the
Russian bloc and the Anglo-American bloc. We must be friendly
to both and yet not join either. Both America and Russia are
extraordinarily suspicious of each other as well as of other countries. This makes our path difficult and we may well be suspected
by each of leaning towards the other. This cannot be helped.'

'Our foreign policy,' Nehru continued, 'will ultimately be
governed by our internal policy. That policy is far from being
communistic and is certainly opposed to the Communist Party in
India. Nevertheless, there is a great and growing feeling in India in
favour of some kind of a vague socialist order of society. There is
much goodwill for America and expectation of help from her in
many fields, especially technical. There is also a great deal of sympathy for the work of the Soviet Union and the remarkable change
that this has brought about among the people. The Soviet Union
being our neighbour, we shall inevitably develop closer relations
with it. We cannot afford to antagonize Russia merely because we
think this may irritate someone else. Nor indeed can we antagonize
the USA.'

This is a significant document in the making of India's foreign
policy and it is to be hoped that soon it will be published in
entirety. It is comparable in some respects to Eyre Crowe's famous
memorandum of 1 January 1907 about British foreign policy. But
there is a vital difference. Eyre Crowe was summarizing and
expressing a tradition of policy which was that of an established
Power, fashioned over hundreds of years, whereas Nehru was
shaping virtually *de novo* a foreign policy for a new state. Perhaps a
closer analogy would be with the prescriptions of the authors of
the Federalist papers or with Washington's famous Farewell
Address of 1796. Be that as it may, Nehru's note to K. P. S. Menon
did suggest some standards by which India's foreign policy may be
judged; it was also notable for its omissions, particularly for its lack
of any mention of Pakistan. The leaders of new states, just as those
of old ones, have their blind spots, their instinctive preferences and

prejudices—and for leaders of new states these prejudices and preferences usually stem mostly from the independence movement.

Newness is a very ambiguous and evanescent quality[1] and the
myth of newness—fervent belief in the importance of newness as
such—sometimes may be more important than the fact. This can be
illustrated from the last twenty years of India's foreign policy when
sometimes by accident and sometimes by design India repeatedly
has been cast in the role of paradigmatic new state, the natural
leader of the new states—a role which India has been somewhat
equivocal about in practice and which has had its liabilities as well
as assets. For a number of years it was widely assumed that India
led and could count on the support of the new states. Since 1962
this is no longer assumed to be axiomatic; but India has not
entirely abandoned the idea that she could and should play a
leading part among the contemporary new states. Some of the
ambiguities of newness were very evident in Nehru's conception
of India's foreign policy as from the earliest days when he began to
speak publicly about international matters he was at pains to stress
that, though free from historic hatreds such as had bedevilled
European politics, all Indians were the heirs to a great and glorious
heritage.

Much of Nehru's writing, especially two of his books, reveal-
ingly entitled *The Discovery of India* and *Glimpses of World History*,
are suffused with such ideas. The second of these two books was
originally composed in the form of letters from prison to his
young daughter, and thus formed part of the education of India's
present Prime Minister. Spreading a shared notion of national
history is an important aspect of the arduous task of nation-
building, and in a very real sense Nehru was the principal purveyor
of modern India's national history, certainly of India's place in the
modern world: Nehru's ambiguities became official India's ambiguities. Not only did his deep sense of history, of the past pulsating
in the present, accord with Nehru's own idiosyncratic philo-

[1] I have explored this theme more widely and thoroughly in 'New States and
International Order' in *The Bases of International Order*, edited by A. M. James,
Oxford University Press, forthcoming.

sophical–historical disposition, before and after 1947, but to stress that independent India was the principal heir and successor state to the former British Raj (as well as to a complex civilization stretching back many millenaries) while Pakistan was secessionist, was of some psychological and practical value to India. It implied that India had arrived at independence with unimpeachable credentials, while Pakistan had not. This view, or something very akin to it, seemed to be widely accepted by the great majority of the world diplomatic community until the 1960s. The implicit psychological rejection–dismissal–of Pakistan is something which has been present in India's policy ever since 1947; is obvious, at least to outsiders; and is at once evidence for and a source of tension between India and Pakistan. It is now less easy for India to sustain such a view when it is believed that Pakistan and China are colluding together against India. It is recent history, post-1947 history, and now particularly post-1962 history, much more than the history of the deeds and inspiration provided by Ashoka, or Kautilya or even by Gandhi, which now principally shapes Indian foreign policy and Indian thinking about international matters. The heydays of high-sounding oratory and prophetic universal utterances about foreign policy are now over. Nehru's successors are preoccupied by day-to-day concerns, whatever long-term goals are proclaimed. For them, and even for his daughter, much more than for Nehru himself, politics, including foreign policy, is the pressing needs of the present, and of the possible.

The significance of shape and size

India is a country, almost a sub-continent, of vastness and variety. But present-day Indian nationalists assert that behind the immense variety of terrain, population and cultural patterns lies an abiding unity. It is an article of national faith to claim that this unity is in being and becoming, *in esse* and *in posse*. It is intrinsic to the paradoxical endless adventure of nation-building. (Paradoxical because the nation is at once built and needs building; endless because these processes seem perennial, once launched.) Undoubtedly though, among the many ambiguous warrants for nationhood, the national

257

territory is a principal requisite. And territorial shape and size, indeed locational factors generally, must be considered to be relative constants in shaping any country's foreign policy–even though changes in the relevant balances of power and in utilizable military technology can force important changes concerning situational significance.

India has 3,500 miles of coastline, 9,400 miles of land frontiers and 1·26 million square miles of land area. To know further that this vast area encompasses geographical conditions, climate, scenery and peoples, more diverse even than those of Europe or of Africa, immediately implies that there will be politically divisive and unifying factors simultaneously at work, as in those two continents. But the significant difference is that India is now deemed to be a single political shape, a single country, a single nation, which neither Europe nor Africa is. Current political and moral fashions define and decree that nation-states and not continents shall be the basic units of political organization, and of foreign-policy making. That India should be, and show itself to be, a nation-state, actual and incipient, ancient yet modern, old yet new, thus conforms with currently dominant world fashions. Clearly defining and securing widespread international recognition and respect for what Indians regard as their national territory is thus an important, inescapable, and integral part of nation-building, and of Indian foreign-policy making.

India spreads 2,000 miles from the towering Himalayas in the north to where the tip of Cape Comorin juts out into the Indian Ocean and the rest of South India points towards Ceylon. India also stretches some 1,850 miles from the Rann of Kutch (where West Pakistan's disputed south-east boundary meets India) in the west, to where Assam is virtually enclosed by China, East Pakistan and Burma in the east. Territorially India is the seventh largest country upon the contemporary world political map. It is, approximately, thirteen times as large as the United Kingdom, eight times the size of Japan, a third of the size of Canada and one-seventh that of the Soviet Union. India is territorially big; but great size alone has never been sufficient in itself to constitute great-Power status, and sometimes in international history it has not even been an indispensable requisite (remember the former eminence of the Portuguese in the sixteenth century, the Dutch in the seventeenth, and the British in the nineteenth century). The stability of the political system, economic and military strength, relations with immediate neighbours and even more those with other great powers are all important determining factors.

It has often been said that foreign policy begins at the frontiers. It is no mere coincidence that India's most troublesome international problems concern her relations with Pakistan and with China, the two countries with which she shares most of her land frontiers. India's international boundaries are those of the former British Raj—with the exception of her boundaries with Pakistan and those which have been re-drawn *de facto* by war—these, of course, constitute large and important exceptions. It should be remembered, too, that it is only within the last hundred years, and often within only the last twenty years, that the originally European notion of demarcated and agreed linear boundaries, up to which a centrally organized political system exercises general administrative and jurisdictional control, has begun to shape political realities in Asia. What were once rather remote frontier regions, areas of indeterminacy, zones of transit at most, have become defined and apportioned politically by stressing the importance of linear frontiers, national frontiers.

For India independence began literally with the making of many new land frontiers—by the process of partition of former British India. This vivisection of a sub-continent was an act of political surgery which resulted, in a matter of days, in several hundred thousand deaths and in the creation of several million new refugees. It split up families and launched two new states into world affairs simultaneously: as ambivalent towards each other and as initially weak and uncertain of each other as two severed and unequally proportioned Siamese twins.

India is four times as large as Pakistan in area; its population is about five times as large, and its industrial base is probably ten times bigger. Yet it cannot really be said that India has displayed towards Pakistan that magnanimity which, as Burke once said, is not seldom the truest wisdom of politics. This is not to say that India has not been provoked. Frequently she has, but some of this is attributable to her own stubborn inflexibility and excessive self-righteousness in dealings with Pakistan, especially concerning Kashmir.[1] The complex Indo–Pakistan story since 1947, a record which registers some agreements, is basically one of mutual antipathy: again with Kashmir as a principal persisting emblematic issue.

The Kashmir dispute is deeply rooted, indeed entangled, in different interpretations of the meaning and significance of the partition of the sub-continent between India and Pakistan in 1947. It is now also profoundly involved in the power rivalries of several of the great Powers, as well as being significantly affected by the complexities and volatility of Kashmir's own political climate. Any adequate assessment and understanding of India's interest in Kashmir also has to take into account Kashmir's own complex and chequered internal history, as well as extraneous factors. Kashmir has a predominantly Muslim population and yet this very fact apparently impels Indian governments to regard (to the surprise and perplexity of many foreigners) its retention as a principal symbol of India's secular statehood. This retention is also often represented as stopping the main floodgates to further bloody communalism within India. The retention of the Kashmiri Muslims within the Indian Union is thus represented as an earnest that all the fifty million or so Muslims in India are welcome as Indian nationals, and that India is truly a secular state.

Yet when all the complex interwoven elements and interests which attach India to Kashmir are added up there is an extra element of passion–one might call it obsession–about Indian fascination with Kashmir that cannot be fully understood merely by being attentive to the varied and varying arguments Indians advance in favour of their cause. The retention of Kashmir (or,

---

[1] I have discussed this theme more thoroughly in my book *India and Pakistan*, Routledge and Kegan Paul, forthcoming. See further my article on 'Kashmir' in *International Relations*, 3(2) October 1966, pp. 111–28.

rather, what is left now that Pakistan occupies 'Azad' Kashmir, and the Chinese have part of Ladakh) has become one of the articles of Indian national faith, tested in and consecrated by war. There are events in the life of nations that are traumatic and thereafter shape the outlook, the fears and expectations of the leadership, and of the nation at large–they become part of the national heritage. 1947, 1962 and 1965 were crisis years in India's history–involving, successively, partition, the war with China, the war with Pakistan. In each of these crises the adhesion of Kashmir to the Indian Union was an issue at stake.

In the late 1940s and early 1950s it was plausibly argued by India's government, which mostly meant in effect by Nehru, that it would be enormously expensive, and unnecessary, actively to patrol all India's frontiers. In any case frontier policing and patrolling were regarded as the sport of the former imperial Power, not that of a new nation-state. Within this mantle of national innocence reposed essentially one great hope and one great exception. The hope was that shows of goodwill and trust towards China would be reciprocated. The great exception was that Pakistan could not be trusted. Over time events have shown, so many Indians now believe, that the hope was too optimistic and the belief about Pakistan has been amply, and unhappily, justified. In the 1960s Chinese and Pakistani opposition to India has run parallel and has often resulted in deliberate collusion, so Indians claim, thus enormously compounding India's security problems. Pakistan's and China's irredentist and other activities against India thus become linked in Indian minds.

Indeed, whatever Pakistanis regard as irredenta almost all Indians therefore regard as a threatened piece of national homeland. Strictly this need not always be so, as Pakistan could covet contiguous pieces of Iranian, Afghan, Chinese or Burmese territory too; but in practice the territorial claims (apart from resisting Afghan support for Paktoonistan) that have principally preoccupied Pakistan's policy-makers, and certainly her only expansionist claims, have been those directed against India. Arguments about claims to the Rann of Kutch, to Gurdaspur, Murshidabad,

Tripura, even about Kashmir, mean very little, and indeed are not much understood in the world at large; but they mean a lot to politically aware and nationalistic Indians and Pakistanis. Both India and Pakistan in their dealings with each other protest, of course, that they are unaggressive, and non-expansionist; one has only to study the confusing background to the Kashmir war of 1947, or of 1965, to see how easily each side can construct a plausible case; but to the present writer it does seem clear that since 1947 it is Pakistan which has been territorially revisionist and India in practice has not. Even now, or especially now, after the wars of 1962 and 1965, India is territorially a *status quo* rather than a revisionist Power, more concerned not to lose any more territory to either Pakistan or China than to prosecute actively moves designed to secure the whole of Kashmir for India governance or even to try to recover the portion of Ladakh which has been lost. Indian soldiers now stand sentinel along India's frontiers; but they perform guard-duties and are not spearheads for her advancing armies.

If Pakistan were left to herself India could deal with her quite adequately and reasonably; it is the intrusion of outside powers which has hindered and/or prevented Pakistan's recognition of the full implications of the partition—so Indian spokesmen substantially claim, in diverse ways. The, usually unstated, implications of this official Indian outlook are that Pakistan should be isolationist, or should accept in its relations with India a position of permanent inferiority, or at best a junior partnership; and in particular it implies that no great power should actually or apparently favour Pakistan against India. In effect these have been operative assumptions in Indian foreign policy ever since 1947 and go a long way to explain the vicissitudes in her relations with Great Britain, with the United States, with the Soviet Union and especially with China.

India's northern frontiers, those with China, are very long, and the issues are very complex.[1] It is convenient, in discussing briefly

[1] The literature of this subject is already immense and can best be approached through the voluminous correspondence published by the Chinese and Indian

their significance, to regard them as four sectors from west to east:
 (i) The boundaries of the outlying dependencies of Kashmir (i.e. Gilgit, Baltistan and Ladakh);
 (ii) The Punjab, Himachal Pradesh and Uttar Pradesh boundaries;
 (iii) Nepal, Sikkim and Bhutan;
 (iv) The North-east Frontier.

Also we shall note, again very briefly, how frontier disputes become entwined with other issues. For it is, of course, China's rising military power and obtrusive and challenging presence all along India's northern frontiers which has transformed India's security problems and indeed almost the whole context and concerns of her foreign policy.

(i) Kashmir frontiers

These in effect face two ways: north towards Sinkiang and east towards Tibet. Where the frontier adjoins Sinkiang, looking north from Gilgit and Skardu, this territory is now in Pakistan; and while the Chinese did in their maps issued in the mid-1950s shade part of that area as theirs, not only have they taken no military action there, but, as a Sino–Pakistan *entente* began to unfold, from early 1963 onwards, the Chinese have shown a willingness to demark this boundary, and the rest of Kashmir's northern frontier, by mutual agreement with Pakistan – in the face of Indian protests. Where India's frontier adjoins west-south-west Tibet (that is the large bulge which comprises Ladakh) the whole is claimed by

---

governments, and with the help of a good atlas. For two brief accounts of the manner of argument and issues at stake (which I have relied on heavily here) see Sir Olaf Caroe, 'The Geography and Ethics of India's Northern Frontiers' in *The Geographical Journal*, 126, 1960, pp. 298–308. Sir Olaf served for over forty years in the Indian Political Service in the days of the British Raj; throughout the whole of the Second World War he was Secretary of the External Affairs Department of the government of India, and, when British rule ceased in 1947, he was Governor of the North-West Frontier Province. It should be remembered that this survey of his was made in 1960, before the wars of 1962 and 1965. See also W. Kirk, 'The Inner Asian Frontier of India' in *The Transactions of the Institute of British Geographers, 1962*, pp. 131–68.

India, and is now in part occupied by China. The Chinese have
built a road across the north-east or Aksai Chin portion of Ladakh,
thus linking Tibet and Sinkiang. The Indians insist that this road
has been built across their national territory and that Chinese
claims were originally advanced clandestinely and by trickery and
were implemented and have been maintained by military force.
Chinese maps until recently concurred with the frontier lines for
Ladakh shown upon Indian maps. They included in India the
regions of Aksai Chin and the Changchenmo valley, now claimed
by China, altogether some 12,000 square miles. It is thus only in
recent years, since 1954, that the Chinese have altered their maps to
support their occupation of the region through which their link
road (built, apparently, between 1954 and 1958) from Sinkiang to
Tibet passes.

Ethnically Ladakh is Tibetan and Buddhist (unlike Gilgit and
Baltistan, which are Muslim); but it has a long history of association with India. Indeed, history rather than geography dictates the
nature of India's claims here. Not only Ladakh but Gilgit and
Baltistan also are all north of the main axis of the Himalaya, and
thus do not conform with the general claim that the Himalaya
crest line is India's frontier. Chinese governments (that in Taiwan
as well as the Peking government) ever since 1949 have asserted
that no part of the frontier between India and 'the Tibet region of
China' has ever been properly delimited, that a permanent settlement awaits upon a formal agreement, and that claims based
apparently on so-called historic rights and ancient traditions or
upon arrangements made by the British are imperialistic or neo-
imperialistic rubbish.

(ii) The Punjab-Himachal Pradesh sector

This sector (the only one of the four discussed here which is strictly
only a Sino–Indian border), where the boundary of the Indian
states of the Punjab, Himachal Pradesh and Uttar Pradesh march
with the Ari district of Tibet, has two very distinctive geographical
features: the Himalaya is here cleft by the river Sutlej, and in many
parts there is a double range of almost parallel snow peaks, the higher

mostly being nearer to India, but the lower range is the water-shed. Rival claims are made by India and China to part of the upper valleys lying between the two ranges and to the passes over the lower, which is the more northerly and is, as we have already noted, the watershed. The largest of these upper pastures between the ranges is the Nilang–Jadhang area, very close to the sources of the Ganges at Gangotri. This Gangotri region is among the holiest of all ground reverenced by Hindus, and is visited yearly by thousands of devout pilgrims–and this fact explains much of the fierce outburst of Indian passion when the territorial claims of the Chinese against India erupted into the open. And not only does this area have sacred significance for many million Indians but also it contains most of the main ages-old routeways and passes for trade and transit between India and Tibet.

In the 1954 Sino–Indian Treaty of Trade and Friendship concerning Tibet (which came at the end of four years of a slowly developing *détente* and after several months of intense secret negotiation by Indian diplomats in Peking) India in effect abandoned any historic rights in Tibet, receiving in return nothing more substantial than Chinese promises of eternal friendship with the Indian people, and the Panch Sheel principles. Since the Sino–Indian dispute erupted into the open it has become clear that there is sharp disagreement about the ownership of the six passes specified in Article IV of the 1954 Treaty. For, despite the famous, or now notorious, Panchshila, or Panch Sheel, clauses, which laid down five abstract principles for international good behaviour, India then also conceded that Tibet was an integral part of China. After four years of public dithering about whether Tibet was a suzerain of China or should come under full Chinese sovereignty, Mr. Nehru had in effect conceded full Chinese sovereignty–a change in the Himalayan and indeed Asian international order which in fact prefigured changes of enormous consequence for the Asian power constellation. Having conceded that Tibet is part of China, India subsequently has had to live with the unfavourable military and other aspects of this (e.g. the flight of the Dalai Lama, the influx of Tibetan refugees, the loss of trade with Tibet) and has come tardily and at high cost to recognize that the 1954 agreement, far from inaugurating a peaceful settlement in perpetuity, was but an early, yet major, Chinese move in what now looks like a protracted Sino–Indian struggle along the whole of the Himalaya–and elsewhere.

In this specific Punjab–Himachal Pradesh sector the Indians contend that the six passes specified in the 1954 Treaty cross the watershed, which is the natural and traditional frontier and that shown in maps, and that their explicit mention in that treaty, without any *démarche* to claim that they are part of Tibet throughout their length, infers that their southern end is within India. The Chinese case is that the 1954 Treaty does not deal with frontiers at all, that the people in the areas south of these passes are of Tibetan stock and that Tibetan records show them to have paid taxes to Lhasa.

Clearly these are complex and, as presently advanced, incompatible contentions. It is true that the 1954 Treaty does not deal explicitly with frontiers. But it should also be noticed that the Chinese claim that people who are ethnically Tibetan must be within China is audaciously simple. For all along the Himalaya peoples have met and mingled, and in many areas are very closely entwined. Indeed many of the mountain peoples, Akas, Daflas, Abors and Laolaktics, for example, are no more clearly 'Indian' than the varied Tibetan communities are clearly 'Chinese'. Buddhism, or Hinduism (Indianism), or Communism, or Democracy, do not conform to precise physical boundaries and the current attempts to affix 'Indian' or 'Chinese' labels on them are dictated mostly by current exigencies, by the arbitrary conveniences and the impassioned preferences of policy-makers in New Delhi or Peking.

(iii) Nepal, Sikkim and Bhutan

The main feature about this sector of the frontier to remember is that Nepal is an independent state (since December 1955 a member of the United Nations) and that Sikkim and Bhutan are protectorates of India, a situation inherited from the days of British rule but rephrased and reaffirmed after 1947 in bilateral treaties. From being in their different ways under the hegemony of India, all three states have now become, though again in distinctive ways, pawns of Sino–India rivalries.

In Nepal,[1] Hinduism and Buddhism meet–Buddha was born at Rummindei in Nepal–and Nepal is a Hindu state of some ten million people. It is culturally a part of the Indian world. Politically it is inescapably caught up in Sino–Indian rivalries. India must always be as much concerned over the integrity of Nepal as Britain has been over the Low Countries, perhaps more so for the Himalaya is Nepal's heartland and frontier as well as India's frontier.

Sikkim and Bhutan, both smaller states,[2] are regarded by some Indians as potential victims of what they describe as China's intention to play a 'five-finger exercise' at India's expense. Having acquired the palm of the Himalayas–Tibet–between 1950 and 1954, China wants, so this theory goes, to add five fingers–Ladakh, Nepal, Sikkim, Bhutan and Nefa. Even though this does not represent the full measure of China's declared irredenta it is a programme which could only, if implemented, result in India's increased discomfiture. There is no agreement as to how, when and why China might continue to do this–whether precipitantly or by waiting patiently until India's guard lowers, whether openly or covertly, by means of encouraging each small state to assert its independence of India or by promoting actively, what it has already shown some interest in, a confederation of small Himalayan states.

What is certainly now regarded by Indians as an especially vulnerable area within this sector of their northern frontier is where the northern tip of East Pakistan protrudes towards Nepal to leave only a narrow neck of Indian territory linking up with Assam and the eastern parts of the Union. Indian concern, involving as it does both internal and external policies, was heightened when a peasant revolt broke out in the Darjeeling district of west Bengal in March 1967 under the leadership of extremist elements

[1] See Peter Lyon, *Neutralism*, Leicester University Press, 1963, pp. 95–6.
[2] *Ibid.*, pp. 96–7.

in the pro-China Communist Party of India. Many Indians believe that this revolt may be the first of many to be incited, in part at least, from China. The area involved, one of about thirty-five square miles around the small towns of Naxalbari, Kharibari and Phansidewa, is of great strategic significance, as Naxalbari is only four miles from Nepal, fourteen miles from East Pakistan and sixty miles from the Tibetan border. This narrow strip is sometimes evocatively called India's 'Polish corridor' since it was carved out during Partition to provide continuous land links with Assam and the rest of India's eastern territories. If this vital corridor were ever severed India would become two discontinuous parts, as Pakistan is, with all the problems and complications that accompany such a situation.

By October 1967, Western press reports claimed that Indian security forces were looking for a revolutionary leader who had been a principal in fomenting the Naxalbari disturbances. The fugitive was Kanu Sanyal, leader of the Kisan Sabha, an extremist group of agricultural workers who demand that landless peasants be given farms. The Indian Home Minister said publicly several times in the middle months of 1967 that his government had no definite information that the Chinese were directly involved.

But officially approved Chinese attitudes were unmistakable and unequivocal. The Chinese press enthusiastically praised the Naxalbari revolt as a model to be imitated by Indian Communists. An editorial in the Peking *People's Daily* said on 5 July 1967:

> The Indian revolution must take the road of relying on the peasants, establishing base areas in the countryside, persisting in protracted armed struggle, and using the countryside to encircle and finally capture the cities. This is Mao Tse-tung's road ... Armed struggle is the only correct road for the Indian revolution; there is no other road whatsoever. Such trash as 'Ghandism', 'the parliamentary road' and the like are opium used by the Indian ruling classes to dope the Indian people ... renegades and revisionists are running dogs of US imperialism and Soviet revisionism and stooges of bourgeoisie.

(iv) The North-East frontier

It is in this sector that the largest amount of disputed territory lies. The area whose possession is contested amounts to almost 40,000 square miles, roughly 400 miles long and 100 to 75 miles wide, about the size of England without Wales. This was one of the areas in which China made major incursions in October 1962 and where she could conceivably threaten India along a broad front sweeping down through Nefa, beyond her advance in 1962, to the oil installations and tea estates of Assam. The territorial claims of the Indian government in the Nefa are no different from those of the previous British Raj, and postulate that the McMahon line (which China substantially has accepted where it depicts the Sino–Burmese frontier, though refusing to recognize it as a valid demarcation of this portion of the Sino–Indian frontier) marks the frontier now and has done ever since 1914. But whereas the British were often satisfied with 'indirect rule' in remote frontier regions the Indians have felt themselves obliged to establish effective administration right up to the very limits of what they regard as their territory, thus actively involving the tribal peoples concerned in the governance and in many administrative rules and regulations which ultimately stem from or are the responsibility of the central government in New Delhi. The process of spreading a nation-wide order thus itself prompts some local resistance and opens out new opportunities for one's enemies.

Though not strictly a part of the Nefa frontier it is convenient here to say something about Nagaland and the Mizo Hills area—both lying at the eastern extremities of the Indian Union and thus south of the eastern end of the Nefa—because here again we can see where domestic and international problems entwine. Thirty or forty years ago there were no people known as Nagas or Mizos, there were only Angami, Ao, Rengma, Konyak and others, tribal groups all busily engaged in recurrent mutual hostilities with neighbours. Naga was a mere category label used by foreigners to describe a mixed collectivity of very small culturally distinct groups. It is the accidents and pressures of the past twenty-five years or so which have moulded these diverse peoples into incipient nations. Today the inhabitants of the Naga (or Mizo) Hills are aware of themselves as Nagas (or Mizos) and on that account they constitute organized political forces of consequence. The Delhi government is determined that consciousness of being Naga or Mizo should not become politically more important than being Indians. Yet those elements within the Nagas and the Mizos who want independence from India (and so far these are minorities) look expectantly to China and to Pakistan, India's enemies, for help. Once again India's immense problems of instituting and maintaining a nation-wide order converge with her foreign policy problems.

There is one further matter which is at least metaphorically linked to the theme of India's size. That is the question: what is India's diplomatic size, standing, stature in the world? The rough-and-ready ratings made by contemporary leaders and journalists reflect self-esteem and reputation: how a state is regarded by its own populace and by foreigners, what roles it fashions and carries out for itself in the world.

Nehru's views on this subject were always somewhat vague and equivocal, but nevertheless managed to convey his conviction of India's great importance in the world. In March 1949 Nehru was saying publicly that India was potentially a great nation and a big Power; in the Indian parliament on 30 September 1954 he made a qualified claim that India was the fourth world Power—after the US, the USSR and China; after 1962, and the reverses suffered from China, he stopped making such statements directly, and since his death the subject does not get discussed very directly and prominently in India. National narcissism has given way to mild national egophobia. In the late 1960s there is a general recognition among Indians that their country's reputation and standing has slumped somewhat since the mid-1950s; but this is matched by an equally vague and general but probably much stronger feeling that her proper role is among the top six Powers of the world. And as well as these verbal claims and vague hopes there is the less controvertible evidence of action. The size of its diplomatic establishment, the number of missions maintained overseas, activity in international organizations and international conferences–are all evidence of diplomatic stature and ambitions. There is no doubt that India plays the role of a Power of size and consequence in world affairs and seems likely to continue to try to do so, straitened economic and other circumstances notwithstanding. After all, India today is weaker and poorer, but much more active internationally, than either Germany or Japan.

India's economy

Economically India is still basically an inward-oriented economy, and, what is more, India's share in world trade has been declining since independence and its burden of indebtedness is increasing. It is thus not surprising that increasing attention has had to be given to the economic aspects of foreign policy.

India's poverty is proverbial. It is also pervasive, a present-day fact and persisting. But poverty is not an ineluctable law of nature and India has had ever since 1947 a government dedicated to the proposition that material improvement for the whole nation is a common good and goal and that India must ascend a ladder of ever-increasing prosperity. Any future Indian government that is likely to take office will avow similar ambitions. While it is certainly true that India is still some way from the cherished and now frequently avowed target–that of achieving self-sustaining economic growth–the fact that India has made remarkable economic advances, in relation to the scale of her problems and her past economic history, is not widely known or understood. With an overall gross growth rate of about 4 per cent during the period of the first Five-Year Plans, 1951–66, India certainly has not entirely stagnated economically. By comparison with most other countries at roughly comparable stages of development (say Japan between 1868 and 1914 or Britain between 1760 and 1810) India has done quite well, and her rate of growth in the first fifteen years following independence is significantly better overall than what was achieved in the previous 150 years of her economic history. But there is no escaping the fact that by the standards of contemporary demands and of popular journalistic criticism India's overall economic performance, viewed in the mid-1960s, has disappointed her own nationals and her friends and well-wishers abroad. Agriculture is still very much India's largest industry, supporting 70 per cent of the population and constituting half of the annual national income.

In this regard the size of India's population, and its rate of increase, is a burden not a blessing. India had in 1967 as much as 12·8 per cent of the world's population, but only 2·2 per cent of the world's land area. The population was 439 million in 1961, when the last ten-year census was taken. Between 1951 and 1961 it went up by 78 million, and the total exceeded 500 million during 1966. The rate of growth continues to be high and is about 2·5 per cent per year. Because of this fast rate of growth, about 40 per cent of the population is below the age of fifteen years. In large part this population increase is due to a considerable fall in the death-rate, which is in large measure attributable to better sanitation and medical services. Just as the causes of the problem are domestic so the remedies must be principally domestic, even though the United States and other countries have provided some assistance for birth-control schemes, and food supplies from the United States, Canada and Australia (not the Soviet Union, despite Indian requests) have alleviated famine in the late 1960s.

Today, as was often not the case in the past, no great state can have the greater part of its populace in acute poverty and yet be recognized and respected as a great Power. This is one of the currently dominant moral truths embodied in Henry Wallace's phrase that this is the century of the common man. Technological advance, great steel mills, nuclear power plants are not enough; the efficiency of a modern state is unavoidably judged today in terms of the goods and services it provides for its whole citizenry.

Providing, or at least encouraging favourable conditions for the provision of, food is the most fundamental test of a political system's capacity to provide goods and services. By this test India fares unfavourably, for this is notoriously a country which is recurrently afflicted by mortal famines. It is important to recall

272

that famine is no new phenomenon in India and that acute food shortage cannot be solely attributed to the shortcomings of India's post-independence central government, still less to the niggardliness and malfeasances of foreign food suppliers. Famines did not flow in with India's independence. But an ancient and familiar scourge is not made more welcome by its familiarity. Rather it is now felt to be one of the crucial tests of India's developing 'modernity' to bring famine to an end for ever. Self-sufficiency in agricultural productivity is an avowed goal of present Indian government—said to be achievable by 1971, but present indications are that this is unlikely. For India has had to import a lot of food in the 1960s, raising problems of finance, foreign exchange, transport, distribution and national pride. But much of these imports could have been avoided by better Indian management. Half the food produced in India is wasted by rats, rot, birds and insects, according to an FAO report published in 1967. That loss, in financial terms, is equal to about twice India's annual central governmental budget. (And this is to say nothing of the 'sacred cows' which literally and metaphorically are very numerous shibboleths, residues of traditional culture impeding modernization.) To end dependence, reliance on foreign food suppliers, is a basic ambition of India's leaders. The hope, the intention, is that increased production of food, and population control, will soon enable the government to regard food acquisition as not a foreign policy problem at all. Foreign policy begins, and ends, at home.

India is at once the recipient of the largest quantity of foreign aid in the contemporary world, and, among those who receive aid, the donor of the most assistance to others. This second point is less well known than the first, but it is important to Indian self-esteem as well as to her diplomacy and strategy. India's aid programme is small when compared to those of the more affluent countries, but it represents a significant sacrifice in view of her own critical needs. The bulk of India's aid has been concentrated upon the three Himalayan neighbours—Nepal, Sikkim and Bhutan—where she is either a major or the sole contributor of foreign assistance. It is not accidental that India's aid programmes to these countries has increased as China's interest in them has also increased.

This short chapter is not the place to discuss the amount of aid received or dispensed by India, nor to discuss the range and character of foreign-assisted projects, the diplomacy of aid giving and receiving, the politics and economics of encouraging favourable public and private investment. There are already many detailed books on these subjects,[1] though the connection between India's economy and her foreign policy is seldom treated frontally and centrally.[2] What must be stressed, however, is that the economic aspects of foreign policy have become increasingly important to India in the 1960s and seem almost certain to remain a preoccupation in the late 1960s and 1970s. The main modalities of Indian foreign policy have changed: soaring rhetoric, advising the world and promoting anti-colonialist enterprises now have to give ground to military matters and to more concern with economic intelligence and management. The differences between the Asian Relations Conference which met in New Delhi in 1947 and the second UNCTAD conference which met in New Delhi in February 1968, symbolize this shift of emphasis.

India's economic planning now comprises and contemplates a series of Five-Year Plans from 1950-1 to 1975-6. These Five-Year Plans are represented by India's leaders as decisive steps towards the goal of self-generating economic growth and peaceful social change, towards a self-reliant economy. In fact, the notion of a self-reliant economy is nowhere closely defined by the Indian government. But it apparently means, principally, an ability to do without foreign aid, the absence of an acute foreign exchange problem, and no persistent need for food imports; or if food is

[1] Michael Kidron, *Foreign Investment in India*, O.U.P., 1965; K. R. V. Rao and D. Narain, *Foreign Aid and India's Economic Development*, Bombay, 1963; S. Chandrasekhar, *American Aid to India's Economic Development*, New York, 1965; A. H. Hanson, *The Process of Planning, a study of India's Five-Year Plans, 1950-64*, O.U.P., for the Royal Institute of International Affairs, 1966.

[2] One notable exception is Warren F. Ilchman, 'Political Development and Foreign Policy: The Case of India' in *Journal of Commonwealth Political Studies*, Vol. IV (3), November 1966, pp. 216-30.

imported it assumes that there will be eventually an ability to pay for it with foreign exchange earned by buoyant Indian exports. Substantially increasing autarky, if never complete autarky, is thus the government's avowed aim. Recent years of being a mendicant for food probably has heightened the government's desire for self-sufficiency, even though the realization of the ambition is still a long way off, perhaps much farther off than 1971, which has been for some time the announced goal for the achievement of complete self-sufficiency in foodstuffs, just as the mid-1970s are said to be the time when general economic self-reliance will be achieved. In fact, the fourth Five-Year Plan should have been ready in its final version in 1965. But in late 1967 it was still in draft form and Indian hopes of a self-supporting economy by the mid-1970s seemed remote. Indeed, Moraji Desai, India's Finance Minister, said in Tokyo in August 1967 that India would need at least $1 billion a year in foreign aid for the next decade in order to ensure a satisfactory economic growth, that is a rate of 5 per cent per annum. Desai added that: 'Today, some 40 per cent of the aid we get has to be used for paying interest and amortization charges on past debt', and nearly one-quarter of India's total export earnings had to be spent on similar purposes. For economic assistance India looks primarily (with Soviet aid the only notable exception) to the Aid-India Consortium of ten nations which was organized under the auspices of the International Bank for Reconstruction and Development first in 1957, and which, with the World Bank's affiliate, the International Development Association, comprises Austria, Belgium, Canada, West Germany, France, Italy, Japan, the Netherlands, Britain and the United States. India is thus a considerable, mostly passive, part of the international economy.

India's political system
India is a uniquely large parliamentary political system, with a uniquely large electorate, which has already expressed its collective will at four general elections, in 1951, 1957, 1962 and 1967. The electorate also elects not only the central parliament in New Delhi, but also sixteen state parliaments, each constituent parts of the

Union of India. These are matters of which Indians are understandably proud; but how does being a parliamentary and federal political system affect India's foreign policy? It does so not so much in matters of substance but in the style of foreign policy and in the manner in which foreign policy matters are discussed and dealt with within India. Parliamentary government encourages but does not ensure a civilian, publicly justifiable foreign policy. Parliaments are intended, when they are taken seriously, as in India, to nourish habits of public discussion and debate concerning matters of high policy, and nowadays to serve as a permanent reminder that parliamentary democracy means representative and responsible government. Parliaments are, of course, literally places for talk, and Indian foreign policy too is mostly a matter of talk either at home or abroad. In most public affairs there comes a point when you proceed from talk to action. But for parliament and for the Ministry of External Affairs in India foreign policy remains essentially a matter of saying what you propose. Any action which is taken is usually that of another or of several arms of government. If you go to war, it becomes a matter for the armed forces as well as for the Cabinet and the Ministry of External Affairs. If it is a matter concerning trade then it comes before the Ministries of Trade and of Finance. The only actions that the Foreign Minister and/or his professional diplomats ever take are to write diplomatic notes, to sign treaties, and to travel to other countries for conferences and discussions (an infinite capacity for taking planes is sometimes said to be a contemporary definition of genius). Indian foreign policy, perhaps more than that of any other contemporary Power of consequence, has been characterized by the ascendancy of words over deeds, of avowals over actions. One partial explanation of this political loquacity is that this may be a legacy of the experience of India's leaders during the struggle for independence against Britain. For to speak publicly against the British Raj was, in a sense, to take action–to court arrest and to face charges of sedition and prospects of imprisonment, and thus to demonstrate one's patriotism. But the legacy of these verbal battles, however heroic they were in many ways, has been unfortunate inasmuch as it has encouraged the illusion – which some commentators have said is endemic in 'the Hindu mind' – that words are deeds, that defiance, and denunciation, protest and proposals are in themselves a policy. Much, some would say too much, of Indian foreign policy can be seen as a reflection or continuance of the tactics of the independence struggle, in which words, demonstrations and negotiations took precedence over bullets and battles.

The prestige of parliament was cherished by Nehru, who had a Gladstonian regard for the prestige and procedures of parliament, for the courtesies of debate – and for civilian diplomacy. His regard for parliament – broadly shared by his Union cabinet colleagues and successors – and for foreign policy debates in parliament was the domestic counterpart of his preference for civilian diplomacy. Foreign policy while Nehru was Prime Minister was, for better or worse, largely the expression of one man's vision, will, statecraft, and of his personal political ascendancy throughout India. Since Nehru's death India's foreign policy-making must be assumed to be much more of a collegiate matter; much more a product of the Union cabinet's corporate will, of the bargaining and compromises which inevitably attend cabinet government, and a consequence of the fact that neither in cabinet nor in parliament has any of Nehru's successors, not even his daughter, approached his former eminence. But how *precisely* the central executive of Indian government operates and affects the formulation and conduct of foreign policy in post-Nehru India we do not know.

Until recently the domestic opposition, or rather oppositions, within India to foreign policy as actually practised by the government was (were) notable in general only for its (their) weakness and ineffectiveness. This era may now be coming to an end in foreign policy just as it has more certainly in domestic politics. The waning of the Congress Party's former ascendancy was dramatically demonstrated in the general election of February 1967 and though Congress has retained control of about half the state governments the future of India's internal political order is unsettled and likely to be stormy in the years immediately ahead. So long as the Congress Party retains control of the Union government there will be broad continuity in foreign policy, that is in so far as foreign policy is shaped by domestic considerations; if Congress were to lose power, as a result of electoral defeat, then any conceivable successor government which took power would almost certainly only continue substantially, whatever its rhetoric, the present much more introverted and more modest foreign policy – more modest, that is, than that of the 1950s.

In part this greater introversion may perhaps be ascribed to the increasing 'Indian-ness' of Indian political life. India's foreign policy to date has been formulated and conducted by the English-language-educated, Westernized, predominantly secular, élite (at the pinnacles of national politics and of administration). The future continuity of policy, and the national cohesion of the country, may well depend considerably on the political future of this élite. The present Commander-in-Chief of the Indian Army is the last of the Sandhurst-educated officers; and the present top grades of the Indian Administration and Diplomatic Service are the last generation of former ICS men. Already there are signs of the emergence of a new élite, more localized in experience and outlook, securing power first at the state governmental level and then wielding power at the central of Union governmental level. Foreign policy is always principally an affair of capital cities; Indian foreign policy is Delhi-centric. But whether foreign policy dialogue and action from New Delhi will in future be determined by an English- or Hindu-language-educated élite; how, to put it more generally, the vast social and political changes currently in motion within India will affect foreign policy, if significantly at all, we do not know.

Parliamentary government is an imperfect form of government. But, all in all, it is the least imperfect of all imperfect governmental forms. It is not proof against revolution; but its continuance is an indication that revolution is unlikely. All governments have a multiplicity of objectives: to stay in power, to enhance prestige, to spread prosperity ... and many matters more. There are no firm, simple and certain criteria by which a citizen (still less an outside observer) can judge in an informed and sophisticated manner the overall foreign policy that is practised by a government. Even for those Indians who agree with this sceptical thought their praise and criticism of their country's foreign policy will not stop; nor should it.

Non-alignment

India's foreign policy is non-aligned. This at the very least means no membership in formal military alliances. It means much more too, but these meanings change. No adequate assessment of India's non-alignment could be made without careful analysis of the many apparent ambiguities and inconsistencies of argument and action – such as the avowals of independent uncommitted judgement and yet the examples of strong partialities at particular times; the disavowal of military force and yet its employment in Goa and in Kashmir; the clear presumption by many Indians that India is or should be the natural leader of the Afro/Asian and of the non-aligned worlds and yet the palpable failure of India energetically to provide decisive leadership in the UN, at Bandung, at Brioni in 1956, at Belgrade in 1961 or Cairo in 1964. But the record is not, of course, entirely one of equivocation. For although hesitancy has been a hallmark of much of India's diplomacy the record of mediatorship and of Indian peace-keeping in Indo–China, Suez, the Congo and Cyprus must be accorded due place too. But a, perhaps *the*, central fact of Indian policy (which still badly needs adequate analysis at book length) is that it has been strongly influenced by the major Powers, especially by the policies of the super-Powers. Indian foreign policy has been reactive much more than it has been innovatory. Soviet and American policies have shaped much of the substance of what is meant by Indian non-alignment.

What advantages would India have gained, or might gain in the future, by abandoning non-alignment and adopting an explicit alliance policy? We cannot say with surety. So much would depend on the central or world balance of power and the factors which occasioned such a move by India. What does seem clear is that so far the Indian government has never even considered the possibility of entering a military alliance very seriously. It may

279

have flirted with the idea of an alliance between 1962 and 1965, after the shock of the Chinese attack. But the experience of standing alone against Pakistan in September 1965 while condemned or treated with diffidence or disdain by the United States, Britain and Russia, while China issued ambiguous threats, not only served to restore India's self-respect but also apparently confirmed most Indians in their belief in the essential rightness of what they regard as self-reliant non-alignment. An alliance with the United States alone undoubtedly would have worsened India's relations with Russia; and a formal alliance with both the United States and with Russia so far has never been a practical possibility. If this is so, then non-alignment in some form or other for India, at least since the mid-1950s, has been not a luxury, a lotus-land of illusion, but a necessity, however much debate and disagreement there may be about the best tactics to pursue.

Current Indian stress on 'national interest' as the complementary principle of non-alignment draws attention both to the currently fashionable preference for self-professed realism and also, incidentally, to a recurrently employed simplistic stereotype of foreign policy analysis. The so-called theory of 'national interest' either suggests an idea as undeniable as it is vague – that the government of each nation-state is self-regarding and tries to act in terms of what it regards as the national interest – or else the theory tries to oppose the notion of national interest to other apparently seductive goals or aims, e.g. that the foreign policy of states is, or ought to be, dictated by ideology, by its economic strength, its ruling or other élites, or, most rarely – even in India – by moral considerations. To say that India conducts its foreign policy on the basis of national interest is in itself to say nothing very clear and certainly to say something too simple. There is no reason, in logic or experience, to believe that one factor will always be paramount: for India or for any other country's foreign policy. The importance of any one obtrusive factor can only be understood if one has analysed all others in their context of time and place; assertive simplifications mean something, if they mean anything at all, only in context.

280

Indian non-alignment is what the current government says it is. Outside observers may think it is, or is not, 'truly' non-aligned, but in matters of nomenclature, as Humpty Dumpty once shrewdly observed, the only question is: Who is to be master?

India's importance and the question of nuclear weapons

One of the central problems perplexing the Indian government in the late 1960s is the question whether India should or should not manufacture nuclear weapons. The government's policy as officially described and defended, certainly right up until the middle months of 1967, is that India will not produce nuclear weapons, though she has the ability to do so. But undoubtedly the issue has been debated within India with much more seriousness and concern since China detonated her first nuclear device in October 1964, and with an increasing number of protagonists for an Indian bomb as China has continued to develop her nuclear capability. My own view is that India will eventually decide to produce a nuclear bomb; but this is a conjecture, and even if it proves to be true the exact consequences for India of doing so in political, economic and strategic terms cannot be foreseen. Much will depend on the timing and context in which India makes her first detonation: whether she is the next, that is the sixth, nuclear Power or follows several other new nuclear Powers; whether the decision to 'go nuclear' militarily is prompted primarily by the failure to get guarantees from the super-Powers – guarantees, that is, which have been earnestly sought – or from distrust of guarantees *per se*; whether a first detonation is regarded as a significant achievement in itself or as a mere prologue to an extensive nuclear weapons programme.

Whether India will in fact become an independent producer of nuclear bombs thus cannot be foreseen. But, whether India does or does not become a military nuclear power, debate concerning the issues involved will be of continuing importance. If India does decide to produce a nuclear bomb she will have to consider what costs – political, moral and strategic as well as economic – she has incurred in so doing; and if she decides not to produce she will have to consider what has been foregone in not producing a bomb; negative decisions are still decisions. What is then clear and certain is that the debate in India about nuclear matters is now on and will continue, in the 1970s and 1980s no less than in the 1960s.

It is a many sided, highly controversial, often unavoidably conjectural debate; for what is in effect being discussed is the whole style, significance and substance of India's foreign policy–not only here and now but in the unknown future. In presenting their arguments some Indians emphasize the security aspects, some the moral, some the economic implications and others the domestic or the diplomatic considerations involved. We may here, for the sake of clarity and simplicity, represent the main arguments as being for or against an Indian nuclear-weapons programme, though it should be remembered that the actual discussion and debate within India is much more diverse, less stylized, than might be suggested to some readers by this enumerated form of presentation. The present outline merely lists the main arguments currently made for and against an India nuclear-weapons programme (without any specific attributions or attempts to weigh the support for or changing emphasis given to any one or more of the points) but even this presentation, it is hoped, will illuminate something of the nature and complexity of the issues perplexing any present or future Indian government. Many of the arguments used are not, of course, peculiar to India's predicament but are part and parcel of being, or of being potentially, a military nuclear Power. The Indian debate (and it has only really become such since 1964) contains many echoes of earlier and continuing debates: in the United States especially, but also in Britain and in France (the debates about nuclear matters which no doubt went on and continue within the USSR and China are more muted for outside ears). We will put the arguments of the proponents of an India bomb first as they are seeking to change present policy, to act in part at least as innovators.

The main claims of the advocates of an Indian nuclear weapons policy are that:

(1) India is now threatened by a nuclear Power, China; and

without an available nuclear capability of her own she lacks the material and psychological resources to deter China, and to be able to resist nuclear blackmail;

(2) a non-nuclear India does and will inevitably and ultimately depend for her security on either or both the United States and the Soviet Union, and this continuing dependence will not only with time heighten, dramatize and perpetuate Indian reliance on the two super-Powers but it will also restrict her independence of action in world affairs; joint or individual offers of nuclear protection from the United States and the Soviet Union might also encourage China to try further 'nibbling' at India, to distract the super-Powers from other matters and at the same time test their determination to help India, as well as revealing the degree of concord or discord between the two super-Powers; indeed, it may be questioned how reliable and durable is the joint Soviet–American interest in India, and though their co-incidental interests are now obvious on some matters in this time of super-Power *détente* the US–SU relationship is still far from being a workable entente and India should place no strong reliance upon it;

(3) the independent ability to escalate a conflict confers flexible deterrence capability, the only way for India to have a credible deterrent and to escape the discomforts and uncertainties of an alliance policy and/or of nuclear guarantees offered by another Power or Powers is to develop her own independent capability; to possess nuclear weapons oneself is the only way to possess the ultimate deterrent, if such there be;

(4) there can and should be no divorce between deterrence and disarmament in the present-day world, and if India's disarmament plans are to be practicable and acceptable they have got to promote improved and stabilized deterrence; in any case non-alignment implies self-sufficiency in defence;

(5) the nuclear oligopoly of the present five nuclear Powers is more objectionable to India than the nuclear duopoly (or,

more strictly, triopoly, as Britain also is a nuclear Power) against which France and China protested and which they have now in part circumvented; this oligopoly, this potential pentarchy, is especially obnoxious to India (and may have a greater longevity) because one of the new nuclear Powers is a declared enemy and because the constitution of the UN Security Council seems to favour such a pentarchy of the present nuclear Powers;

(6) the trend towards multipolarity, to polycentrism, in the world must be further encouraged; if a *détente* between the United States and China were to set in, with the result that the Peking government obtained a permanent seat on the UN Security Council, then there would be a danger that a new great-Power pentarchy in effect had come into being, there would then be only five Powers with vetoes and with nuclear weapons, and this would be a world in which India would be permanently at a disadvantage and she would be permanently graded below her proper, or potential, role in world affairs; hence it is in India's interest to prevent the stabilization of the world as a nuclear pentarchy, and India's acquisition of nuclear weapons would facilitate this process and maintain diplomatic fluidity; and, besides, nuclear proliferation is not inevitably and axiomatically destabilizing, it may help to stabilize and institutionalize a new and more durable Asia and perhaps a world balance of power;

(7) to be a military nuclear Power is a necessary, if not a sufficient, element of great-Power status; a non-nuclear India will have little or no influence on the policies of the nuclear Powers; China's influence has increased with her development of nuclear weapons, neighbouring small Powers are more anxious than ever before not to offend her and the other nuclear Powers have to take more account of her and pay greater attention to China's words and deeds;

(8) if a principal task in future years is going to be the containment of a revisionist China, then a territorial *status-quo* Power, such as India is, will have a vital role to play in the

erection and maintenance of an Asian balance of power; and India will need nuclear weapons in order to play her most appropriate role as a principal and anchor in such an Asia system;

(9) it might do great damage to India's domestic progress if the level of national self-confidence were to sink dangerously low because of dependence on other Powers for security purposes; and the acceptance of a condition of permanent inferiority to at least five other Powers—and particularly to China—in diplomatic terms is unnecessary and unworthy of India; national nuclear weapons are a national morale-booster and an important symbol of status in international matters; the national interest should be the government's lodestar and it is in the national interest to acquire nuclear weapons;

(10) the economic costs of an independent nuclear-weapons pro-gramme for India are often exaggerated: India already has an atoms-for-peace programme and so the economic costs of a weapons programme should not be computed as the gross cost of production starting from scratch, but as the net cost on outlays specifically earmarked for weapons pro-duction and then on what is diverted from the atoms-for-peace programme to weapons production, as well as, of course, new nuclear defence expenditures.

The opponents of an Indian nuclear weapons programme utilize some or all of the following arguments:

(1) While it is true that China now threatens India, the threats are principally political-propagandistic and in so far as they are military they are likely to be either analogous to the invasion of 1962 border forays, or will involve China's incitement of guerrilla warfare, so-called 'wars of national liberation', India does not need (even if she had, should not use) nuclear weapons to cope with either of these types of threat;

(2) far from equipping India with adequate deterrence against attack by potential adversaries, to acquire nuclear weapons

285

oneself is to ensure that one's country will become a target for attack in the event of nuclear war, an enemy would immediately want to use its counterforce capability; further-more, Indian cities are much more vulnerable to Chinese attacks mounted from Tibet than are comparable Chinese cities to Indian military capabilities; thus to raise the military stakes in competition with China is to initiate another arms race and to dramatize further that China can hold Indian cities hostage more easily than can India respond in kind to China; it would be expensive for India to mount a counter-city capability which could credibly threaten China's great coastal and riverine cities, even if this were desirable, which it is not;

(3) if India acquires nuclear weapons herself, then Pakistan will desperately seek to do so, and if she succeeds (perhaps with Chinese help, it is sometimes conjectured) then a new and more awesome element of insecurity will have been added to the already troubled sub-continent;

(4) the Indian economy cannot and should not be subjected to the strains of a nuclear-weapons programme; to begin such a programme is to step on to an escalator of ever-higher costs; weapons are not preferable to welfare;

(5) by deciding to produce nuclear weapons herself India would be alienating – temporarily or permanently? – her two most powerful friends, the United States and the Soviet Union, both of which are and are likely to continue to advocate anti-nuclear proliferation measures, and they may in the future provide India with an anti-ballistic missile system (ABM), especially if she foregoes producing offen-sive weapons herself;

(6) nuclear weapons are evil and India should have nothing to do with them; all weapons of war are evil, but nuclear weapons are worst of all.

The debate continues.

What then is India's most appropriate position in the world-wide diplomatic community of states? Is she the last and least of the great Powers, or is she the first of the lesser Powers? If it be said that this is only a matter of definition, it may be agreed that it is indeed a problem of definition, but that it is more besides. What Indians expect of their country, and what other countries, other governments, will in practice regard and act upon as India's proper station in world affairs is important; but what is more important and usually left unstated is the almost world-wide interest that there is in the maintenance of the present Indian Union as such: that India, as presently constituted in size and shape, should remain a member of the international diplomatic system. The preservation of the present Indian Union is an interest common to all those who want to preserve the present international order or something very like it, not least in Asia. One thing that now seems to be widely agreed – at least outside Pakistan and China – is that India's survival as an independent nation-state within her present boundaries (or something substantially like her present shape) is infinitely preferable to a balkanized India. In this very fundamental sense India's future foreign policy will very largely be governed by the character of her domestic politics.

BIBLIOGRAPHY

APPADORAI, A. "The Foreign Policy of India." Chap. 17 in JOSEPH E. BLACK and KENNETH W. THOMPSON (eds.), *Foreign Policies in a World of Change*. New York: Harper & Row, 1963.

GUPTA, SISIR. *India and the Regional Integration in India*. New York: Asia Publishing House, 1964.

JANSEN, G. H. *Nonalignment and the Afro-Asian States*. New York: Frederick A. Praeger, 1966.

LAMB, ALASTAIR. *The Kashmir Problem: A Historical Survey*. New York: Frederick A. Praeger, 1967.

MORRIS-JONES, W. H. *The Government and Politics of India*. New York: Hillary House, 1966. (Paperback ed.: Doubleday.)

NEHRU, JAWAHARLAL. *Indian Foreign Policy 1947-61.* New Delhi: Government of India, 1961.

PARK, RICHARD L. "India's Foreign Policy." Chap. 9 in ROY P. MACRIDIS (ed.), *Foreign Policy in World Politics.* 2d ed. Englewood Cliffs, N.J.: Prentice-Hall, 1962. (Original paperback.)

Report of the Committee on the Indian Foreign Service. New Delhi: Ministry of External Affairs, October, 1966.

Journals:

Asian Recorder (New Delhi)
India Quarterly (Bombay)
International Studies (New Delhi)
Seminar (Bombay)

INDEX

INDEX

INDEX

INDEX

champions collective security and disarmament, 89; decision-making, 84–6; notion of 'capitalist encirclement', 99

Stalin, Svetlana, 79

Strang, Lord, 98

Strauss, Franz Josef, 236–7, 240, 249–250; principle of disengagement plan, 237

Stresemann, Gustav, 36

Suez Canal crisis, 14, 20, 34, 37–8, 154; Anglo-French action regarding, 36–37, 64, 95, 97, 185, 189; nationalization of, 37–8; peace-keeping by India in, 279

Sukarno, President, 64, 90, 104, 123, 143

Suslov, Mikhail Andreevich, 114

Taiwan, 119, 126, 139

Technology, growth of, 10–11, 19, 50, 101–2, 150, 155, 272

Templewood, Lord, 37, 157; Works, *Nine Troubled Years*, 37 q.

Teng Hsiao-ping, 122, 127

Thailand, 133, 172

Thermonuclear weaponry, developments in, 102

'Third World', 102, 104–5, 120, 123, 142, 212, 222, 236

Thorez, 190

Tibet, 118–19, 263, 265–7, 286

Tito, President, 64, 79, 88

Touré, President Sekou, 103

Trotsky, Lev Davidovitch, 78–9, 84–5

Truman, President Harry S., 24, 44, 53, 101

Tshombe, Moishe, 160

Turkey, 99–100, 107, 162, 172; joins Balkan Pact, 101

U Nu, 123

Ulbricht, Walter, 95

UNCTAD Conference, 274

United Bloc, 112, 116, 140

United Nations, 10, 18, 31, 38, 63–5, 105, 117, 119, 155, 174, 176, 179, 181, 209–12, 236, 279, 284

United States, 10, 14, 31, 33, 98, 172, 209, 237, 249–50, 255, 270, 272, 280; absolutism of, 55; anti-ballistic missiles developed, 60; anti-colonialism, 63; arms race with Soviet Union, 64; becomes world's leading great power, 53; beginnings of aristocracy, 54; China substituted for Soviet Union as principal aggressor, 53; common interests with Soviet Union on avoidance of nuclear war, 152; conflict between government and legislature, 25–6; *détente* with Soviet Union, 60, 62–3; dominance of in Western hemisphere, 42–3; 'feedback process', 40; frontier tradition, 48–51; geographical situation of, 11; importance of public opinion, 26; isolationism of, 55–7; lack of intellectual movements in, 55; military strategy of, 60; national character, principal elements of, 43–8; obligation to assist Germany militarily, 232; policy of containment, 52–3; policy towards China, 65–6; power of Jewish minority in, 44; prestige weakened, 64; relations with Europe, 61–3; religious traditions of, 45–6; shortcomings in policy, 68; space, exploration of, 50; split personality of, 23; structure of government, 20; unbroken success and expansion of, 57–58

Uttar Pradesh, 264

Vandenberg, Senator, 53

Versailles Treaty, 163, 169, 188

298